Train Wreck

The Story of the
Shepherdsville Train Wreck
on December 20, 1917

Train Wreck

The Story of the Shepherdsville Train Wreck on December 20, 1917

by

Charles Hartley

Dedication

This book is dedicated to the families and descendants of those who perished or were injured in the train wreck. May it give them solace that their loved ones are not forgotten.

Table of Contents

Preface

In the summer before the 90th anniversary of the worst train wreck in Kentucky history, David Strange asked my wife, Betty Hartley to refurbish Lloyd Mattingly's model of that train wreck so that it could be properly displayed at the Bullitt County History Museum.

While she worked on the model, I browsed through the information about it that was available at the museum.

David, who was then the museum's director, talked of wanting to do a memorial on the anniversary of the wreck, and coaxed me into producing a short talk about the train wreck for that event. However, the more I learned about the wreck and the people involved in it, the more I wanted to know, and my research took on a life of its own.

By the time of that memorial event, we had produced a small booklet on the wreck to share.

Meeting so many descendants of the train wreck victims at the memorial service caused me to want to learn more about those whose lives were shattered by the wreck.

I continued to gather information about these people, and in 2008 we published a second booklet, The People of the Wreck, together with additions to the first volume.

I thought at the time that my work was done on the subject of the train wreck, but additional information kept coming to light. Finally, David convinced me that we needed to publish one more book on the train wreck, incorporating all of this new information. That book was published in 2009 and contained revised editions of both earlier books, as well as a wealth of additional information discovered in my research or provided by descendants of the wreck victims.

I thought I was finished with the train wreck story, but it seems it was not finished with me, just yet.

In the years since that volume was printed, additional information about the wreck and the people involved in it has continued to appear. Finally, I decided it was time to do a revised edition of the earlier volume in time for the 100th anniversary on December 20, 2017.

This volume contains corrections and revisions to the earlier volume, plus a considerable amount of new information, much of it shared by descendants of those involved in the wreck.

I can't begin to thank each contributor by name for I would surely forget someone; but I wish to express my appreciation to everyone who shared in this endeavor. I simply could not have done it without you.

Finally, I want to thank my wife who has been a part of this from the very beginning, and whose encouragement and support (and hours of proofreading) has been invaluable to me.

Charlie Hartley

Photo Acknowledgments

The sources of many of the images found throughout this volume are identified on the same page with the image. For the others, we provide the following list.

The signal tower photo on page 6, the post card image on page 14, the photo of the Shepherdsville Baptist Church on page 19, and the two photos on page 36 all come from the archives of the Bullitt County History Museum.

The image of the baby, Annie Craven, on pages 20 and 49 is taken from microfilm of *The Evening Post,* of 21 Dec 1917.

According to Dixie Hibbs, original photos of the train wreck, taken by Louisville photographers, Bramson and Piers, were found in evidence folders in Nelson Circuit Court records in 1992. A number of these photos have been reproduced in this book, specifically on pages 17, 20, 22-27, and 158.

The image of Father Eugenio Bertello on page 39 is taken from microfilm of the 21 Dec 1917 edition of *The Louisville Times.*

The image of Frank Daugherty on page 50 taken from microfilm of the 21 Dec 1917 edition of *The Courier-Journal.*

The images of Redford, Carrie, and Redford Cherry Jr. (page 48), Emily Mashburn (page 67), Mabel Miller (page 70), Mack & Amelia Miller (page 71), Frank Nunn (page 76), John & Bettie Phillips (page 80), and Ben Talbott (page 96) are taken from microfilm of the 23 Dec 1917 edition of *The Courier-Journal.*

The image of Arthur Cahoe on page 44 is taken from microfilm of *The Des Moines Register,* 11 Oct 1921.

The photo of Margaret Anne Dodds on page 52 comes from the Miami (Ohio) University 1933 yearbook.

The photo of Henry Zollicofer Hardaway on page 55 is used by permission of Jess Scott.

Photos of Thomas Ice, Kate Cundiff Ice, and Jeffie Ice on page 60 are provided by Clara Rhodes.

The photo of Charles Todd Jesse on page 61 is used by the permission of user "flmeow1" at Ancestry.com.

Photos of the David Maraman family and the Howard Maraman family on page 65 were taken from the photo of the 1917 family reunion, provided by Pauline Bryant.

The image of Tom Smith Miller on page 70 comes from microfilm of *The Courier-Journal,* 11 Apr 1909.

The photo of Garnette McKay Dudley Moore on page 72 is used by permission of the Baldwin Family, via "RobGividen14" at Ancestry.com.

The photo of George W. Moore on page 73 is provided by Olivia Hamilton.

The photo of Lucas Moore on page 73 is provided by John Kelly.

The photo of Jackson Morrison on page 74 is provided by Josh French.

Portraits of Nathaniel Muir and Cora Muir on page 75 are provided by Mary Lou Crum and Nancy Talbott, Bardstown.

Photos of Annie Mitchell Reed on page 83 and Lem Reed on page 84 are provided by Sharon Reed, Bardstown.

The photo of Emory Beamis Samuels, Jr. on page 86 is taken from his college photo at University of Kentucky, 1940.

The portrait of Susie Sheckles on page 88 is provided by Rev. Billy G. Jenkins, pastor of Mt. Zion Baptist Church, Shepherdsville.

The photos of Althaire Simms & her mother, Lottie Wall Simms on page 92 are provided by Chris Wolf.

The photo of Tom Spalding on page 94 is provided by Charles Lamb, Notre Dame Archives.

Photos of J. Thomas Tucker and Maggie McCue Tucker on page 99 are used by permission of Linda Keller, their great-granddaughter.

Photo of William H. Wolfenberger on page 104 taken from *The L. & N. Employee' Magazine* of February, 1932 which is available at the Louisville Free Public Library.

The letters duplicated in Appendix B are provided by Sheila Walden.

The various images of newspaper stories featured throughout the book are taken from microfilm copies of those papers.

Prelude to Disaster

By 1855, the town of Shepherdsville had barely extended its borders since its establishment sixty years earlier. Getting to Shepherdsville from almost anywhere else involved a trip over roads barely passable at times. But with the arrival of the railroad, that was about to change.

On October 8, 1855, the first locomotive reached Shepherdsville on the just completed tracks. It pulled an excursion train that carried Louisville city authorities, members of the press, some railroad officials, and anyone else who could hitch a ride. *The Louisville Daily Courier* reported the next day that work was beginning on the bridge over Salt River.

LOUISVILLE, KY.

TUESDAY, : : : : : OCTOBER 9, 1855.

Nashville Railroad—Opening to Salt River.

Gradually, but still rapidly enough to assure the public of the certain completion of the enterprise, does the Nashville Railroad progress. Yesterday it was completed to Shepherdsville, the county seat of Bullitt, eighteen miles distant from Louisville. To that point an excursion train was run, carrying the city authorities, members of the press, some of the railroad officers, and a number of citizens.

The Louisville Daily Courier, October 9, 1855.

By the following June, daily trains were running between Louisville and the junction with the Lebanon branch, the future site of Lebanon Junction. By 1858, trains were traveling up this line to Lebanon, Kentucky.

Not to be left out, the folks in Bardstown committed the necessary funds, and within two years, an 18-mile line connected Bardstown with the main line at a place appropriately named Bardstown Junction. This line would eventually be extended as far as Springfield in 1888.

By 1870, the railroad made stops in Bullitt County along the main line at Brooks, Hubers, Gap-in-Knob, Shepherdsville, Salt River, Bardstown Junction, Belmont, and Lebanon Junction. In addition, it stopped along the Bardstown line at Chapeze, Quarry Switch (Clermont), Big Spring (Hobbs), and Cane Spring before entering Nelson County. These local trains, generally called Accommodations, had to compete for room on the tracks with express passenger trains that connected Louisville with Nashville and points south, as well as heavy freight trains.

Dangerous Journeys

All of this rail traffic was not without its dangers. Today we frequently hear reports about automobile and truck accidents occurring on our state's highways. Regrettably, far too many of these accidents result in deaths. But in the days before automobiles and trucks filled the roads, such events seldom occurred; that is, until the railroads arrived on the scene.

An early report described a wreck at Bardstown Junction in August 1860 in which an express passenger train ran into the back of a freight train that had not cleared the main tracks. An eye witness described the collision this way: "The express engine climbed into the last car of the freight train, unroofing and demolishing it entirely." Fortunately, no one was killed, but the Adams Express messenger, a young man named Joseph Smithers, was badly

1

bruised and cut when he jumped from the train onto the rocks and crossties.

Then, a later train that night struck and killed a rider on horseback near the site of the previous wreck.

Accidents continued to happen at Bardstown Junction. In July 1867, a misplaced switch caused three passenger cars to derail, bruising about twenty-five passengers. Then in November, a tree fell over the tracks. An oncoming locomotive hit the tree and derailed, taking the express car and baggage cars with it.

Two years later, a local woodcutter, apparently laid down on the tracks in a drunken stupor, and was cut in half that night by an oncoming train about a half-mile north of Bardstown Junction.

In April 1873, the bridge over Rolling Fork River was destroyed by fire, apparently caused by sparks falling from a passing locomotive. It took nearly a week to replace it.

In June 1874, a fatal accident occurred at Belmont early in the morning when a freight train failed to clear the main tracks ahead of an oncoming passenger train.

The freight train was on its way to Nashville when it attempted to take the siding at Belmont to allow the Nashville-bound passenger train to pass. It was a long train of thirty-four cars, and there were already ten cars in the siding.

There were still five cars loaded with corn remaining on the main tracks when the passenger train arrived. The freight's officers had failed to properly set the signal to indicate that they were still on the tracks, and the passenger locomotive crashed into the remaining cars.

The engine, baggage car and express car were thrown off the track. The engineer, seeing the danger ahead, stepped into his engine and clung to the lever, probably saving his life. The fireman, Johnnie Wallace attempted to jump from the train, but was caught in the wreckage, and severely mangled. He died at the scene.

The 1880's were witness to numerous accidents and deaths.

A SERIOUS SMASH-UP

A Freight Train on the L. and N. Road
Runs Into a Couple of Mules,
With Terrible Results.

ENGINEER MINOTT KILLED

The Courier-Journal, October 22, 1882

In October 1882, a heavily loaded freight had just passed Shepherdsville heading north. At that time trains had to pick up speed to climb through the gap in the knobs, especially if they were pulling a heavy load. The engineer, George Minott had just increased his speed when he saw a brace of mules ahead, attempting to cross the tracks.

It was too late to stop the train which struck the mules tearing them literally to pieces, and throwing the engine fifty yards from the track into an open corn field. The entire train followed, and was made a most complete wreck.

The brakeman, Charles Cameron received several injuries and was transported to a Louisville hospital. Engineer Minott was crushed beneath his locomotive, dying instantly.

The railroad had rules governing train movement to help prevent such accidents, and generally they were followed. However, sometimes a breakdown in communication or a neglected duty led to disaster.

Such was the case at Lebanon Junction in August 1883. Normally the fast passenger train from Nashville passed the junction ahead of a particular freight train, but this early morning it was running late. The freight's conductor neglected to check for orders at the telegraph station, assuming the other train had passed. He separated his train into two sections with the intention of switching part onto the siding. The part left on the main track in the gloom of the early morning was nearly invisible to the oncoming passenger train.

When Captain Ben Gifford, engineer of the passenger train, discovered the track was blocked ahead of him, he applied the brakes and gave a danger signal before jumping from the locomotive.

Three cars loaded with coal belonging to the freight and the engine and baggage car of the express were totally demolished, and a number of the other freight cars were thrown from the tracks.

Remarkably, beyond some bruises, none of the passengers were injured; but Captain Gifford sustained serious injuries, and the fireman, David Kidd had to have a leg amputated. The only fatality was a tramp named Sam Perry who was stealing a ride between the bumpers of two rear cars.

> Won't somebody keep a tally of the accidents occurring on the L & N?

A week later, *The Interior Journal* reported, "There was another collision at Lebanon Junction yesterday, in which engineer Tom Pegeon was quite badly mashed. The express was preceded by an engine, which was carrying a flag for it and which had stopped to open a switch at the Junction. Some difficulty was had in doing so and while it was standing the engine of the following train ran into it. Won't somebody keep a tally of the accidents occurring on the L & N?"

This call for accountability did little to slow the growing list of wrecks, injuries and deaths.

A near disaster happened just after Thanksgiving south of the Rolling Fork bridge at Lebanon Junction. An express train traveling at night with three sleeper cars and three coaches filled with passengers was traveling at about forty miles per hour when it struck a broken rail. The engineer quickly applied the air brakes and reversed his engine, bringing the train to a halt. Remarkably, only the tender left the track.

The wreck occurred less than a minute before the train was to cross the high trestle over the river, where death would have awaited plunging passengers.

The following April, a brakeman named Charles Anderson lost his life at Bardstown Junction when he stepped between two cars to make a coupling, lost his balance and fell between the draw-heads where he was crushed. He was 22 years old, and the sole support of a widowed mother and sister.

Another victim was Thomas Rooney who had worked for the railroad as a brakeman for a quarter century. He was helping unload a freight car loaded with bridge iron at Lebanon Junction when the load shifted and fell on him. He later died of his injuries.

Two more serious injuries occurred at Lebanon Junction in 1887. William Clark, an acting conductor, was run over when coupling cars. The newspaper reported that his left leg was crushed and had to be amputated, and that he might not live. Then two months later, Samuel Hicks was killed while attempting to board a moving engine. He had been a brakeman for two months.

Christmas Eve, 1888

On Christmas Eve, train #23, bound for Knoxville via Lebanon Junction, left Louisville at 7:45 that morning. It consisted of the engine, a baggage car and an express package car, a smoker car, and two first class coaches at the rear. It would be making a number of stops along the way.

Meanwhile Train #5, better known as the *Cannon Ball*, was preparing to leave the Louisville depot. It was an express train, and included the engine, a baggage car, and four coaches. It left the station at 8:05, and expected to make no stops until reaching Nashville.

As it was the Christmas holiday season, both trains were heavily loaded. Train #23 was especially loaded with packages for delivery at the various stops along the way. It should have reached Bardstown Junction by 8:52, but had lost considerable time along the way.

At Bardstown Junction it sat on the main track next to the busy depot as the express messenger busied himself collecting and distributing packages. Some passengers had disembarked, but others remained aboard.

The tracks curved just north of the depot, creating a bit of a blind spot for trains approaching the depot.

Suddenly the *Cannon Ball* appeared, running at normal speed. When its engineer, Milton McFerran saw the train ahead, he reversed the engine and applied its air brakes, but it was too little, too late.

His fireman, Charles King chose to leap from the engine in a bid to avoid death; while McFerran remained at the throttle, grimly prepared for the worst.

The Courier-Journal later reported, "The *Cannon Ball's* cow-catcher first lifted the rear platform of the last coach, and the engine, plowing and butting through wood and metal alike, as if it were only paper, split it from end to end, the fragments falling on either side."

It continued forward, halfway through the next coach, before coming to a halt. The sound of grinding and cracking of wood and metal was replaced with "the infernal shrieking of escaping steam" from the ruptured engine.

Had there been anyone in the first demolished coach, all lives would have been lost; but fate had placed an empty coach at the end of Train #23, a coach destined to be added to another train further down the tracks.

But this didn't prevent injuries and even death from occurring. Many of those who had remained in the second coach sustained serious injuries, and were scalded by the escaping steam.

Two were killed outright: Mary Perkins and William Houston, both of Hodgenville; and two would later die of their injuries: Engineer McFerran and Miss Mary Kinnaird of Louisville.

After investigating the incident, the railroad concluded that the conductor and brakeman of #23 were negligent in failing to place warning devices behind their train to warn oncoming trains of their presence, a failure that would repeat itself twenty-nine years later. Also blamed for contributing to the accident was the dispatcher at Shepherdsville who should have warned the *Cannon Ball* that it was closing on the train ahead. All three lost their jobs.

Accidents Continue

The following July, J. W. Carroll, a brakeman, was busy coupling two cars together at the Lebanon Junction yard when he apparently slipped and was dragged beneath the slowly moving train. Both of his arms were mangled and had to be amputated.

More than a year later, in September 1890, James McHugh was working as a brakeman on a fast-moving freight train near Lebanon Junction when, while running from one car to another, he slipped and fell beneath the train. His legs were smashed and he received severe cuts to his head.

He died before reaching the hospital in Louisville.

Then in December, Charles Ross, a farmer living near Lebanon Junction, was walking along the tracks with a friend as a train approached behind them. The train's engineer sounded a warning whistle, but the men appeared not to hear it. At the last instant, Ross's companion leaped from the track, but Ross stumbled and fell beneath the engine, dying instantly.

A similar tragedy occurred in April 1894 along the tracks at Huber's Station. John Henry Huber had retired from business as cashier of The Peoples Bank of Kentucky, located in Louisville, and was living near the railroad station named for his family. He would often come down to the station and take his daily exercise walking up and down the long railroad platform. This particular morning he appeared to have decided to walk along the tracks themselves.

When Engineer William Shallcross, the engineer of train No. 5, spotted him on the tracks ahead, he blew the whistle of his engine, and applied the air brake, but the distance was too short to stop. The train's cow-catcher caught Huber up and tossed him to the side of the tracks. Although he was little disfigured, death had claimed him.

Three years later, in September 1897, Benjamin Lloyd was a brakeman working a north-bound freight that was making switches at Lebanon Junction. He lost his footing and fell across the tracks where a freight car's wheels passed over him. He was dead when his fellow workers found him.

The following August of 1898 witnessed the death of Learner Davison, then the oldest active Methodist preacher in Kentucky. Davison, who had earlier served as pastor of the Methodist Church in Shepherdsville, was on his way to Brooks Station in Bullitt County to preach at the church there. Exiting the train, he started across the track to a buggy that awaited him. He never heard the fast Nashville bound train that struck and killed him.

Gap in Knob, December 23, 1899

T. C. Coleman, a Louisville businessman with ties to the railroad, had been responsible for getting a small railroad station located near his home in Bullitt County. Because of its location between two knobs (small rounded hills), it bore the name "Gap in Knob."

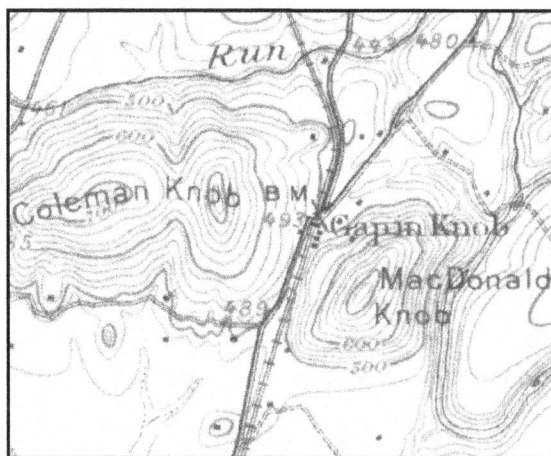

Topo map of Gap in Knob, 1907

Two days before Christmas in 1899, Coleman, now in his mid-seventies, was seated in his accustomed seat at the very rear of the last coach of the evening passenger train that included three coaches, all seats filled, with numerous folks standing in the aisles.

The elevation at the gap required that trains approaching the station from either direction had to climb a rise to reach the gap. Additionally, the track north of the station curved around the side of the knob, reducing visibility, especially in the late afternoon near sunset, and especially on this cloudy evening with a mist of rain falling.

As the train slowed to a stop at his station, Mr. Coleman rose from his seat and offered it to Miss Susie Simpson and Mrs. Cora Carothers.

Meanwhile, a freight train with 49 cars was making its way southward. It left the Louisville station about eleven minutes after the passenger train, and had been slowly gaining on it.

John Davis, engineer of the passenger train, stood looking back for his signal to proceed, and saw one last passenger, a young lady named Ora Shepherd, standing on the coach step, apparently waiting for assistance.

Then Davis saw the headlight of the freight train rounding the curve behind him. At the same time, a gentleman who had gotten off the train saw the freight, and called to Miss Shepherd to jump off. She did not understand him, and he jumped up on the step of the car, caught her, and pulled her off.

Davis quickly opened his throttle and his train began to move forward. It had moved about two coach lengths when the shock came.

As soon as George Chestcheire, the freight train engineer, caught sight of the passenger train, he shut off steam and applied his brakes to little avail. The freight engine struck the coach with considerable force, smashing the rear end, and knocking out the lights as well.

The jolting passed through each of the coaches, creating considerable panic and confusion. Ed Croan suffered whiplash, injuring his neck and back as well as his lower body which was battered against the fruit basket in his lap. Mary Richmond received injuries to her shoulder, arms, and side. W. D. McClain was thrown from the coach in which he was sitting out upon the track, falling upon his back. Several others received injuries including John Sharp and Joseph Thompson of Louisville, as well as Miss Simpson whose hand was slightly injured.

But Miss Simpson's injury was forgotten as she stared in horror at her seat mate. The rear panels of the coach, splintered and jagged by the force of the freight train, had caught Mrs. Carothers and crushed her against the seat in front, where she was bound as in a vice. Death came instantly.

Ironically, three of its passengers, Alice May, Ben Talbott, and Judge Frank Daugherty, would find themselves in a far greater disaster just before another Christmas 18 years later.

A New Century Begins

Before dawn on Tuesday, November 3, 1903, Engineer William Farrar brought his freight train northward in a heavy fog. He strained his eyes in vain for the signal light at the south end of the Shepherdsville bridge, but the fog was so thick that he could not see even ten feet away.

Meanwhile Engineer Jeremiah Corkery was bringing his freight southbound over the bridge, as the light he had seen in the thinner fog north of the bridge gave him the right of way.

Signal tower at south end of bridge.

The bridge at Shepherdsville was double tracked, but did not admit two trains passing at the same time because the rails were laid close together, and the engines as well as the cars that followed them would lap on the approach a short distance before reaching the bridge proper.

Suddenly Farrar spotted the southbound locomotive which had cleared the bridge, but mistook it for a reflection of his own engine in the windows of the signal tower.

He proceeded forward and struck the side of the other train's cars containing coal, other freight, and in one car, cans of gasoline.

By the time everything was done, seven cars of the southbound train and eight of the northbound train had left the tracks. Engine No. 231, which drew the north-bound train, was thrown down the embankment, and came to rest with its pilot in the river. On top of the engine the water tank came to a stop, and a coal car was thrown on top of both the engine and water tank, resulting in a smash-up that required several days to straighten out.

But more serious at the moment was the leaking gasoline which was ignited by an overturned lantern. For a time, it appeared that the cars remaining on the tracks were in danger of burning, but the fire was finally contained.

Engineer Farrar had remained with his engine as it plunged into the river. He was badly battered and bruised, but sustained no broken bones.

As dawn broke, the bodies of two crew members of the northbound train were discovered. Dead were Fireman William Brown, and Brakeman Luckett Brown, who were not related. Additionally, Brakeman Ed Riney, whose overturned lantern had started the fire, suffered serious burns.

Then, nearly two years later, Orlean Lee was walking along the tracks near his Belmont home. Lee, who was 84 and very deaf, did not hear the approaching train that took his life.

In May 1906, a deadly accident occurred in Louisville when a wheel flange broke on the Knoxville Express just minutes before it was due at the depot. Nine were killed and twenty-one injured including two from Lebanon Junction; Eugene B. Ray whose right leg was fractured in three places, and Murray Samuels whose leg was fractured in two places below the knee.

According to the train's conductor, Peter C. Renaker, when the flange broke the front end of the ladies' coach and the rear end of the smoker were thrown against a row of box cars backed up on the siding. The engineer, John B. Keyer stopped the train as quick as possible, but was unable to stop the cars from derailing. He would relive the horrors of this wreck, and much more, eleven years later.

In the years to follow, Bardstown Junction saw more than its share of accidents. In January 1907, Chrissie Lee Bell, a brakeman, was killed there when he stumbled while throwing a switch and fell beneath a moving train. Then in July, William King, a conductor, was in charge of a work train, and was standing on the rear platform of the caboose when a stuck switch caused the car to leave the tracks, knocking King to the rails below. Two cars passed over him, killing him.

Two years later, near Bardstown Junction, Mrs. Mack Jones and Mrs. Yetta Patterson and their two children were waiting in their wagon for the northbound train to pass. As its caboose passed them, they started to cross the tracks only to be struck by a southbound train. The newspaper reported that they suffered multiple injuries, but fortunately no one was killed.

Time, Timetables and Scheduling

As railroads spread across the nation, making accurate train schedules for east-west routes was a nightmare. Each community decided for itself just what time it was, and something had to be done.

It was 1869 when the Rev. Dr. Charles Ferdinand Dowd, the headmaster of Temple Grove Seminary in Saratoga Springs, New York, came up with his idea of dividing the nation into standard time zones. The next year he submitted his plan, complete with a map of the country, to the railway managers at a convention; but it wasn't until 18 Nov 1883 that his plan for four time zones was adopted by the railroad industry.

According to that plan, all of Kentucky and Tennessee fell in the Central Time Zone, and would remain there for many years to come.

By 1917, train scheduling on L. & N. tracks across the South was handled in one of three ways: timetables and train order, manual block scheduling, and automatic block scheduling. According to a report from the Interstate Commerce Commission, more than 80% of their tracks were controlled with timetables.

Timetables established a train's expected location along its route. For example, the weekly morning train from Springfield to Louisville was scheduled to leave Springfield at 5:55 a.m., arrive at Bardstown at 6:40, join the main tracks at Bardstown Junction at 7:25, reach Shepherdsville at 7:33, and arrive at the Tenth Street station in Louisville at 8:20. There were two problems with this. First, passenger trains often got behind on their schedules for a variety of reasons; and second, they weren't the only trains running.

One report indicated that there were 44 scheduled trains daily on the route from Louisville to Lebanon Junction, and that didn't include extra trains added to the schedule when necessary.

Train conductors and engineers were expected to know about any other trains scheduled to be on the same tracks during their scheduled run. Trains on the Springfield run mentioned above were expected to give way to fast or express trains. To do this, they carefully timed their arrival at stations with sidings, so that they could take the siding and allow the express train to pass. Such sidings were available at Bardstown Junction, Shepherdsville, and Brooks.

Trains on the same tracks were required to maintain a minimum of ten minutes distance to avoid collisions. Since they could not anticipate when another train was going to be off-schedule, they depended on telegraph operators along the way to advise them.

Imagine two trains, both heading southward out of Louisville toward Lebanon Junction. Train A leaves at 9:00 a.m. and is scheduled to arrive at Bardstown Junction at 9:50 where it will leave the main tracks and go toward Bardstown. Train B leaves Louisville at 9:20 a.m. and should reach Lebanon Junction at 10:04, traveling at a speed of slightly less than 60 mph. At this speed, it will reach Bardstown Junction at about 9:42. If both trains are on schedule, train A will have just cleared the track ahead of train B.

However, this violates that ten minute rule. The dispatcher in Louisville is aware of this. He knows that at the speed train B is traveling it will reach the Brooks station at about 9:33, just 5 minutes behind train A. For this reason, he issues a train order to train A to take the siding at Brooks and allow train B to pass. That order is dispatched via telephone or telegraph to stations down the line where it is given to the conductor of train A at the first available station. At least, that is how it was supposed to work.

The automatic and manual block systems worked differently. In each one, the tracks were divided up into blocks of distance, and one train was not allowed to enter a block if another train was still in it. Generally, the ends of blocks were located at telegraph stations, and the telegraph operator would inform the next station down the line that a train had entered the block. He would then close that block until the other operator informed him that the train had cleared the block. (For more details, see Appendix L.)

Trains could still be ordered to take sidings to allow faster trains to pass.

In 1917, the southbound tracks from Louisville to Lebanon Junction were still controlled by timetables and train orders.

Adversaries

In most cases, those injured, or the families of those killed, sought compensation from the railroad. The compensation sought was frequently much greater than the railroad was willing to pay, and these cases ended up in court. By this time, the railroad was well represented by a battery of lawyers, and the cases often reached the state's highest court before being settled.

In May 1917, John Robert Hoagland and Jimmy Morrison were walking along the tracks that passed Hoagland's farm near Bardstown Junction. John Robert was almost 12, Jimmy was 14. For some reason, John Robert was too near the tracks, and was struck by a northbound freight train. He was dead at the scene. His father, Thomas W. Hoagland, would later reject the compensation offered by the railroad, and the case would go to trial in December.

Winter Storm

Christmas was fast approaching, the first Christmas since America had entered the war; the war to end all wars. The first flakes of snow began falling in Louisville around nine o'clock in the evening on Friday, December 7th. By Sunday morning there were reports of sixteen inches on the ground in the city, with drifts as high as six feet in places.

The temperature was rapidly dropping during the storm, and dipped below zero by Sunday, where it remained for several days. In outlying areas such as Shepherdsville, reports of fourteen degrees below zero were reported.

In the city, streetcar service ground to a halt, as hundreds of workers struggled to remove the snow from the tracks. Railroad traffic continued, but was frequently hours off schedule.

In Shepherdsville, the local newspaper, *The Pioneer News*, reported that "traffic was almost entirely suspended, as the wind blew at the rate of 40 miles an hour, which drifted the snow in many places to a depth of from 5 to 15 feet."

Freezing temperatures caused the Ohio River to form ice. By Wednesday, at Madison, Indiana the river was already covered with ice. It was believed that similar conditions would exist at Louisville soon.

CITY IN GRIP OF BLIZZARD, NEARS ZERO

Courier-Journal headline, December 9, 1917

However, as the weekend arrived, the temperatures moderated a bit, raising some hopes for a quick thaw.

Away from the city, roads were mostly gravel or dirt, and all were nearly impassable. Trains were the main means of transportation from towns like Shepherdsville, Bardstown and Springfield. With Christmas almost upon them, folks in these places were anxious to get to the City for last minute shopping, or to take care of postponed business.

Finally, by December 19th, things were almost approaching normal, as folks anxiously watched the sky and checked themometers.

It looked like tomorrow would be the day to travel to the City.

Union Station

Tenth & Broadway, Louisville
Photographer: Jack Boucher
Historic American Buildings Survey
(Library of Congress), Date: August 1979

Union Station was formally opened on September 7, 1891 by the Louisville and Nashville Railroad.

It would be the point of arrival and departure for those traveling to Louisville and returning home.

December 20, 1917

The morning of December 20th broke bright and clear.

Before dawn, Len Riney, Carl Perkins, Sie Lawrence, Marvin Williams, and perhaps others gathered at the Springfield depot to take the train to Louisville. It was scheduled to pull out at 5:55 a.m. and arrive at Bardstown at 6:40; making one scheduled stop at Woodlawn with possible stops at as many as five other places along the way.

At Bardstown the sun was just breaking the horizon, and the depot was crowded with folks anxious to board the train. Among them were Nat and Cora May Muir and their son George who were traveling to the City to buy last-minute Christmas presents. Waiting nearby were Redford Cherry with his wife Carrie and their young son, Redford Jr., also planning a day of Christmas shopping. With them were Alice May Pulliam, Ben Talbott, and Judge Frank Daugherty, all three of whom had been aboard the Accommodation in the 1899 wreck at Gap-in-Knob.

When the train arrived, these boarded along with many others including Judge Nat Halstead and his daughter Natalie, Town Marshall John Phillips with his wife Bettie and their daughter Ella, Mack and Amelia Miller, and Louisa Hurst with her baby and the baby's nanny, Annie Reed.

The cars were getting crowded, and would fill up even more as the morning ride continued.

Along the way the train picked up Emory Samuels and Harry Mack Samuels, third-cousins whose family gave their name to the Samuels community. Maggie and Forrest Overall also boarded, having ridden down from High Grove.

Two other young people, Josie and Hollis Bridges, also boarded at Samuels.

The train stopped briefly at Clermont and Chapeze where the lawyer Ben Chapeze boarded. He was heading to Shepherdsville to the courthouse.

At Bardstown Junction, a number of folks came aboard. They included, among others, George, Ottie, and little Virginia Duke. George planned to stay in Shepherdsville for the day while Ottie and Virginia went on to Louisville to shop. Also aboard was Thomas Hoagland and little Jimmy Morrison. They were stopping in Shepherdsville for Hoagland's trial against the railroad for his son's death.

The train paused briefly on the south side of Salt River to pick up passengers, including Mattie Harmon, and the Daniel Nutt family who had arrived there in a surrey in time to catch the train to Louisville. Little Claud Nutt, who was seven, was excited about getting to go to the City with his folks. Also boarding there were Carrie May Simmons with her daughter Susan and Susan's nanny, Susie Sheckles. They planned a big day of shopping in Louisville.

At Louisville, the train emptied quickly, with everyone eager to attend to the day's activities. All these, and many more would return to the Tenth Street Depot later for the journey home.

Late that afternoon, as time approached for the train's departure, the depot rapidly filled with those planning to board it. The train porter, Ernest Chase busied himself helping James Carrico, the baggage master and express messenger, load packages and luggage in the baggage car while the train's crew made their preparations. They included Engineer John Keyer, Conductor Mahlon Campbell, Flagman Lawrence Greenwell, and Fireman E. J. Masden.

The Accommodation train, #41, included the locomotive, a baggage car, a smoking car, and the rear-most passenger coach. Many of the men selected the smoking car, while most of the women chose to ride in the other coach.

Among the first to arrive were Tom Spalding and Mary Alethaire Simms. They were returning home to Springfield from school, and had missed the morning train by minutes. Joining them for the trip to Springfield was Elizabeth McElroy. She had taken the train from Shelbyville to Louisville earlier in the day, to meet the evening train. The three friends would sit together on the way home. Tom Schaefer, who was about their age, may have joined them.

Louisa Hurst chose a seat there for herself and one for Annie Reed, her son's nanny. However, a friend of hers soon boarded the coach and wanted to sit with Louisa, so she told Annie that she would hold the child, and Annie could find a seat in the other coach.

Ben Talbott and James Thompson likely sought seats together so they could discuss what they'd learned at the income tax school held annually for deputy revenue agents while it was still fresh in their minds.

Lucas Moore, a field agent for the Bureau of Crop Estimates, was there, along with Frank Nunn, a ticket accountant for the railroad who was traveling to Nazareth in anticipation of holiday travel by the students there.

Nearby sat Eliza Craven with her baby in her arms and her young son Raymond at her side. She was taking the children to visit relatives in Washington County for the holidays while her husband Tom remained behind to work.

Alice May Pulliam arrived at the depot with numerous packages, Christmas presents she was carrying back to Bardstown from her aunt and uncle to their kinfolks.

Garnette Moore and her sister Emily Sturges had elaborate plans for a family house party for the Christmas holidays in Bardstown where Garnette lived. They had come to Louisville for the day, and planned to meet Emily's daughter who was arriving from Cincinnati by train. Although the daughter had not arrived as expected, both sisters boarded the train for Bardstown. However, at the last moment Emily decided to remain in Louisville to meet her daughter, and take the train the next morning.

Mabel Brown Miller had been in Louisville for two days. She was heading to Bardstown to spend Christmas with her family.

Conductor Campbell learned from the dispatcher that the fast train out of Cincinnati was running behind schedule. It had been scheduled to leave Louisville at 3:00 p.m., but now had orders to run an hour and a half late which meant it was now scheduled to depart at 4:30, just before sunset.

Campbell's left on schedule at 4:35. The express train, #7, pulled out at 4:53, eighteen minutes later, which meant that it needed to make up 23 minutes by the time it reached Bowling Green. According to the rules, the two trains should never have been closer together than ten minutes.

	#41	#7	minutes apart
Louisville	4:35	4:53	18
FX	4:47	5:05	18
Strawberry	4:53	5:09	16
Brooks	5:06	5:18	12
Shep.	5:18	5:24	6
Bard. Jct	5:27	5:28	1

If the dispatcher had seen the anticipated travel times for the two trains side-by-side according to their regular schedules as shown on the previous page, he would have known instantly that the ten-minute barrier would be breeched, and would have ordered #41 to take the siding at Shepherdsville.

But #7's late arrival and departure was not listed on any time schedule, and was one more thing he had to take into consideration along with all the other trains passing through the Louisville yard that evening.

And, of course, all this would depend on the two trains maintaining their schedules.

But due to heavy rail traffic, #41 took an extra four minutes to reach the FX switching station, passing it at 4:51. Then #7 reached that point at 5:08, three minutes past its schedule, but reduced the time gap between the trains to just 17 minutes.

The operator at the FX station reported both times to dispatcher, J. W. Sams.

At the Strawberry station, 2.7 miles further, the trains were about fifteen minutes apart. The station operator there failed to promptly report the times to the dispatcher, who, being busy, failed to request them.

By now Dispatcher Sams had become aware of the closing gap between the two trains, but rather than call the Strawberry station to determine exactly how close they had been when passing there, he elected to call the operator at Brooks instead, and tell him to tell Campbell that #7 was by FX at 5:08, and if he could not go to Bardstown Junction on time it would be a good idea to take the siding at Shepherdsville.

Written orders were automatically shared with both the conductor and engineer, but this was only a verbal message to be shared with the conductor. As such it was a cautious suggestion rather than a direct order.

W. E. Sanders, the operator at Brooks, passed this message on to Conductor Campbell when #41 reached that station at approximately 5:12. According to the logbook, they spent only a minute at Brooks before leaving for Shepherdsville at 5:13. Almost exactly ten minutes later, No. 7 passed Brooks.

Campbell passed this information on to the train's porter, Ernest Chase, but apparently didn't have time to share it with the engineer.

The train paused again at Hubers, then very briefly to drop off someone along the way, and finally at Gap-in Knob, before heading into Shepherdsville.

We speculate that Alice May Pulliam and others remembered the wreck there eighteen years earlier; and were relieved when the train continued its journey south.

During one of those brief stops, Campbell asked Chase if he had informed the engineer of the need to take the siding at Shepherdsville.

It's not clear whether he had expected the porter to relay the message, or not; but when Chase responded that he had not, Campbell decided to continue to Shepherdsville and get more information there.

SPEED IN MPH	#41	#7
Louisville to FX	16	16
FX to Strawberry	27	40.5
Strawberry to Brooks	34	49.3
Brooks to Shep.	25	50
Shep. to Bard. Jct.	25.3	57

According to their schedules, #41 was to travel from Brooks to Shepherdsville in 12 minutes; while #7 was to take only half that time; bringing them to within four minutes of one another.

If both trains were on schedule, the previous chart indicates what their average speeds would be from place to place. While #41 would slow down to about 25 mph after leaving Brooks, #7, which had no scheduled stops before Lebanon Junction, would be increasing speed as it passed Shepherdsville.

After Brooks, #7 would be rapidly gaining on #41, especially since the latter was likely losing even more time with stops along the way.

This postcard image, circa 1906, shows the Shepherdsville depot on the right, and a northbound train on the left. The siding tracks lay in the middle, and the railroad bridge over Salt River in shown in the distance.

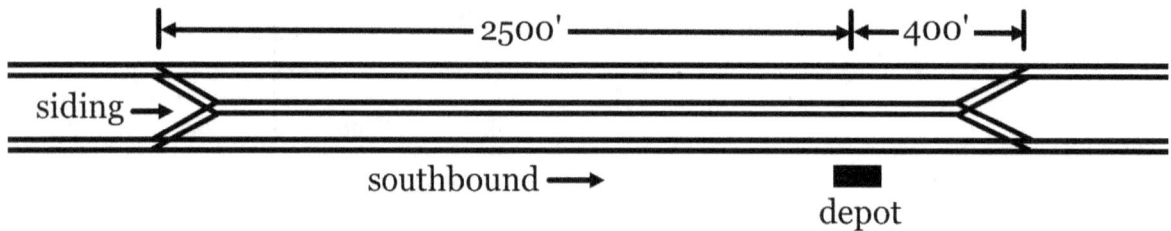

As shown here, at a point 2,500 feet north of the Shepherdsville depot the main tracks were spread to provide for the middle passing track, which was 2,900 feet long, and extended 400 feet south of the station which sat on the west side of the tracks.

Dispatcher Sams' "suggestion" would have taken #41 into the siding nearly a half-mile before reaching the depot. Campbell's decision to not do so, left his train on the main southbound track.

Meanwhile in Shepherdsville, Circuit Judge David A. McCandless closed that day's court session so folks living south of the river could get to the depot to catch the evening train home if they wished.

Among them were Ernest Woodward and George Duke who had been sitting together during the Hoagland trail. Woodward was the lawyer for the railroad, and Duke was the railroad agent at Bardstown Junction. Duke had invited Woodward to spend the night with his family, and Woodward gladly accepted the invitation.

The men who had been selected for the Hoagland trial jury were mostly farmers from all parts of the county. Knowing they had to be back in the courtroom the following morning, many of them likely planned to stay in Shepherdsville in one of the boarding houses or with friends.

The list included William Ashby, John Armstrong, Albert Fisher, James Hough, Albert Smith, Iley Jones, George Swearingen, Henry Bohlsen, Fred Swearingen, Solomon Elzy, Claude Anderson, and William Combs. Many would find themselves involved in rescue operations later that evening.

Father Eugene Bertello, a Catholic priest who resided at Chapeze, was in Shepherdsville at Troutman's undertaking establishment. He had a very sick parishioner living south of the town and planned to take the train to visit him. As the train approached Shepherdsville, Father Bertello and Henry Wathen were heading to the depot together when a friend drove up in a buggy and called to Wathen to make his trip in the buggy instead of the train. Bertello bade him a pleasant journey and prepared to board the train.

Young Roscoe Tucker stood on the depot dock. He had an armful of newspapers that had come in earlier in the day. He hoped to sell most of them to folks on the arriving train, and he was alert to the sound of #41's whistle in the distance as it approached the town.

Just then Mr. Duke mentioned that his wife and daughter were on the approaching train. Realizing that she and her daughter would likely be tired and not appreciate company that evening, Mr. Woodward begged off, and said he would enjoy their hospitality at a later date.

However, Duke insisted that Woodward at least step aboard long enough to meet his wife and daughter, and he agreed to do so.

	#41	#7	minutes apart
Louisville	4:35	4:53	18
FX	4:51	5:08	17
Strawberry	4:56	5:11	15
Brooks	5:13	5:23	10
Shep.	5:25	5:29	4

This chart shows the actual times that each train either passed or left the various stations up to Brooks. If both trains followed their scheduled speeds from Brooks to Shepherdsville, they would reach that place just four minutes apart.

In the investigations that would follow, there was considerable debate as to when #41 reached Shepherdsville. The dispatcher's log showed the time as 5:24, but this was reported and recorded several days later, and its accuracy was doubted.

It is far more likely that it arrived no earlier than 5:25, and possibly a minute or so later, due to the three stops it made along the way.

Meanwhile #7 passed Brooks Station at 5:23, a time verified by Conductor John C. Willett of train No. 13 which was on the siding at

Brooks. It did not stop, but blew the right of way, four short blasts. The right of way was given its engineer by the usual signal of changing a red to a green light, and he blew two short blasts in acknowledgment and went on his way.

By this time the sun had long since disappeared below the horizon, and darkness was upon them.

The Accommodation's locomotive pulled past the depot to the point where the passenger coaches were next to the depot. Some 15 to 20 passengers exited the cars, and perhaps half that many replaced them.

Meanwhile, the station's telegraph operator, Jesse Weatherford went to help unload perhaps a half dozen mail bags, and other packages. This took him about 50 feet away from the depot.

Upon arriving, Conductor Campbell had hurried to the depot and called the dispatcher in Louisville to learn where #7 was.

He was informed again that #7 had passed the FX station at 5:08, and that he should take the siding at Shepherdsville.

Weatherford was returning to the depot when he met Campbell who told him they were taking the siding.

By this time the dispatcher had learned the time that #7 passed Brooks, and he tried to call the Shepherdsville station, but no one was close by the phone to take his call.

Campbell told the porter to run and tell the engineer to pull forward and back into the siding. This he did, and rode on the locomotive up to the switch.

Meanwhile, William Wolfenberger, engineer of #7, glanced at his watch and noted that it was a few seconds past 5:27 as he passed the Gap-in-Knob station about two miles north of Shepherdsville. He would be traveling at about 50 mph according to his schedule.

About a half mile from the Shepherdsville station, Wolfenberger sounded the station signal, a single blast from his train's whistle. He then blew four blasts for orders.

Peering into the darkness and haze, he could dimly see a green signal light. Following his signal whistle, the light should have changed to red and then immediately back to green if the way was clear.

While this was the rule, he knew that oftentimes a station operator would give the proceed signal before it was called for, and believed that this was the case now.

At about 200 yards closer, he again blew the signal for orders. He also slightly reduced speed to about 45 mph. Fog or smoke from #41's locomotive caused the signal light to disappear and then reappear a moment later, adding to the confusion.

When #41's locomotive reached the switch, Ernest Chase, its porter, jumped off and waited for the last car to pass before throwing the switch to enable the train to back into the siding.

At that moment, Weatherford was almost back to the depot when he looked up and saw #7's light, fast approaching.

He dashed the remaining distance to the depot, threw the switch to change the light to red, and then grabbed a red lantern and began waving it frantically.

After Chase threw the switch to shift the rails, he too saw the approaching train. He jumped a nearby fence to escape.

Wolfenberger was less than a hundred yards from the depot when he saw the light change to red. He applied his emergency brakes, and closed the throttle, but it was too little, too late.

Those who remained on the dock at the depot watched in horror as the huge locomotive ran past them.

By the time it reached #41, its speed had been reduced to perhaps 25 mph, but its great weight and momentum imploded the back of the rear passenger car, sending fragments of wood and glass forward into the car and its passengers. It continued forward shattering the sides of the car. The roof dropped down on passengers' heads.

The locomotive continued through the length of the car, shattering it completely. It scattered splinters and broken glass debris and bodies to both sides of the track. Other bodies were trapped on the massive engine when it smashed into the next car, and plowed half way through the smoker car.

The force of the collison shoved the rest of #41 forward approximately 800 feet, and crushed #7's tender and locomotive together, as well as rupturing the locomotive, as shown below.

Photo of #7's locomotive the morning after the collision.

Although #7's momentum stalled about half way through the smoker car, the whole car was damaged as it was pushed forward into the baggage car which was also damaged as it was caught in a vise between the smoker and the engine. Parts of both cars fell down the side of the track into a small underpass at what is now Second Street near the Ridgway Library. Later, bodies would be found in this wreckage.

In the midst of this carnage, unnoticed by anyone at the time, a small bundle was cast from the train, flew threw the air, and landed beyond a fence in a snow bank. It would be discovered later that evening.

Dead and dying bodies lay scattered everywhere; some on and some under wreckage.

Wolfenberger and his fireman, Charles E. Gossem, crawled out of their locomotive. Shocked by the carnage before them, Wolfenberger shouted, "For God's sake do what you can for these people while I run to the station and summon all the doctors in Louisville!"

As the roar of the collision echoed throughout the little town, those on the dock stared speechless, unable to grasp the reality of what lay before them. Then, seemingly as one, shouts and exclamations were heard from every quarter, and people rushed to the scene to offer whatever assistance they could to the victims.

Among those first on the scene was Dr. S. H. Ridgway who lived a short distance from the wreck. He was joined by the town's other physicians and a host of others as they sifted through the rubble in the dark, listening for sounds of life.

A supply of Christmas candles was discovered in the baggage car and they were used by the searchers to cast beams of light in the gloom.

One by one, as victims were found, the bodies of the dead were laid out on the dock. Survivors were moved to nearby homes to receive needed care.

The bodies of David and Howard Maraman were laid side-by-side on the dock with the other corpses. Then someone noticed that Howard's fingers were moving. Though he was severely injured, he would survive.

When word of the tragedy reached Louisville, immediate steps were taken to organize a relief train. It was comprised of a day coach, a sleeper, two baggage cars and a fast locomotive. Calls were broadcast for physicians and nurses, and by 6:30 the train left for Shepherdsville with eleven Louisville doctors and several surgeons and within half an hour pulled up at the station at Shepherdsville.

In the rush to prepare the relief train, and perhaps in L & N's determination to take charge of the scene, a potential opportunity for rescue was overlooked. Dr. Underwood, surgeon of the B & O, Southern, and K & I railroads, would later comment that K & I had a hospital car that was "a veritable operating room on wheels, and has every bit of equipment needed for any purpose. Had the car been dispatched, probably several lives would have been saved." It's not clear if this would have been true or not.

The next day's *Louisville Evening Post* described the scene this way:

"Within five minutes after the accident had happened, the commotion of the first shock had passed and the work of rescue was under way and the dead and injured were being removed. The dead were laid out in a line on the platform of the station and the injured were removed to the homes of the people of Shepherdsville, that quiet town being converted by the accident into a sort of general morgue and hospital. The larger buildings near the station were filled with the injured and dying. Many of those injured in the wreck died as they were being taken to places of safety.

"The little brick Baptist church, an imposing structure for a town of that size, was turned into a morgue and many of the dead were later removed there.

Shepherdsville Baptist Church, dedicated in May 1910

"As the bodies were lifted from the wreckage they were viewed by the physicians on duty and a hasty examination of their injuries made. Where the cases were urgent they were given immediate attention, but where the injuries were such that a few minutes would not endanger life they were passed on. The dead were laid to one side.

"The most seriously injured were taken into the baggage room first and first aid was given them. They were then removed to the homes of people nearby. Shepherdsville opened its doors wide to the injured, and there was no lack of facilities for housing the injured.

"When the relief train reached Shepherdsville the physicians found that much of the preliminary work had been done by the local physicians and by the people of that city, and the doctors and nurses on the relief train applied themselves to completing the preliminary work and to preparing the injured to be removed to the hospital in Louisville. The relief train, in addition to the sleeper, carried cots and stretchers. A thorough search of the town was made by employees of the company, under direction of W. F. Sheridan, superintendent of the Louisville division of the L & N, who with other officials of the company, were on the relief train, and all of the injured were placed on stretchers and taken to the train. It left there shortly after 10 o'clock and arrived in Louisville at 10:55 o'clock. It was switched off at the Y in South Louisville and sent around to Sts. Mary and Elizabeth Hospital, where preparations had been made to receive the injured."

The body of Mrs. Hurst was later found on top of the engine of #7 with her baby clasped tightly in her arms.

Susan Simmons, who survived the crash, could not locate her mother, and she became frantic, and then hysterical. When Mrs. Simmon's body had not been located after two hours, two men were deputized to find her. After searching the length of the track, in each bit of wreckage, they found her body beneath a mass of wreckage near #41's engine. It was dangerous work extracting her, as wreckage kept falling on the shoulders of rescuers.

When Mrs. Simmons was brought to the morgue, the last of the bodies to be found, her daughter could not be consoled.

The Louisville Herald reported the next day, "The most serious phase of the disaster was caused by the fact that one half of the second coach fell a distance of about twelve feet into an underpass over a roadway leading from the west to the east section of the town. Many of the victims were crushed to death in the fall, and others who had escaped injury in the main crash were injured by the fall."

The photo on the next page shows part of the wreckage above the underpass.

Some passengers on the Flyer (#7) assisted in the search and rescue operation. In particular, Miss Margaret Woods, a trained nurse described at the time as the "lady with the brilliant red hair," who worked diligently to aid the injured, along with William E. Russell who worked in the railroad's legal department. [See Appendix C.]

Word spread by telephone and telegraph down the line to Samuels, Bardstown, and then Springfield. Frantic calls were made, seeking information on loved ones. In Bardstown, anxious relatives awaited news that was too slow in coming. Automobiles filled with many of them made their way along muddy roads toward Shepherdsville and Louisville.

In Shepherdsville, Mrs. Mattie Glenn enrolled names of the dead as rapidly as they were identified. She stood at her post, a tall dry goods box near the center of the room, from the time the first body was brought in until 3 o'clock Friday morning. Relatives seeking information went to her. When loved ones were found among the dead, she consoled and comforted them.

Photo of the wreckage above the underpass; Trunnell Hotel on the right.

A Miracle

Two versions of this story have been told. In one Curran Troutwine was walking a short distance from the track when he spotted a small bundle in the snow. Curious, he investigated and discovered a baby wrapped in its blanket. The baby girl's face and head were scratched a bit, but otherwise she appeared to be just fine. Curran took her to the nearby Trunnell Hotel where the child quickly won the hearts of all the women who came to shower care and love on her.

In the second version which was published in *The Evening Post,* Mrs. Henry Grunwald noticed the object lying on the ground. She went to it and saw it was a baby. The little one was apparently dazed by its experience, and was not making a sound but was found to be unhurt. The newspaper published a photo of Mrs. Sola Trunnell holding the baby. The copy we have from microfilm is of very poor quality, but the baby is shown here.

While the baby's identity was a mystery at the scene of the disaster, Thomas Craven of Louisville was hunting for his family. The first that he knew of the fate of his family was when he read the morning newspaper. The names of his wife and children did not appear in the first casualty list, but Craven hurried to the hospital. There he found his wife seemingly near death, his son dying, and his daughter missing.

When word reached Louisville about the mystery child, Thomas left his wife's bedside and traveled to Shepherdsville where he discovered his baby girl alive and quite well.

Mrs. Craven was thought by most to be sure to die from her injuries. Perhaps the sight of her daughter gave her the determination to survive.

Meanwhile, the first relief train arrived back in Louisville at 11 p.m. It backed into the siding near Sts. Mary and Elizabeth Hospital at 12th and Magnolia Streets and ten policemen were required to hold back the frantic relatives and friends who had rushed there, seeking word on their loved ones. The injured were carried on stretchers by soldiers from nearby Camp Taylor from the train to the waiting hospital.

The Louisville Evening Post reported the next day:

"The women were taken to the north wing and the men in the south. Waiting hands took the stretchers from the grasp of the bearers, and the elevators worked with clocklike regularity in lifting the most serious cases to operating rooms on the floors above.

"Here and there a brother or sister, a father or mother, with face drawn pale, gazed at some stricken relative as the stretcher bearers marched through the driveway. A dull moon overhead added to the gloom, and the silence was broken only by a choke or sob as men and women gave vent to their feelings.

"Men stood with bared heads in the archway as the soldiers bore the apparently lifeless forms to the doors of the building.

On both sides of the steps persons familiar with residents of Nelson and adjacent counties made possible the identification of many.

"A stretcher would be borne to the steps where it changed hands from the soldiers to doctors inside the doors. The blanket would be lifted from the faces of the injured and friends or relatives would sob 'That's John' or 'That's Mary.'

"Thirty-nine injured persons were admitted to the hospital, while many persons who were in the wreck and who were brought there on the relief train, called for taxicabs and were taken to hotels."

About midnight a second train was dispatched to bring the dead to Louisville. It returned at 3:45 a.m. with the bodies which were taken by army ambulances to the undertaking establishment of Lee E. Cralle at Sixth and Chestnut streets.

Sam Conner, a real estate man of Bardstown, who knew almost every one in that section, went to Cralle's soon after the arrival of the bodies and made positive identification of most bodies. Relatives began pouring in by the scores and soon all the lower floor rooms at the undertaking establishment were crowded.

Frank Nunn's wife was waiting at the Louisville depot for word on her husband's fate. Finally when a phone call to Shepherdsville confirmed his death she fainted and had to be carried to a table in the lobby, where military physicians had difficulty in reviving her. A taxi was called and she was taken to her home in a hysterical state.

The body of Frank Nunn was mangled beyond recognition. Identification was made by his clothing and the contents of his wallet.

Joseph Hurst arrived at the hospital in an automobile with his brother, reaching there an hour before the relief train. When the first relief train arrived, he stood and silently watched the suffering women brought in on stretchers.

Finally his wife was brought in. The covering was lifted from her face. He couldn't identify her at first because of terrible marks on her neck and chest. His son was also almost unrecognizable. A half hour later he was informed of their deaths.

The last relief train carried most of the bodies of those killed to Louisville. The remainder were handled by the two undertaking establishments in Shepherdsville, Troutman Bros and Maraman Bros.

These included Forrest and Maggie May Overall, cousins of High Grove; Mrs. Carrie May Simmons of Shepherdsville; David. H. Maraman of Shepherdsville; Mrs. Katie Ice, Bardstown Junction; Emory Samuels, Deatsville; Flagman Lawrence Greenwell, New Haven; Thomas Schaefer, Chapeze; J. W. Stansbury, Bardstown Junction; Father E. A. Bertello, Roman Catholic priest, Chapeze; and little Jimmy Morrison of Bardstown Junction.

After the last relief train left for Louisville, wrecking crews cleared the tracks for traffic, removed the locomotives, and burned up the debris. A pathetic feature was the broken bits of dolls, child's furniture, and other Christmas presents that lay strewn along the tracks.

Wreck Photo

The Aftermath

The scene of the accident was thronged with people throughout the next day (see photo below). Search was made in the debris for lost articles. Two gold watches were found and turned over to Coroner C. A. Masden. Later a woman's double case gold watch with a short chain was recovered and placed in the keeping of Jailer Franklin Monroe. Rumors circulated that looting of the dead and wounded had been committed causing considerable anger by spectators at the scene.

The report spread was that three men had been arrested for such offenses. Coroner Masden and other officials of Bullitt County denied the story, and a reporter's visit to the jail turned up just two prisoners; one arrested for drunkenness, the other for fighting. Neither had anything to do with the wreck.

Jailer Monroe said, "I found three satchels that had been placed in a pile and took possession of them. An official of the L & N railroad called at my home for one of them. It contained $200, railroad tickets, and other articles. The two other satchels are in my possession and have not been opened. They will be delivered to the proper persons."

Coroner Masden and Sheriff Rouse had placed a guard over each body until it was identified and claimed by relatives or sent to Louisville on the last relief train. Masden gave no credence to the stories of looting. He was a brother-in-law to David and Howard Maraman in the wreck.

The next day a special funeral train was formed shortly before two in the afternoon. At 3 o'clock a long line of gray army ambulances rolled noiselessly up to the Tenth-Street depot in Louisville. The caskets were placed on the special train in a baggage coach nearest the engine. Behind this coach were three others filled with relatives and friends of the victims who were accompanying their dead back home.

Jack Dalton wrote in *The Courier-Journal*, "Women heavily veiled and men were in the coach behind the baggage cars, no tears in their eyes and no words spoken. Men whose wives or other relatives had been killed, tried to ease unstrung nerves by smoking incessantly. One man toyed idly with a tin horse which had lost an ear. He was Thomas Craven, whose baby son was killed. Others just stared vacantly. Apparently the train crew had received orders to proceed slowly. It moved out of the gray mist under the depot shed into the clear air. It gathered speed slowly, never exceeding twenty miles an hour. Workmen in ditches removed their hats as the train passed."

At Shepherdsville, the train collected the coffins of bodies that had been prepared there. At Bardstown Junction, the bodies of J. W. Stansbury, Virginia Duke and Miss Katie Ice were received by family and friends. Then at Samuels, the train gave back the body of Emory Samuels.

The next stop was Bardstown. Seventeen taken from the funeral train there were the bodies of Nat, Cora, and young George Muir; John and Bettie Phillips; James Thompson, Mack and Amelia Miller, Ben Talbott, Sr., Redford C. Cherry, his wife Carrie, and their young son, Redford, Jr.; Mrs. Joseph Hurst and baby Raoul; Emily Haycraft Mashburn; Alice May Pulliam and Lillian Miller. The bodies of others arrived earlier in hearses furnished by Louisville undertakers.

Then the train moved on to Springfield where the bodies of Thomas Spalding, Mary Alethaire Simms, and Elizabeth McElroy were removed.

Wreck Remains

Sts. Mary and Elizabeth Hospital remained the abode of many of the injured, some for months.

Howard Maraman spent nearly a month there before returning to his home near Shepherdsville and the grave site of his dead brother. Dan Nutt finally returned to his home in mid February where he and his son mourned the death of Stella, wife and mother.

T. W. Hoagland returned to his home July 4th after six months in the hospital. He received several breaks in the wreck, left leg broken below the knee, knee cap broken, elbow crushed, face cut all to pieces, head mashed, right side hurt, with several other parts broken. The fates of others, some unrecorded, were similar to these. It would be some time before the emotional wounds began to heal as well.

Others would never leave there alive.

Besides Mattie Harmon, W. C. Johnson, Mabel Brown Miller and Raymond Cravens who all died in the hospital on the day after the wreck, Henry Hardaway died on Christmas Eve, Silas Lawrence of Springfield died January 2, and Joshua Bethel Bowles died three days later.

Wreckage Beside the Underpass
(More Wreckage Photos on Next Two Pages)

Another tragic event was indirectly caused by the train wreck.

William House of Colesburg had already experienced considerable heartache in the year and a half prior to that evening. Two of his six sons, Jerome and Charles, had died, and then his wife also died in November.

William had a brother in Louisville who had been watching over the two youngest boys temporarily, and William was in Louisville that day to get the boys and take them home for Christmas.

They boarded the No. 9 train that evening which was scheduled to leave Louisville at 5:15 and would reach Colesburg on the main line at 6:36, if it stayed on schedule.

By the time the train reached Shepherdsville, the track was already blocked by the wreck. William and his boys left the train and he finally found a way to get them as far as Lebanon Junction where he left them with a friend so they could warm up while he made his way home to Colesburg.

Once there, he started a fire in the fireplace to warm the house before his sons arrived. Then he went to retrieve his sons. They went on to Colesburg where they found their home on fire. The house was destroyed, another victim of the train wreck.

Locomotive #230, which was #7 that evening, was restored and returned to service. Richard E. Prince took this photo of it in 1948.

Locomotive #18, twin sister to #17 shown here, was #41 that evening. This photo was taken by Thomas T. Tabor in 1923. Both photos are used with permission.

Assessing Blame

Blame for the wreck was swift, and widespread. The editor of *The Courier-Journal* exclaimed two days later that people were "being transported in old-fashioned wood coaches, long demonstrated to be death-traps for passengers," and, "at Shepherdsville we have, in the form of a horror unmatched in the annals of local railroading, an illustration of what happens when a fast through train [with cars of steel construction] strikes a kindling-wood Accommodation loaded with patrons."

The railroad was quick to acknowledge responsibility, with their president, Milton H. Smith issuing a statement to that effect.

"Standing in the presence of the gravest catastrophe in the Louisville & Nashville Railroad company's history—the collision at Shepherdsville—I feel, speaking for my associates and myself, utterly unable to adequately express how deeply we deplore the deaths and injuries, and how profoundly we sympathize with those to whom have come these sufferings and bereavements. They and the general public are entitled to know just how the calamity came about, and this they shall know to the fullest, but I am sure the thinking men will realize that we cannot make a statement until a complete investigation has been made, lest possibly premature judgment do someone an injustice. In the meantime, however, in order that the Louisville & Nashville Railroad company, which has never knowingly contested a just claim, may do what it can in the way of compensation, I desire hereby to definitely acknowledge legal liability in the case of the death or injury of all passengers and to suggest a method of ascertaining the amounts to which each is entitled I propose and request that the Hon. A. O. Stanley, the governor of Kentucky, appoint a committee of three men of integrity and high standing, one each from the counties of Bullitt, Nelson and Washington, to whom shall be submitted all claims, settlement of which the company and the claimants cannot agree upon, their decision to be final. This will save the claimants the delay and expense of litigation, will insure a certain and just termination of their rights, and will guarantee their receiving the full amount awarded, instead of dividing it with others. This proposition is not dependent upon acceptance by all claimants, but is open for three months to all who may desire to avail themselves of it. Respectfully, MILTON H. SMITH, "President, Louisville, Ky. "E. S. Jouett, General Attorney."

Smith's statement, as printed in *The Tennessean*, a Nashville paper, on 23 Dec 1917.

But at the same time, it had its agents out trying to limit the financial damage, particularly in the Bardstown area where so many prominent families suffered death and/or injury in the wreck. See Appendix M for details of some of their efforts.

L. & N. Wreck Probe

According to the Christmas Day issue of *The Courier-Journal*, the railroad almost immediately convened an examining board of railroad officials. They determined that "Conductor Campbell and Flagman Greenwell of #41 disobeyed the rules in failing to protect their train by the use of proper signals between Brooks and Shepherdsville where the schedule of the train was not being maintained, and at Shepherdsville while endeavoring to get on the sidetrack out of the way of #7."

Further, they stated, "William Wolfenberger, engineer of train #7, violated the rules in not approaching Shepherdsville prepared to stop before passing the semaphore signal unless he got a signal to proceed. In approaching a station it is the duty of an engineer to absolutely stop his train before reaching the semaphore unless he receives an affirmative and positive signal that he may proceed. This signal to proceed is made in only one way–that is, there must be displayed a red light, which changed into a green light, and this change must be made in view of the engineer. Upon this occasion the green light (which was the proper signal to be displayed in view of #41, standing at the station as it was) constituted a stop signal for Engineer Wolfenberger," and indicated that Wolfenberger "testified that while he realized it was for him a stop signal, he supposed that it would be changed, and kept running, expecting that change, but never receiving it until just before he reached the station."

The examining board took pains to make it clear that the station operator, Jesse Weatherford, was doing his duty when he left the station telephone to assist with baggage at the train, rather than remaining at his post to receive messages; and that "it was proper under the rules for the operator to place the signal at green, and it would have been equally improper for him to change that signal back to red until train #41 had passed out from the station 200 feet or more. In the meantime the green signal maintained in that position constituted for Engineer Wolfenberger just as positive a duty to stop as if it had been red." Weatherford had been criticized in the press for not being at his post at the time of the wreck. A complete transcription of the newspaper's report may be found in Appendix D.

Coroner's Inquest

On December 29, a coroner's inquest was held in Louisville to determine the cause of death of those injured in the wreck who had been transported to Louisville and died there. The inquest jury found that "if the verbal order to 'head in' at Shepherdsville given to Conductor M. W. Campbell had been observed the wreck would not have occurred."

According to a newspaper report of the inquest, "Considerable interest was attracted by the testimony of Jesse Weatherford, the operator at Shepherdsville for the past six years. Weatherford said that the first information of #41 which he had was a message from Operator Sanders, at Brooks Station, asking him whether 41 was in the clear. He said he first saw the train a mile and a half away. When it arrived Conductor Campbell asked him what to do about #7. At that time no orders for #7 had been received by Weatherford, and the train crew, he said, agreed that the best thing to do was to take the siding. He accordingly put up the board, indicating that #41 was on the track, and helped with the unloading of the baggage. When he finished he saw the headlight of #7, seized a red lantern and tried to flag it, but it was too late."

The newspaper reported that chief interest was given to the testimony of Engineer Wolfenberger. According to the paper, he testified, "We passed Gap in the Knobs, it was a few seconds past 5:27 o'clock, as near as I can recall. I sounded the station signal, one blast from my whistle, when we were about a half mile from Shepherdsville. Then I blew four blasts for orders. I could see the signal only dimly, and it was green, our signal to proceed if we had seen it change from red to green. I did not see it change, as it appeared green when I first saw it."

He continued, "Oftentimes an operator gives us the signal before we call for it, and I believed it had already changed from red to green, meaning for me to proceed."

After hearing all the testimony, the jury ruled that the "collision resulted primarily from the carelessness of Conductor Campbell and Flagman Greenwell, of train #41, with contributing carelessness on the part of Engineer Wolfenberger and Operator Weatherford at

Shepherdsville." See Appendix E for a transcript of *The Evening Post* story.

Bullitt County Grand Jury

A special Bullitt County grand jury was convened at Shepherdsville in early January, that determined that "the system of operating trains in use by the L & N, especially between Louisville and Bardstown Junction and through Shepherdsville, to be unsafe and dangerous when an accommodation train doing local work and making many stops, is followed so closely by a fast through train making no stops," and placed the blame for that on "the officers of the company, whose duty it was to promulgate such rules and regulations as would insure safety to the traveling public."

The grand jury further blamed the company for having the Shepherdsville station operator, Jesse Weatherford, leave his office to help with baggage, rather than remain at his post at the telephone to receive messages and instructions. The jury found that Conductor Campbell of the Accommodation should have headed into the siding upon arrival, rather than wait for additional instructions on the main line. They debated, but could not agree on whether the flagman of the Accommodation, Lawrence Greenwell, was at fault for not protecting the rear of his train with fusees and torpedos.

The grand jury further found "that William Wolfenberger, the engineer on #7 was guilty of gross, wanton and willful negligence in approaching Shepherdsville at such a great and excessive speed. He knew that the #41, even if running on the scheduled time, could only be a short distance ahead of his train. He was an old railroad man and knew that the local travel was always heavy just before the holidays. Therefore, the great loss of life was in a measure due to his fault as well as the others heretofore mentioned."

"Indictments against the Louisville & Nashville Railroad Company, B. M. Starks, general manager of the road, W. F. Sheridan, division superintendent, and F. J. Fishback, master of trains, charging "creating and maintaining a common nuisance," and against William Wolfenberger, engineer, charging involuntary manslaughter, were returned" by the grand jury. Read the complete grand jury report in Appendix F.

Kentucky Railroad Commission

On January 10-11, the State Railroad Commission held its inquiry into the wreck.

It seems clear from newspaper reports that the commission chairman, Laurence B. Finn, believed that the wreck was due in large part to the absence of an automatic block system along the route between Louisville and Bardstown Junction. Such a system would have automatically informed Wolfenberger that a train was sitting on the main line in front of him.

On the first day, besides witnesses from railroad management, the panel heard from J. W. Sams, operator at Louisville; Engineer J. B. Keyer, of #41; Ernest Chase, porter on #41; W. E. Sanders, operator at Brooks, and Jesse Weatherford, operator at Shepherdsville.

Testimony of Chase, Weatherford and Sanders was the same as that at previous hearings and they were not kept long on the stand.

According to a *Courier-Journal* report on January 11, Engineer Keyer said at one point, "I don't believe the accident would have happened if we had received orders to 'head in' at Shepherdsville. I never saw Conductor Campbell after we left Louisville and I know nothing about the information he received at Brooks."

Once again, company officials testified that Weatherford was following orders when he left the station telephone to assist with baggage.

The second day was largely taken up with the testimony of William Wolfenberger. At one point he insisted, "Had #41 been given orders to 'head in' at Shepherdsville, or had I been informed that I was to pass #41 at Shepherdsville, or had the dispatcher taken into consideration the fact that I was gaining on #41, the wreck would not have occurred." [*The Courier-Journal*, January 12]

The newspaper reported, "In substance, other testimony given by Wolfenberger was the same as introduced at the inquest here to the effect that engineers on fast trains had to maintain high speed when approaching stations in order to 'make' time; that it was a common occurrence for operators to give 'clear' signals before the engineers called for them, and that he had thought the 'clear' signal had been given while a haze of smoke obscured his vision temporarily."

Two other engineers, who were present at the scene of the wreck, were called to testify. Both John Ford, who was a passenger aboard the Accommodation, and H. R. Johnson, who was at the Shepherdsville station, gave testimony that supported that of Wolfenberger.

When Ford was asked, "What's the custom of engineers in regard to signals at such places as Shepherdsville?" he responded, "Sometimes the signal is given by the operator before it is called for, and sometimes the engineer has to call for the signal twice." [*The Louisville Times*, January 11]

The newspaper reported that "Ford also testified that engineers on fast trains seldom come toward such stations under control. Johnson said, in his opinion, had #41 gone on to Bardstown Junction instead of attempting to take the siding at Shepherdsville, #41 would not have been struck. This statement corroborated one previously made by Wolfenberger. Other statements made by Engineer Wolfenberger were corroborated by Johnson and Ford."

The Kentucky Railroad Commission issued its report at the end of January. In perhaps the most comprehensive statement yet, it laid blame eight different ways.

1. "That the train dispatcher at Louisville did not perform his full duty; in that he did not specifically order trains #41 and #7 to pass each other upon the evening of December 20th, at Shepherdsville."

2. "That the operator at Strawberry failed in his duty in that he did not promptly report the passing of trains #41 and #7 to the train dispatcher."

3. "That the operator at Brooks failed in his duty; in that he did not promptly report the passing of trains #41 and #7 by the station at Brooks."

4. "That Weatherford was confused, no doubt, by the complicated rules relating to his duty as operator, ... and that being confused he exercised woefully bad judgment in looking after the baggage instead of staying in his office 'when trains are due and standing at the station.' But we find that the rules were calculated to mislead him. Also his conduct seems to have the approval of the officials of the company, notwithstanding the fact the rules provide that 'the telephone and telegraph service must always be regarded as first in importance.' ... We find also that the strong presumption is that at the time #7 sounded the station whistle he should have been in his office and that the signal green should have been changed to red."

5. "That the conductor and flagman of train crew 41 failed in their duty; in not placing fusees on the track or torpedoes on the track, or protecting the rear of train 41, when 41 was running late under such circumstances that it might be overtaken by #7."

6. "That Wolfenberger failed in his duty; in that he did not bring his train under control at Shepherdsville, when he was 'in doubt' as to whether or not the signal had been changed from 'red to green' in his sight."

7. "That the rules of the company in many instances are too vague and indefinite and that employees on some occasions are permitted such latitude in their discretion that it is not compatible with safety and that under the rules of the company the same acts may either be commended or condemned."

8. "That the management of the Louisville and Nashville Railroad Company has not adequately equipped its system with the necessary safety devices."

It is significant that, while they declared that Wolfenberger had "failed in his duty," they also said, "we find that his failure to do so was under such circumstances as were calculated to mislead any engineer of extraordinary prudence and skill; and that it would have required more than human intelligence for him to have anticipated that the green signal thus displayed at Shepherdsville indicated a danger signal which should require him to stop." The entire Kentucky Railroad Commission report may be read in Appendix H.

An Engineer's Perspective

Jason Kelley, writing for the *Locomotive Engineers Journal* in January 1918, gave an opinion from the perspective of an engineer.

He wrote, "When a wreck like that at Shepherdsville, Ky., takes place, conditions are brought to light that are apparently amazing to the State Inspectors, and the public in general, but the men in the service are facing these conditions every day and night in many places, fully conscious of the possibilities, even surprised that the inevitable disaster does not take place more often, and the nerve-racking effect of it all is reflected in the careworn look of the engineer at the end of a trip on one of these so-called flyers, on roads where the mechanical aids and general system of train operation are wholly inadequate for that class of train service."

Appendix G contains all of Mr. Kelley's comments on this topic.

Interstate Commerce Commission

On January 28, in his report to the Interstate Commerce Commission, H. W. Belnap, Chief of the Bureau of Safety, stated, "The direct cause of this accident was the failure of the conductor and flagman of train 41 properly to protect their train. Knowing that they were on the time of train 7, and that it could not be far behind, the action of these two experienced employees in failing to protect their train is inexcusable."

He continued, "A material contributing cause of the accident was the failure of Engineman Wolfenberger properly to observe the train order signal at Shepherdsville and so control his train as to stop before passing the signal, as required by rule.

"A large measure of responsibility for this accident must rest with the operating officers of the Louisville & Nashville Railroad for their failure to provide proper means of spacing trains in this territory."

He was especially critical of the inadequacy of the rules used to control trains on that stretch of road. He charged that "The Louisville & Nashville Railroad in its annual reports to the Interstate Commerce Commission has repeatedly stated that this section of the road from Louisville to Bardstown Junction was operated under manual-block rules. It is clearly disclosed by this investigation, however, that such protection is not afforded, and furthermore it is evident that such protection was not intended to be given."

Mr. Belnap's entire report may be read in Appendix I.

Criminal Court Cases

In April, in the Bullitt County Circuit Court, the railroad was found guilty of "maintaining a common nuisance" and fined $8,420. [Bullitt Circuit Court Order Book 7, page 334]

The railroad appealed their conviction to the Kentucky Court of Appeals, and in October the conviction was overturned. In its judgment, the court stated "In order to sustain a penal prosecution against a railroad company for running its trains in city or country at a higher or even dangerous rate of speed, either upon a street or in approaching a crossing, it must be shown that such running of the trains was attended with a failure on the part of those operating them to give the necessary and usual signals of their coming."

"Since it was neither alleged in the indictment nor proved by the Commonwealth that the running of such trains was without the customary and necessary warnings of their approach," the judgment against the railroad was overturned. The Court of Appeals judgment may be found in Appendix K.

The Bullitt County indictments against Wolfenberger were continued to the August term. Then on 7 Aug 1918 the jury found him not guilty on the first indictment. Since the second indictment was based on the same evidence as the first, that indictment was dismissed at the request of the Commonwealth Attorney, J. Lewis Williams. [Bullitt Circuit Court Order Book 7, pages 333, 364]

Civil Court Cases

The railroad was able to settle many of the damage claims out of court, but a number of the larger claims required them to go to trial.

This was the case with the Muirs, Mabel Brown Miller, Emily Mashburn, and Lillian Miller, all who were killed, and J. E. Smith who was injured, all of Bardstown.

Recognizing that these were likely to be difficult and expensive trials, the railroad had its lawyers try to take advantage of what might be a loophole in the law that would prevent them from being sued by these people.

With the nation at war, the federal government had taken control of the nation's railroads shortly after the wreck occurred, and it was the contention of the railroad that since the government was in charge of the railroads before any of these had filed suits, and since the federal government, under law, cannot be sued without its consent, these suits could not proceed.

To do this, they had to move the cases from state court in Nelson County to Federal District Court, which combined all of them into one judgment.

It was the decision of that court that the railroad's arguments were flawed, and the cases were returned to Nelson County Circuit Court for settlement.

To read the entire court record of this case, see Appendix J.

Life Goes On

Except for those who lost their lives in the wreck, even with the physical and emotional scars, life for those who remained had to go on.

Arthur Burns and Mamie Ice were married on Christmas day, just five days after her mother's death.

Jackson Morrison printed an announcement in *The Pioneer News* that he could no longer keep his shoe shop in Shepherdsville, but would still do work in his home.

In February, numerous legal suits against the railroad were filed in Bullitt County. Most would be settled out of court. Also in February, the pocketbook of Mrs. H. H. Mashburn was found. Perhaps it had been buried under snow during that difficult winter. Late that month, perhaps to build good will, the railroad installed a telephone at the Shepherdsville depot for the convenience of the public.

Then in May, Miss Fanny Bell Melton, assistant teacher at Bardstown Junction, was slightly injured at the Shepherdsville depot when the Bardstown train in which she was riding, was thrown from the track, and two coaches came near overturning. Fortunately, no one was seriously injured.

The Louisville and Nashville railroad paid out thousands of dollars in compensation to those injured, and to the families of those killed in the 1917 wreck. Not all payments are known, but some that are include $12,500 to Arch Pulliam for his wife's death, $13,000 to Rev. Mashburn for his wife, $32,000 for the deaths of the Cherry family, $15,000 for the death and injuries suffered by the Craven family, $25,000 to the Mack Miller family, $16,000 for the

Overalls, and over $32,000 for the Muir family.

The horrific shock of the death toll at Shepherdsville would not bring an end to accidents along the tracks.

Nearly six months later, on June 9th, train #7 was running 25 minutes late, and at about 50 mph when it wrecked at Huber Station. Although many were hurt badly, there were no fatalities this time.

According to the newspaper report, "the steel coaches, although hurled with terrific force against the sides of a deep cut, did not collapse, and the occupants were shaken about like dice in a box as some of the coaches turned over and over."

A full quarter mile of track was destroyed as the coaches were piled onto the northbound track in the upcoming path of troop trains just minutes away. Fortunately, they were stopped in time.

Four had to be hospitalized including J. B. Arnold of Lebanon Junction, J. B. Oliver of Louisville, Mrs. Emma Wendell of Indianapolis, and W. C. Sanders of Wythville, Virginia. Mr. Arnold's injuries included three broken ribs, severely strained right knee, and head badly bruised with a cut on his right cheek. These were typical of the injuries sustained by others on the train.

The cause of this wreck appeared to have been either a broken flange, broken axle bars, or spreading tracks, typical problems often found to be the cause of accidents.

Nine days later, tragedy struck again, this time near Bardstown Junction. Passenger train

#24 was northbound that morning along a straight stretch of track when an automobile containing five people attempted to cross the tracks. The automobile stalled on the tracks, and the driver had gotten out to try to crank it when the locomotive hit it.

Four of the five passengers were killed instantly. The fifth, Letitia Lee died at the hospital in Louisville. The others were Mrs. Emma Shelton, John Henry Lee, seven-year-old Ethel Lee Howlett, and Sarah Elizabeth Lee, Letitia's month-old baby.

The 1917 wreck has remained an event of interest down through the years. It has been written about a number of times, and Lloyd "Hog" Mattingly of Lebanon Junction hand-crafted a model of the wreck that is remarkably true to the event as told in newspapers. Mr. Mattingly's other work includes a model of Paroquet Springs Hotel, located in the Convention Center in Shepherdsville, and other models on display in the Museum.

Mr. Mattingly's train wreck model was refurbished by Betty Hartley and is now on display on the second floor of the Bullitt County Courthouse, overlooking the actual scene of the wreck.

Descendants viewing the train wreck model.

On the 90th anniversary of the train wreck, a memorial service was held at the Court House overlooking the wreck site. Well over a hundred descendants of wreck victims were present.

And on August 11, 2009, a historical marker commemorating the train wreck was dedicated. Located next to the Ridgway Library, and across from the site of the wreck. It is shown below.

Nearly a hundred people have been identified who were aboard the Accommodation at Shepherdsville on 20 Dec 1917.

The newspapers of Louisville, Shepherdsville, Bardstown, and Springfield all reported lists of those killed in the train wreck. The earliest reports, such as the one shown below, had fewer than 40 deaths, but that number quickly rose, and varied from report to report.

By merging all of these reports together we have a list of fifty-one individuals reported killed in the wreck. However, there are some discrepancies in the individual lists.

In an attempt to create a definitive list we examined both death certificates recorded in Bullitt and Jefferson counties, and stories in the newspapers that positively identify individuals by name other than just on the lists of dead.

THAT hideous thing that threatens civilisation can be defeated only by the united effort of every civilised individual. If you can't fight you can help by joining the Red Cross.

The Courier-Journal.

THE Louisville world is in need of the service you have to offer— listen to the calls made to you by the want ad spokesman.

VOL. CXXVIII. NEW SERIES—NO. 17,887—   LOUISVILLE, FRIDAY MORNING, DECEMBER 21, 1917.—TWELVE PAGES.   PRICE TWO CENTS

39 DIE IN CRASH OF L. & N. TRAINS AT SHEPHERDSVILLE

We find death certificates for thirty-seven that were recorded in Bullitt County at the scene of the wreck. They include the following people, listed in alphabetical order: Eugene Bertello, Hollis Bridges, Josie Bridges, Mahlon Campbell, Carrie Cherry, Redford C. Cherry, Redford C. Cherry, Jr., George Duke, Virginia Duke, Lawrence Greenwell, Joseph Raoul Hurst, Louisa Hurst, Kate Ice, David Maraman, Emily Mashburn, Elizabeth McElroy, Amelia Miller, Lillian Miller, Mack Miller, Lucas Moore, James Morrison, Cora May Muir, George Shadburne Muir, Nat. W. Muir, Frank L. Nunn, Estelle Nutt, Forest Overall, Maggie Overall, Bettie Phillips, David Phillips, John T. Phillips, Alice Pulliam, Emory Samuels, Thomas Schaefer, Carrie May Simmons, James W. Stansbury, and Ben Talbott.

Additionally, although we find no death certificates for Garnette McKay Moore, Mary Alethaire Simms, Thomas Spalding, or James Thompson, each is identified in an obituary in at least one newspaper that identifies him or her as

having died at the scene in Shepherdsville. That brings our total of dead at the scene to forty-one.

A Louisville newspaper article names Mr. N. H. Thompson as one who died on the relief train on the way to Louisville. No death certificate or other death record has been found for him. He would be number forty-two.

These died at the hospital on Dec 21 and have death certificates: Mattie E. Harmon, William C. Johnson, Mabel Brown Miller, and Raymond Thomas Craven who was identified in The Louisville Herald as the forty-sixth victim.

Henry Z. Hardaway has a death certificate that shows he died on Dec 24. A newspaper article identifies him as the forty-seventh victim.

Silas Lawrence of Springfield died on Jan 2 at the hospital. He was identified in The Springfield Sun and Kentucky Standard as the forty-eighth victim.

Joshua Bethel Bowles died on Jan 5 at the hospital, reportedly of blood poisoning. He was identified in *The Courier-Journal* as the forty-ninth victim.

J. B. BOWLES SUCCUMBS; WRECK DEATH LIST 49

——•——

Blood Poisoning From Injury Causes Bardstown Man's Death.

——•——

The forty-ninth victim of the Shepherdsville wreck died at Sts. Mary and Elizabeth Hospital yesterday. He was J. B. Bowles, a saddle horse breeder, of Bardstown. His death was due to blood poisoning which resulted when a shattered ankle became infected.

Mr. Bowles' wife, Mrs. Mary B. Bowles, was at his bedside when he died. She had been in constant attendance upon her husband. His parents, who were members of pioneer families of Bardstown, now live in North Carolina. Mr. Bowles had won many stakes and ribbons with his horses at shows in Madison Square Garden, New York, the Kentucky State Fair and other nation-wide exhibitions. One of his prize winners was Fairway. He formerly was a member of the State Board of Agriculture and had been prominent for years in the conduct of the State Fair.

That leaves us with Joseph Marks and J. W. Thompson who were each listed in at least one newspaper among those killed. However, neither has a death certificate that places him in the wreck, nor is there any other account of either one's death. As you will read later, we suspect that Joseph Marks did not die as a result of the wreck. As for J. W. Thompson, we suspect that

he and James Thompson, named above, are one and the same.

Thus we conclude that there were, in fact, forty-nine who died as a result of the crash.

We have attempted to learn more about all of these people. In some cases, information has been relatively abundant; in a handful of other cases it has been almost non-existent. We have searched census records, marriage records, military records, birth and death records, and court records to write a sketch of each one. In some cases we have been fortunate to talk with descendants who have given us a family perspective of the lives of these folk.

What follows on the next pages are brief sketches of each of the people we have identified as being aboard the Accommodation that evening. In the sketches we have tried to relate what little is known from newspaper accounts of the day about each person, as well as a summary of what we have learned about their ancestry, and for those who survived the wreck, what became of them afterward.

Regrettably, there are a handful of them who have proven to be too elusive for us. For most of the others we have been able to provide a bit more detail. Since the last publication of this story we have learned still more about many of them, and that information has been added to this edition.

We are grateful to those who have provided insight and additional information beyond that available in the written records. We are especially grateful to the family members who shared stories handed down from one generation to the next.

The People of the Wreck

More than a hundred people were involved in this terrible tragedy. In this section, we will take a closer look at each of them.

Father Eugenio Bertello

Eugenio Angelo Luigi Bertello was born 11 Jun 1885 in Torino (Turin), Italy to Eugenio and Lucia (Ponzio) Bertello. He had at least one sister, Anna Eugenia Catterina Bertello who was two years older.

Twenty-two years later, in the summer of 1907, Eugenio said good-bye to his family, and began a journey that would bring him to America. He traveled to the coast at Genoa, and there, on 8 Jul 1907, boarded the Cretic, a passenger ship destined for New York. Nineteen days later, Eugenio spotted the Statue of Liberty through the harbor mist. He was processed at Ellis Island like so many other immigrants, and then made his way to Chicago to the Church of Assumption school where he completed his education.

He was ordained to the priesthood in Louisville on 19 Dec 1908, and assigned to minister to several small churches in rural Bullitt and Nelson Counties, including St. Margaret at Pitts Point, St. Eugene at Bardstown Junction, St. Gregory at Samuels in Nelson County, and St. John near Deatsville.

Father Bertello found a promising nucleus of Catholic families at the thriving little village of Chapeze, and received permission to build a church there. According to Mrs. Ivy T. McBride, "He was granted special permission to live and to say mass in the home of Mr. Ben Chapeze during the building interim. Mr. Chapeze had donated the land and lumber for the building

purpose, and [Father Bertello] was also furnished funds by his dear old Italian mother. It was a small, but very lively church within." Father Bertello gave it the name Church of the Holy Redeemer.

He was one of the most popular priests who ever had charge of churches in the Chapeze neighborhood. He took active part in activities of young folks and was a welcomed addition to social events. He was a stocky man of

Father Bertello
(image from microfilm)

vitality and enthusiasm, according to one report, who spoke broken English when he delivered simple, strong, wholesome sermons. On his declaration of intent to become an American citizen in 1913, he described himself as 5'6" tall, weighing 154 lbs, with black hair, brown eyes, and a scar on his upper lip.

According to Mrs. McBride, Shepherdsville had been without a Catholic church prior to 1912, with mass being said either in a private home or at a skating rink across from the railroad depot. When the rink burned down in 1903, mass was said at the court house. However, under Father Bertello's leadership, a church lot was donated by Henry Clay Bowman, father of Emma Maraman, an early active parishioner. The church was dedicated on 1 Sep 1912 by Bishop O'Donaghue.

Father Bertello continued to live at Chapeze, and traveled to his various ministries, often on his small pony named Keno.

In the year leading up to the train wreck, he was involved in three other accidents, one a runaway, and two involving automobiles. In the last one, in June, his automobile turned over, pinning him beneath the car. For weeks after the accident his condition was serious and for several days recovery was doubtful.

However, as Christmas approached, he was back at his duties. With but five days before Christmas, life was slowly getting back to normal after a fierce winter storm. A blanket of snow still rested on much of the landscape reflecting the remaining rays of a setting sun.

Father Bertello was in Shepherdsville at Troutman's undertaking establishment. He had a very sick parishioner living south of town and planned to take the train to visit him. As the train approached Shepherdsville, he and Henry Wathen were heading to the depot together when a friend drove up in a buggy and called to Wathen to make his trip in the buggy instead of the train. Bertello bade him a pleasant journey and prepared to board the train.

Mere minutes later, Father Eugenio Bertello was dead.

In the archives of the Sisters of Charity at Nazareth, we read that "Father Eugene Bertello had been on the train but about three minutes when the accident occurred. He was carrying the Blessed Sacrament to some sick person. When attention was attracted by his groans, he was found clinging with his arm to the hot boiler. His face was much disfigured as he was badly scalded." He died at the scene.

One can only imagine the grief and profound sadness that filled the home of his parents when the church's representative delivered the sad news of his death.

After Father Bertello's tragic death, he was succeeded by Rev. Joseph McAleer until 1920, and thereafter by Rev. Leo Smith until 1924.

On January 28, 1920 there was a damaging fire at Chapeze, but the furnishings were saved, and the damaged building soon repaired. However since St. Aloysius in Shepherdsville was becoming the center of Bullitt County missions, Father Smith dissembled the living quarters and church contents at Chapeze. Father Pitt, who succeeded Father Smith sold the Chapeze building to a private owner in 1942 and it still stands as a private residence.

St. Aloysius stands today as a legacy of the efforts of Father Eugenio Bertello to minister to the needs of those of the Catholic faith in Bullitt County.

Joshua Bethel Bowles

James William Bowles and his brother John Bethel Bowles had been prisoners of war during the Civil War. John died while trying to escape the prison camp, but James survived. Following the war's end, he returned home to Kentucky, and the next April (1866) he married Annie Fredericka Pope in Nelson County.

Annie was the only child of Godfrey and Nancy (Minor) Pope. Her father, who had been publisher/editor of *The Louisville Sun*, was killed during the Mexican War.

James and Annie obtained their passports in May and, along with James' sisters Margaret and Mary Elizabeth, left for a tour of Europe. They had reached Paris when Annie gave birth on 28 Feb 1867 to a son they named Joshua Bethel Bowles after James' father, a prosperous farmer turned merchant and banker in Louisville.

Following their European trip, James brought his wife and son back to Louisville where he was involved in real estate. Together they would add seven more children to the family including Nancy, Grace, Mary Guthrie who died as an infant, Julia, Frederick, Octavius, and Mary Caperton Bowles who married William Dale and lived to be a hundred years old. But that first son, Joshua Bethel Bowles, is our subject.

Young Joshua grew up in Louisville, but family ties to Bardstown led him to meet Margaret Eleanor Nicholls, better known as Madge. They were married in Bardstown on 16 Mar 1893, and made Nelson County their home.

Tragedy struck the Bowles family in the last half of the 1890's. First, in November 1896, Joshua's young 15-year-old brother Octavius Shreve Bowles suffered an appendicitis attack, and died despite an emergency operation.

Then in 1899, Joshua's sister Nancy died after giving birth. Her husband, Major William F. Lewis, was an army surgeon stationed in Cuba at the time. Her mother had traveled to Baltimore to be with Nancy during the birth. When Nancy died two weeks later, her body was returned to Louisville for burial in the family plot. The baby, little Fredericka, was raised by her grandparents who moved to North Carolina following James' retirement in 1903.

Meanwhile, Joshua, or J.B. as he was apparently known, turned his hand to breeding saddle horses and became one of the leading breeders in Kentucky until the advent of the motor car. Hardly missing a beat, J.B. began breeding Holstein cattle and was head of the Kaintuckee Holstein Company. He was one of the wealthiest and best known citizens in Nelson County, and was at one time secretary of the Kentucky State Fair, and also a member of the State Board of Agriculture.

Since he was traveling without Madge, he was in Louisville either on business or perhaps shopping for Madge's Christmas present on the day of the accident. We're not certain whether he was in the coach or the smoker car when it happened.

He was one of those taken on the relief train to Saints Mary and Elizabeth Hospital. There he lingered a bit more than two weeks before succumbing to his injuries on January 5th.

News reports differ on the nature of his injuries. On 11 Jan 1918, *The Pioneer News* of Shepherdsville reported he died of blood poisoning when a severe ankle injury became infected. This combined with internal injuries to bring on his death. However, *The Springfield Sun* reported on 10 Jan 1918 that "Mr. Bowles suffered only bruises about the body. No bones were broken, but he suffered seriously from the shock, and it is thought this contributed more largely to his death than anything else, although it was thought probable he might have suffered some internal injuries." Finally, his death certificate lists the cause of death as shock and internal injuries.

Grave Inscriptions

Joshua and Madge Bowles had no children. Following his death, Madge lived for a while at home. With her were her parents, John and Annie Nicholls, in the 1920 census. Sometime later she married Dr. James C. Montgomery and they lived in Hardin County. Madge died on 19 Nov 1950 in Elizabethtown.

Joshua's parents and remaining siblings, were living in Waynesville, North Carolina with their daughters Grace and Julia, and their granddaughter Frederika Lewis when James died in 1921. Annie lived until 1928. The two sisters, Grace and Julia, continued living in Waynesville until their deaths in 1938 and 1957,

Bowles Family Monument
Cave Hill Cemetery

respectively. Joshua's brother Fred married Isabelle Williams in North Carolina, and they moved to Florida to live. Mary Caperton married William Dale, and they lived in Columbia, Tennessee which was their final resting place.

Following their deaths, all the siblings, but one, were returned to Louisville to join their parents and grandparents in the family plot at Cave Hill Cemetery, together again.

Henry Bowman

Henry Bowman was seven years old when the Civil War began; and eleven when the Thirteenth Amendment ended the institution of slavery in Kentucky. But people of his race soon

discovered that freedom would not mean equality in American society for years to come. Segregation was a fact of life in 1917, and when Henry boarded the train in Shepherdsville he moved directly to the front end of the combination smoker and colored car. Quite possibly this saved his life.

Henry's parents were Basil Bowman and Lida Crigler. He and Bertha Hardin, daughter of James and Sarah Hardin, were married in 1878. They had ten children, three of whom would not live to see the 1910 census. Henry and Bertha lived on a small farm near Bardstown Junction. Their eldest son, John Henry Bowman lived nearby with his wife Nellie (Simmons) Bowman, and two daughters. The other two boys, George and Howard were living at home. George worked for Standard Oil; Howard was a section hand for the railroad.

Howard had married Susie Lillian Murphy the previous year, and they were proud of their baby boy they named Charles.

When the wreck occurred, Henry suffered serious injuries. It was reported that he suffered either a broken hip or a fractured leg, and body bruises. However, he didn't make it to the hospital in Louisville until the next day, for as he said, he was "afraid to trust the train."

The following February, *The Pioneer News* reported that Henry Bowman was suing the railroad for his injuries, and asking for $10,000. The paper later reported that the case had been dismissed and settled, with no indication what he actually received.

In April, their son George was called to active duty and reported to Camp Taylor in Louisville. He would serve until released in July 1919.

That Fall (1918) tragedy struck again. Henry and Bertha's son Howard was hospitalized and died that September. Then in December, his widow also died, leaving the infant child for Henry and Bertha to rear.

With George returning home, and John Henry nearby to help with the farm, and the grandchildren around to bring them joy, life would go on.

Henry Bowman died at home on 13 Mar 1931 at the age of 77. George continued to live at home with his widowed mother until her death ten years later.

James & Margaret Bradbury

James Madden Bradbury was one of four brothers and a sister born to John and Frances (Mathis) Bradbury. His grandfather was Henry Bradbury who was a native of England, and a teacher by trade; and his great-grandfather, John Bradbury, was one of the first two professional naturalists to explore any part of the Louisiana Purchase (the other being Thomas Nuttall).

The brothers included George Henry, William Oscar, and Charles Preston Bradbury. Della Mae Bradbury McClure was his sister. Of these, George was a farmer and a postman, delivering the mail to his section of Bullitt County for many years. William was a professor at the Bryant & Stratton Business College in Louisville; and Charles, or C. P. as he was known, was a teacher, a school superintendent, a county attorney, county judge, and one-time State Representative. Della Mae married Thomas B. McClure, a farmer.

James started out as a farmer, likely a dairy farmer, before taking a job with the Ewing Dairy in Louisville. He married Margaret Belle Patterson in 1909. She was the daughter of John B. and Elizabeth Patterson of Lexington.

James' brother, William Oscar Bradbury, died of typhoid in 1910, leaving his wife Myrtle and daughter Frances Vera.

James and Margaret had a daughter Evelyn May in 1910, but before her sixth birthday she died of bronchial pneumonia. They were not to have any more children.

James suffered another lose when his father died a month later, in February 1916, at the age of 81.

It is uncertain if James and Margaret rode the train from Louisville, or boarded it at Shepherdsville to head home; but it seems likely that they were in the forward smoking car since they escaped the worst of the injuries. The reports of James and Margaret's injuries in the train wreck vary from paper to paper, but generally it appears that James suffered some internal injuries and his condition was considered serious for a time. Margaret seems to have suffered some scalp injuries as well.

When James completed his World War I draft card in September 1918, the Bradbury's were living in Louisville where James was working for D. H. Ewing's dairy. They were still there in the 1920 census, but by 1930 they had moved to Oldham County where James was once again farming. This didn't last, as they were living in Lexington during the 1940 census; and were there in 1956 when James died at the age of 78.

Of his other siblings, his sister Della Mae died in 1939, leaving her husband, T. B. McClure, two sons, Clyde and Woodrow, and a daughter Mildred Frances Cornell. Della was 59.

His brother Charles lived until 1964, following a long and distinguished career.

Ironically, James' older brother, George H. Bradbury, was killed on 19 Sep 1936 when he tried to cross the railroad track ahead of an oncoming train near Belmont, KY. He was 74, a retired postman.

Hollie and Josie Bridges

Hollie and Josie Bridges attended a commercial school in Louisville, and rode the train from their home in the Samuels precinct of Nelson County to Louisville each day for classes. Their parents, Tom and Nannie Bridges expected them home on the evening train from Louisville in time for supper. They wouldn't make it. Instead Tom had the grim task of collecting their caskets at the Samuels depot the next day.

This Bridges family had roots in Bullitt County. Joel Thomas Bridges was born there in 1868 to John and Paulina (Tucker) Bridges; Nannie was born two years later to James M. and Susan (Hill) Lee. They were married in Bullitt County in January, 1892, and their first child, Bessie was born in December. Next was a son, Fayette Hewitt Bridges, who was born in 1896. He was followed by a daughter, Josie, who was born in 1899. She was followed a year later by a son they named Hollie.

In November 1911, Tom and Nannie witnessed Bessie's marriage to John Cotton. John and Bessie would have at least four children: Dixie (1912), Edna Ray (1915), Russell (1919), and Bessie (1924).

Fayette Bridges was inducted into military service on 15 Aug 1918, and sent to Indianapolis for training. Sometime after that, he married Laura Fardette, probably in Pittsburgh where she lived. They had a son named Robert Elwood Bridges in 1922, in Pittsburgh. By 1930 they were living in St. Louis.

Tom and Nannie moved to the Zoneton Road area in Bullitt County where Tom died in 1930. Nannie lived until 1954 with her daughter and grandchildren nearby.

Charles Arthur Cahoe

In their effort to report on the wreck as quickly as possible, the newspaper reporters were surprisingly accurate in gathering names and medical conditions of those involved. In one instance, however, careless penmanship may have led to the misidentification of Arthur Cahoe of Loretto. His last name was printed in several papers as Tahoe, rather that Cahoe.

The papers all reported that he had a gash on the front of his head, and other minor injuries.

From various census records, we believe that Charles Arthur Cahoe was a son of Gonza and Isabelle Cahoe. He survived his injuries, and we discover him in Maynard, Fayette County, Iowa in the 1920 census. There he was working as a farmhand for a farmer named Ross Ashbaugh.

Ashbaugh died in July 1921, and in October his wife Effie was charged with poisoning him with arsenic. Cahoe was charged as well. Despite the sensational headlines and newspaper articles, Mrs. Ashbaugh was acquitted in December. Then in January, all charges against Cahoe were dropped.

Arthur and Effie were married in April 1923. They would have two children, Shirley and James, before Effie died

Arthur Cahoe

in 1934. Sad to say, the children were taken from Cahoe and placed in foster care due to his frequent drinking.

Arthur Cahoe died in 1965 in Iowa, and is buried beside Effie in the Mount Olivet Cemetery in Waterloo.

Mahlon Campbell

Mahlon Campbell was born in Mumfordville in 1869 to Henry and Ellen Campbell. Henry was a carpenter by trade. By the time Mahlon was ten, the family had moved to Louisville, and were living on West Jefferson Street, just a few blocks from the railroad tracks. We can imagine his fascination with trains as a boy might have led him to work for the railroad as a man. Census records tell us that he was already a train conductor by 1900.

Mahlon married Elizabeth "Lizzie" Klages in Louisville in July 1891. She was a daughter of Henry and Mary (Meyers) Klages. They were not to have any children of their own, but events in the year leading up to the accident profoundly changed their lives.

Elizabeth's younger sister, Margaret had married William H. Kraft and they had two boys, Mahlon and Leroy. Margaret developed pulmonary tuberculosis and her family was forced to watch her waste away until her death in September 1916. William was left with two young children to rear. It may have been too much for him because he committed suicide a year later.

The two boys, then ages ten and seven, came to live with their Aunt Lizzie and Uncle Mahlon. Just as they were beginning to settle into their new home, tragedy struck their young lives again when Uncle Mahlon was killed in the train wreck.

Elizabeth Campbell received some compensation money from the railroad and used it to buy a house located at 1911 West Broadway in Louisville. There she brought the boys to live. Living there also according to the 1920 census were Elizabeth's brother, Charles Klages, and her sister Josephine with her husband and two children.

Young Mahlon and Leroy grew to adulthood in that home, and Elizabeth lived there until her death in February 1953 of congestive heart failure. She was buried in Cave Hill Cemetery next to her husband; together again.

James Marion Carrico

James Marion Carrico was born in 1883 to Thomas and Maggie (Mullican) Carrico, the eldest son in a large farm family in Marion County. With seven brothers in the family, James decided to leave the farming to the others, and went to work for the railroad as an express messenger.

By 1900 there were four principal parcel express companies: Adams Express Company, Southern Express Company, American Express Company, and Wells Fargo. In 1913 the Post Office introduced its parcel post service, which offered major competition for the express companies. But despite this, private railway express business increased steadily through the end of World War I.

James apparently spotted the approaching train at Shepherdsville, and leaped from the baggage car in time to save his life. He did suffer several broken ribs and some bruises from his jump.

James was living in Springfield when he married Mary Grundy, daughter of Charles Lee and Lucy (McMakin) Grundy, in 1923. They would have no children.

James continued to work as an express messenger until his retirement. They had moved to Louisville as early as 1935, and James died there in 1957. His body was returned to Springfield for burial in the St. Rose Cemetery.

Mary continued living in Louisville until her death in 1963.

Walter Augustine Carter

Frank and Susan (Mattingly) Carter already had two sons, Carroll and Ambrose, when Susan gave birth to twins in December 1899. They were named Walter and Mary.

As a young man, Walter Augustine Carter found employment at Nazareth College as a dairyman, an occupation he knew well from working on his parents' farm. He was on his way there when the wreck occurred.

The next day, *The Louisville Times* reported, "Walter Carter, of Cloverport, was dreaming he was in a railroad wreck and awoke suddenly to find his head jammed through a window. He was taken to Sts. Mary and Elizabeth Hospital with a deep gash in his scalp."

After he recovered, he returned to his job at Nazareth. He was there in the following September when he completed his World War I draft registration, recording his birth as 6 Dec 1899. He would not see his nineteenth birthday.

In November he became ill with pneumonia, one of many who would succumb that winter. He died on November 16 back at Sts. Mary & Elizabeth hospital, a victim of pneumonia in both lungs.

His twin sister Mary never married. Twenty years after the death of her brother, she died of pulmonary tuberculosis.

Benjamin Chapeze

Ben Chapeze followed the tradition of his namesake grandfather, becoming a noted attorney in the region.

Ben was born in 1863, the son of Adam and Mariah (Smith) Chapeze. His father and uncle, also named Benjamin, were in the distillery business at Chapeze Station, a community named for the Chapeze family which began there with Ben's grandparents, Benjamin and Elizabeth (Shepherd) Chapeze. (Elizabeth was a daughter of Adam Shepherd, for whom Shepherdsville is named.)

Ben Chapeze was educated in the local schools including Pitts Point Academy, and finished his education at St. Joseph's College at Bardstown. He began the practice of law in 1888, and was elected Bullitt County Attorney two years later.

He seemed to be a confirmed bachelor until Lizzie Marion Newman caught his eye. Lizzie had arrived with her parents and siblings from England around 1882, when she was but a child; but that child blossomed into a beautiful woman, and they were married in June, 1900. Their daughter, Elizabeth Marion Chapeze was born a year later.

Then tragedy struck the family. According to a Newman family member, Lizzie Marion Newman Chapeze died on 30 Mar 1903. Ben was devastated, but set at once to be the best father he could be for his infant daughter. His sister, Flaget Chapeze helped to rear the child. Later, the newspaper's editor would write, "his deep devotion to his motherless daughter has won and held the admiration of his friends."

He was in Shepherdsville as the attorney for Thomas Hoagland in Hoagland's case against the railroad in the death of his son earlier in the year. On the day of the wreck, the case was called, the jurors selected, and testimony begun. Then, with the day drawing to a close, the trial was continued to the next morning. Chapeze and Hoagland went to the depot in Shepherdsville to await the arrival of the Accommodation train so that they could sleep in their own beds for the evening. It was not to be.

While Hoagland suffered serious injuries and had to be hospitalized, it appears that Ben Chapeze's injuries were less severe. He said he remembered nothing of the wreck at all, except that when he woke up he was at the home of a friend, Francis Moore in Shepherdsville. With both the plaintiff and his lawyer unable to proceed with the case, the Hoagland case was postponed until the next term of court.

Chapeze would continue his law practice following the wreck, but kidney disease would bring an end to his life in September 1925. The week after his death, a good friend, Wallace A. McKay wrote a tribute to his memory. It included these words:

"Mother Nature never created a man of purer heart or one freer from guile. He believed and practiced that forgiveness is the crown jewel placed in the heart of man by the hand of God. He thought no evil of any man. He carried his heart on his sleeve and trusted many who took advantage of him. He carried no resentments and harbored no malice. He worked and worked in an earnest effort to serve his friends and his clients without a thought of his personal comfort and ofttimes without thought of his pecuniary need. He had no diversion and no hobbies. He took few, if any, vacations and indulged in few pleasures or recreations. His hobby was his law books and his diversion was to find some new case in the reports to help him with some law suit for a client or to solve some vexed problem of the law. Ben Chapeze had a good legal mind which he trained and polished by studious applications and hard work.

"He was never too busy to serve a friend or too tired and fatigued to help out those in trouble or distress. He was not an old man, only a little past the prime of life and his death will leave an aching void in the hearts of a great number of friends who admired and loved him for his many sterling qualities of head and heart.

"He worked until the last and died as he wanted to die, in the harness, having remained in his office in Louisville, busy all day, until he left for the depot to make his last journey to his old home in his beloved county of Bullitt. Peace to his ashes; honor to his memory, rest to his weary soul."

Ernest Chase

Ernest Chase spent almost his entire adult life as a porter for the L. & N. Railroad, but he likely never forgot the close call he experienced in Shepherdsville, nor the sight he witnessed after the wreck.

Ernest was born in Glasgow Junction (now Park City) in 1895 to Eugene and Lillie (Rhodes) Chase. As a teenager, he helped work the family farm, but by the time he registered for the World War I draft in June 1917, he was already working for the railroad as a porter.

He hardly had time to get over the wreck when he was called to active duty and reported to Camp Taylor in April. Three months later he was aboard a ship bound for Europe where he spent nearly a year working in a supply depot. He returned from Bordeaux, France in June 1919, with the rank of corporal.

Returning to America, he went back to work for the railroad. Then, in February 1921, he married Ellie Smith, daughter of William and Addie (Patterson) Smith, in Clark County, Indiana, and they settled in Louisville. They would have no children, and after 34 years of marriage, she obtained a divorce in 1955.

Ernest Chase died at Veterans Hospital in Louisville in November, 1965, and was buried in Eastern Cemetery, bringing to an end a life of hard work in the segregated society in which he found himself.

The Cherry Family

Redford Columbus Cherry was born in 1871, the third son of George W. and Frances Martha (Stahl) Cherry. While much of the family remained in Warren County, including brothers

Henry Hardin Cherry (president of Western Kentucky State Normal School; now W.K.U.) and Thomas Crittenden Cherry (superintendent of Bowling Green public schools), Redford made his way to Bardstown where he was appointed court stenographer before being admitted to the bar.

He married Carrie Lucile Barkhurst in Bardstown in June 1901. They would have three children, Alice, Bess, and young William Redford Cherry.

Mr. Cherry served as city attorney for the town of Bardstown, and was afterwards elected Nelson County Attorney, a post he still held at the time of the wreck.

Carrie Barkhurst Cherry was born in Bardstown in 1878 to George W. and Mary Alice (Wood) Barkhurst. At her death, the local newspaper described her as "a splendid type of womanhood and a fine Christian character." It went on to say that "to her the greatest joys of life were in the home caring for and ministering to the wants of her husband and children."

While the newspapers identified their son as Redford C. Cherry, Jr., his Uncle George Barkhurst gave his name as William Redford Cherry on his death certificate. The boy was but five years old.

The Cherry Family

Redford and Carrie had taken their son to Louisville on a Christmas shopping trip, leaving Alice and Bess with their grandmother. The newspaper obituaries in Bardstown described the trip, saying that young Redford "had gone with his parents to Louisville to see Santa Claus where he had passed the day in looking at the Christmas windows and making purchases for his two sisters at home and for parents and friends."

All three died at the scene of the wreck in Shepherdsville.

After the train wreck took the lives of their parents and brother, the orphaned girls went to live with their maternal grandmother, Alice Barkhurst. Both Alice and Bess later attended and graduated from Randolph-Macon College in Virginia, the nation's oldest Methodist college.

Alice married Herman Kerns Tramell, an attorney, and they lived in Jellico, Tennessee for many years. At her death in 2003, she was 100 years old, and survived by her daughter Alice in Atlanta, and her son Redford who was a Baptist missionary in Peru.

Bess married Marshall Mahan Siler and they lived in Knoxville, Tennessee, and had two children, Caroline and Marshall Jr. Bess was 85 when she died in Knoxville in 1990. Her daughter, Caroline married Robert Hill; and her son Marshall married Janice Edwards of Louisville while both were attending the Southern Baptist Seminary. Marshall Jr. was a Baptist minister.

Had they lived, Redford and Carrie would have taken pride in the accomplishments of their children and grandchildren, but it was not to be.

Ed Clarkson

The good news is that Ed Clarkson seems to have survived the wreck, even though he received injuries to his back and head. The bad news is that this is all we know about him.

He was reported to be from Cloverport, but no one there seemed to know him. A diligent search of *The Breckenridge News*, a local paper in Cloverport turned up his name only once when it wrote on December 26th, "The other victim from here was Ed Clarkson, so far the *Breckenridge News* has been unable to ascertain anything about his condition."

The Louisville Times reported on December 21st that his condition was serious with injuries to his back and head. This was repeated by *The Courier-Journal* the next morning, and *The Kentucky Standard* of Bardstown two days later.

And then silence; no further mention of his condition, except that it appears he must have survived his injuries.

There were Clarkson families in that area, but we've failed to determine that Ed belonged to any of them. The best we can hope is that he later enjoyed a long and prosperous life.

The Craven Family

Thomas Washington Craven and Eliza Marie Montgomery were married in Springfield in March 1909. For a time they lived with his parents, George and Margaret Craven, in Nelson County next door to Thomas' sister and her husband, Ella and Alzo Smith. Eliza's parents were Sam and Alpha (Hobbs) Montgomery.

By the summer of 1917, Thomas was working for the Chess & Wymond Company in Louisville, a company that specialized in making whiskey barrels. He and Eliza, and their two children, Raymond and Annie, were living on Taylor Boulevard.

Eliza Craven
(before the wreck)

As Christmas approached, they decided that Eliza would take Raymond and

Annie to spend the holiday with the Smiths, and Tom would join them later.

When Eliza boarded the train to visit Ella and Alzo Smith, she could not have imagined in her worst nightmare how many terrible blows life would bring her from that moment on.

When the trains crashed, Eliza's body was badly crushed, and her three-year-old son, Raymond's skull was crushed. Both were considered critical when they were placed on the relief train for Louisville.

Annie Craven & Mrs. Trunnell.

What was not known then was that her tiny baby, Annie, who was ten months old that day, was thrown clear of the wreckage into a snow drift. Later when she was found, no one knew who she was. She was taken to the Trunnell Hotel and cared for there.

The image shown here is taken from microfilm of *The Evening Post* of 21 Dec 1917.

The day after the wreck, *The Louisville Times* reported that Eliza's skull was fractured, that her nose was torn off, her upper lip torn half off, and her leg broken.

Tom learned of the accident and rushed to the hospital to learn what had become of his family. There he found his son near death, his wife seriously injured, and his baby girl missing. Young Raymond Craven died early the next morning.

When word came that a baby had been found in Shepherdsville, Thomas rushed there and found his little girl alive and well. He returned to Louisville with the infant and perhaps the sight of her daughter gave Eliza the will to survive.

Indeed, life seemed to go on for the Craven family. Eliza had a son the next year that they named Ival. Then in October of 1919, they had another son they named Edwin Melton Craven. Tragically, this boy was stricken with an inflammation of both the large and small intestine and died shortly after his first birthday.

Once again the family tried to put tragedy behind them. Two daughters, Mary and Violet were added to the family. Then in October 1928 tragedy struck again. Annie, the miracle baby from the train wreck, now eleven years old, was stricken by an attack of appendicitis and died in October 1928.

This last death may have been more than Eliza's frail body could take. Seven months later she was stricken with a brain hemorrhage and died on 18 May 1929.

The family continued to suffer tragedy when Ival Craven, now 31 years old, suffered an epileptic attack, and fell face first into a ditch filled with water, and drowned in 1949.

After Eliza's death, Thomas married again, this time to Margaret Brooks who helped him rear his remaining children. Thomas died in 1963 in Louisville. According to his obituary, he formerly owned Craven's Restauraunt at 29th and Magazine in Louisville.

The photo shown on the previous page of a young Eliza Craven is provided by her great-granddaughter, Judy Simmons.

Frank E. Daugherty

Frank E. Daugherty, was born in 1871 in Bardstown, the youngest of eight children born to Daniel and Sarah Ellen (Slevin) Daugherty.

Frank graduated from St. Joseph College at Bardstown. His first job after graduating was Bardstown correspondent of *The Courier-Journal* and *The Cincinnati Enquirer*. He was barely of legal voting age when elected Circuit Court clerk of Nelson Country, serving one term.

He began the study of law while serving as clerk and was admitted to the bar while holding that office.

He next was elected County Judge in 1897 and served three consecutive terms. After that he was elected Commonwealth's Attorney of the 10th Judicial District and served one term. He was elected State Attorney General in 1923 and served four years. The last public office he held was representative to the Kentucky General Assembly from Nelson and LaRue Counties, serving two terms.

Daugherty was well familiar with the dangers of riding the train between Louisville and Bardstown. In 1899, at Christmastime, he was aboard the local train when a freight appeared through the fog at Gap in Knobs and plowed into the rear of the local train. Injured himself, he had the sad duty to

Frank Daugherty (image from microfilm)

serve as a pall bearer for the funeral of Cora Carothers who had died in the crash.

When the crash occurred at Shepherdsville, Daugherty was sitting with Dr. Dodds of Bardstown Junction. Daugherty suffered a double fracture of the right arm, a broken collar bone, fractured skull and the newspaper reported his right ear was torn off, although later pictures showed it must have been reattached.

Negotiations with the railroad's lawyers results in a payment of $15,000 in compensation for his serious injuries.

At his death in 1951, his obituary reported that he was a past grand knight of the Bardstown Council, Knights of Columbus; and that for years he was the state director of the Kentucky Division of the United States Brewers Foundation.

Daugherty never married, leaving no descendants.

John Gilmore Dodds

On the day following the train wreck, *The Louisville Times* reported, "Dr. J. G. Dobbs, of Bardstown, was sitting with Frank E. Daugherty, former Commonwealth's Attorney, when the crash came."

We find no evidence of a Dr. Dobbs in Bardstown in any of the censuses from 1900 through 1930, nor in any separate newspaper reports during that time period. Instead we do find Dr. John Gilmore Dodds at Bardstown Junction in Bullitt County. We believe he was the gentleman in the wreck.

John Gilmore Dodds was born in 1868 to Josiah C. and Margaret Anne (Hutchison) Dodds in Mt. Joy, Scioto County, Ohio. As a young man, he was working on Matthew Martin's farm in McLean County, Illinois when he journeyed back to Ohio in August 1898 to marry his sweetheart, Clara V. Wolford, daughter of Eli and Juliann (Blake) Wolford. They returned together to Illinois for a time while he studied to become a doctor.

We know that they were living at Bardstown Junction as early as 1907, and that he was practicing medicine there. Their daughter Margaret was born there in 1911.

The newspaper interviewed Dr. Dodds, and printed his statement in which he said, "There was no apparent slacking of the train's speed and no jarring crash. Suddenly the car began to fold up from the giant force pushing from behind. I found myself rolled in a ball in one corner with screaming women and fighting men piled about me."

Four different Louisville newspapers reported on Dr. Dodds' condition following the wreck. *The Evening Post* said his right eye was gouged out; and his condition precarious. *The Courier-Journal* and *The Louisville Times* both reported that his back and ribs were crushed. Finally, *The Louisville Herald* said that his ribs were broken, his scalp wounded and he had deep cuts on his face and chest. While there is some inconsistency in these reports, it is clear that he suffered serious injuries, but he did survive. He must have presented a fearsome sight to Margaret, his sixth year old daughter.

It appears that he spent almost two months in the hospital. On January 18th, *The Pioneer News* reported that "Dr. Dodds, of Bardstown Junction, is reported much better and will soon be out again." And then on February 22nd, it reported, "The many friends of Dr. Dodds will be glad to know he is at home."

Sometime between the census-taking in 1920 and the summer of 1922, the Dodds sold their farm at Bardstown Junction and returned to Ohio. We know this from the kind words printed in *The Pioneer News* in August 1922 by its editor when he wrote, "Dr. and Mrs. J. G. Dodds, of Ohio, formerly of Bardstown Junction, visited friends in Bullitt County last week and attended the Fair. Dr. Dodds is now, as he has always been, a firm friend of the Fair and no one appreciates that fact more than the Secretary of the Fair. Dr. Dodds was a splendid citizen and one we hated to lose and we are not slow about stating that we of the *Pioneer News* are always glad to see Jim when he visits Bullitt. We wish him much success in his native State and trust that he may find it convenient to frequently visit his good friends here, of whom we hope to be counted as one."

We know that Dr. Dodds opened an office in Trenton, Ohio in the summer of 1929, and was there as late as the 1940 census. However, at the time of Dr. Dodd's death in 1945, they were living in Otway, Scioto County, Ohio. Clara lived until March 1960.

The last we've learned about their daughter, Margaret Anne Dodds, is that she graduated from Miami University of Ohio in 1933 with a degree in

Margaret Dodds

education, so she may have become a teacher.

The Duke Family

Ottie and Effie Satterfield were twin daughters born to John and Susan (Monroe) Satterfield in August 1886. In November 1906, when she was 20, Ottie married George C. Duke, son of J. Mills and Polina (Cooksey) Duke. Both families were from Barren County.

By 1910, George was working as a telegraph operator for the railroad at Glasgow Junction (Park City today). In September 1911, they had a daughter they named Virginia Frances. Then sometime before the summer of 1916, George took a job as station agent at the Bardstown Junction station.

On the morning of 20 Dec 1917, George, Ottie, and little Virginia boarded the train. George came to Shepherdsville for the day as part of a legal case that Thomas Hoagland had brought against the railroad following the accidental death of his son earlier. Ottie and Virginia planned to spend the day Christmas shopping in Louisville. They were to meet that evening at the train depot in Shepherdsville to return home.

When the train arrived at Shepherdsville, George boarded it, together with Ernest Woodward whom he introduced to his wife. Woodward was the railroad attorney in the Hoagland case being tried in Shepherdsville.

Woodward planned to spend the evening in Shepherdsville, and left the train before the crash.

It is not clear how Ottie escaped the fatal injuries that took her husband and child. None of the newspaper reports nor their death certificates note the nature of George and Virginia's injuries. Only one brief newspaper note lists Ottie's injuries as serious. However, years later, Woodward would recall that on that night, about ten o'clock, a man, who was working with Woodward to locate and assist the injured, heard someone moaning on top of the engine of the express train. He went up and brought down the unconscious body of Mrs. Duke.

Ottie's older brother, William, who lived in Louisville, came to her aid. It is his name that we find as the informant on the death certificates.

After Ottie recovered from her injuries, she returned home to Barren County, possibly to stay with relatives. There she met Rufus Bell, a wheelwright living in Glasgow Junction. Rufus had recently lost his wife, leaving him with young twin daughters, Lera and Lena. Rufus and Ottie were married in Nashville in 1919.

Ottie was not to have more children of her own, but she was there to help Rufus rear his girls.

Lena married Kelly Sloss and had a daughter they named Carolyn.

Lera married Homer Owens. Tragically, she died giving birth to twins, neither of whom survived.

Rufus died in May 1952 in Warren County. Ottie died in Barren County in March 1963.

John Ford

John Ford worked for the L. & N. railroad as an engineer. He was aboard the train that evening, likely on his way to an assignment elsewhere. With the train as crowded as it was, he may have been riding in the baggage car with James Carrico, the express messenger. This would account for that fact that he only sustained some painful bruises in the wreck.

John was born in March 1869, in Memphis, Tennessee, a son of Bishop Cannon and Carrie (Williams) Ford. He married Ella Alice Humphrey around 1892, likely in Memphis. Their daughter, Bertha was born in September 1893 in Memphis, before they moved to Louisville where John was working for the railroad as a fireman.

In 1900, John, Ella, and Bertha were boarding in Louisville with Kate Masden on Eighth Street. Kate's eldest son Charles was also a railroad fireman, and her youngest son Ezekiel, then just six, would be the fireman on the Accommodation during the wreck.

By 1910, the Fords were living on South Third Street, and he was listed as a railroad engineer.

Their daughter, Bertha Lee Ford, married Henry Sims of Dayton, Ohio in October 1913. The couple went to live in Dayton, and Mrs. Ford made several trips to visit with her daughter.

Then in August 1917, Henry Sims died suddenly of organic heart disease, leaving Bertha a young widow. She returned to her parents' home where she lived until June 1920 when she married Mike King.

Mike and Bertha had two children: John Michael King in 1926, and Elizabeth Alice King in 1932. She was better known as "Betty Alice."

They were living in Estill County in 1932 when Bertha contracted measles, and then pneumonia. The two together brought on her death in September, shortly after her 39th birthday.

We lose track of Mike King after that, but the two children came to live with their grandparents in Louisville.

John Michael King would move to California and marry Lois Ailene Wearne. He died in Yolo County in 1990.

Betty Alice King graduated from Ahrens Trade School in Louisville in 1950 as an honor student. And we believe she graduated from the University of Louisville in 1954 with a major in sociology. After that we lose track of her.

Ella Alice Ford lived until 1943, and John until 1948. They are buried at Cave Hill Cemetery. Pappy, as he was known by the grandkids, would be sorely missed by John who was then in the navy, serving in the South Pacific, and Betty Alice who was still in high school.

Lawrence Greenwell

Lawrence Greenwell grew up in the region of Nelson County along the Knoxville branch of the L & N railroad which passed south to north from New Haven through Nelson Furnace to Boston and Lebanon Junction. His parents were William and Catherine Ann (Culver) Greenwell.

Sometime between 1900 and 1910, he and some of his siblings moved to Louisville. During that time Lawrence joined his brother William to work for the railroad as a flagman.

Lawrence married Jennie Clark, daughter of Joseph and Mary (Watson) Clark, in November 1910 in Clark County, Indiana.

His job as flagman on the Accommodation meant that he was responsible for setting various kinds of flags to alert others to his train's location and condition. Specifically, if his train was stationary on the main train, he was responsible for setting out colored flares, called fusees, and for placing small detonating devices, called torpedoes, along the rail far enough up the track to alert an oncoming train of his train's presence. The torpedoes were fastened to the top of a rail so that the pressure of a locomotive or car would set them off, giving an audible signal to members of a train crew.

We will perhaps never know why Greenwell failed to perform his tasks, but we know from newspaper reports of the time that no flares or detonating devices were set behind Greenwell's train.

In fairness to him, it is possible that he did not know until too late that the oncoming train was so close, or that his train would need to take the siding at Shepherdsville. Again we will never know.

We know that his wife, who provided the information for his death certificate, also sued the railroad for $4,500, perhaps a modest sum compared to what others were asking.

This was a terrible time for the extended Greenwell family. Lawrence's first cousin, once removed, was Mamie Greenwell who had married George Elder O'Bryan, and they had two small boys, Harold who was born in February 1916, and the baby George Jr. who was but two months old and very sickly.

The day after the wreck, Mamie O'Bryan died of peritonitis, complicated by influenza. Then, the following March, George Elder Jr. died of ileocolitis, a form of Crohn's disease.

Elder O'Bryan was left with young Harold to rear, and Jennie Greenwell was alone. In June, they married in Louisville.

Together, they were a family for many years. Elder and Jennie were living in New Hope when she died in 1968. Elder O'Bryan lived until 1971, and his son Harold lived until 1998.

An interesting note: Jennie apparently never forgot her first love. At her death, her remains were returned to Louisville and buried beside Lawrence Greenwell in the St. Louis Cemetery; together again.

Jefferson Davis Gregory

Jefferson Davis Gregory was born in Cloverport, Kentucky in December, 1861 to John and Eliza (Worley) Gregory. He married Alice Adams, daughter of William and Mary (Smith) Adams, in September, 1897, and they were living in Louisville, where they had two daughters, Lena and Grace.

Jeff had always worked with his hands, first on the family farm, and later as a carpenter, a general works engineer, and a construction superintendent, a job he likely held at the time of the wreck. We surmise that he was on his way to Springfield, perhaps to work on a construction job.

He was apparently traveling alone, and was sitting in the smoker car, enjoying his pipe and gazing idly out the window and waiting for the train to resume its journey when the wreck occurred.

Gregory later told a reporter in Louisville, "Cushions, unloosed by the impact, were hurled all over the car. Our coach jerked about some, but did not leave the rails. The sides fell apart like so much paper and after gathering my wits I managed to get out by walking down the aisle to the front of the coach."

He was one of the lucky ones. Beyond a bruised leg and side, he was none the worse for the experience. He arrived at the hospital on the first relief train, and phoned for a taxi to take him home. We can only imagine the relief felt by his wife and daughters when he arrived home.

Jefferson Gregory's remaining years would bring both sorrow and happiness. His wife, Alice died in 1922. However, Lena married Thomas Gilmore, and Grace married Emmett Thompson. Together they gave Gregory eleven grandchildren to watch grow up.

Gregory died in 1945, ten days after V-J day and the end of World War II.

Nathaniel Wicklyffe Halstead
Natalie Halstead

Nathaniel Wicklyffe Halstead, son of Dr. Joseph Singer and Margaret Logan (Wicklyffe) Halstead, was born in March 1853 in Missouri. He moved to Nelson County in 1877, and began the practice of law with Jasper W. Muir.

Nat married Sue Muir in Bardstown in November 1881. They would have one son and six daughters. Sue (Muir) Halstead was a daughter of Dr. James L. and Mary (Carpenter) Muir, and a first cousin to Nathaniel Muir, son of Jasper Muir, who was also on the train with his family.

Nat Halstead was a celebrated criminal lawyer in Bardstown, and was county attorney for twenty-four consecutive years. He was a nationally known fox hunter, for which sport he kept a kennel of pedigree dogs, and a stable of fine horses. He was President of the National Association of Fox Hunters. At his estate "Brenswood" at Bardstown, he and his wife Sue entertained often and lavishly.

Although Halstead was approaching his sixty-fifth birthday, he had every reason to believe that he had many fruitful years ahead. His father and mother were still living in Missouri. Doctor Halstead was 99 and still occasionally practiced medicine. His bride was 87.

Nat and Sue Halstead's only son, Dr. Muir Halstead died in Montrose, Colorado during an operation for appendicitis in November 1914. Each of the six daughters married: Margaret to Earnest N. Fulton; Mary to Fred A. Vaughan; Sue to Clifton Atherton; Dawson to Russell Hager; Martha to Thomas B. Nichols; and Natalie to John Walter Featherstone.

The marriage between Natalie and John Featherstone would not take place until 1920, and on the day of the wreck she was traveling home from Louisville with her father.

Newspaper reports are sparse in reports of their injuries, but apparently Nat Halstead received some burns, probably from escaping steam, and Natalie received some crushing injuries. Both recovered from their injuries, although Natalie's took longer to heal. One report indicated that she reached a settlement with the railroad for $12,000 in compensation for her injuries.

Nat Halstead was in private law practice the last sixteen years of his life. On the morning of May 30, 1924, he arrived at the Bardstown courthouse in preparation to make a plea for his client when he was stricken with apoplexy and died.

His wife Sue lived in Bardstown until her death in 1938, at the age of 81.

Natalie's marriage to John Walter Featherstone was unsuccessful, and they were divorced. She continued to live in Bardstown until at least 1940, and then moved to Louisville where she lived until her death in 1969.

Henry Zollicofer Hardaway

Henry Zollicofer Hardaway, a son of James Leach and Margaret Jane (Cain) Hardaway, was born in Meade County, but made his way to Bullitt County where he met and married Jennie Simmons in February 1884. Jennie was a daughter of William Peyton and Sophronia (Shanklin) Simmons.

Henry and Jennie would have three children: James William,

Henry Z. Hardaway

born in 1885; Jesse Lee, born in 1892; and Mary Ellen, born in 1894.

Jesse Lee Hardaway married Mary Green Lawrence, daughter of Thomas and Elizabeth "Lizzie" (Gilson) Lawrence of Louisville, in 1916, and they were expecting their first child when the wreck occurred.

It is unclear whether Henry Hardaway rode the train from Louisville, or if he boarded it at Shepherdsville just before the crash. Either way, he was headed for his home just south of the river, along Cedar Grove Road. He suffered a broken right leg, a serious concussion, and internal injuries in the wreck, and was taken to Louisville on the relief train. Four agonizing days later he succumbed to his injuries.

Following his death, his son Jesse took over management of the farm. When Jesse and Mary's son was born in June, they named him for his departed grandfather. They would have two more children, Betty and Lawrence. Jesse died in 1949 on the family farm. Mary lived to be 102, dying in 1996.

Jennie Simmons Hardaway lived until 1940, dying on the family farm in October, with her daughter, Mary Ellen by her side. Following her mother's death, Mary Ellen moved to Shepherdsville where she lived until her death in 1971.

James William Hardaway worked as a bank teller for the Peoples Bank of Shepherdsville. He remained a bachelor until 1924 when he married Hester Belle Anderson, a local teacher. After the tragic loss of premature twins in 1926, they would have no children.

James remained with the bank, rising to become its president, a post he would hold until his death in 1961. Hester Belle lived until 1996. She was an active member of the Woman's Club, and very faithful to her church. Of their many gifts of charity is the James W. Hardaway Scholarship that is presented annually in his memory.

Hester Belle Anderson's 1923 college photo, Hester Belle Hardaway in 1979 church directory, portrait of James William Hardaway as President of The Peoples Bank.

Mattie Harmon

Simeon Harmon and Martha E. "Mattie" Jones were married at her parent's home in November 1874. She was the daughter of Patrick and Elizabeth (Roby) Jones who were married in Bullitt County in August 1845.

Mattie gave birth to Malcolm Sims Harmon in 1876. He would be their only child.

Malcolm and Hattie Harris were married, and had a son they named Louis. However, Hattie died in 1903 while the child was an infant. Then in 1907, Simon Harmon contracted a bad case of measles and died.

Together Mattie and Malcolm set their hands to tending the farm and rearing young Louis. Then as Christmas approached in 1917, Malcolm's mother decided to travel with her niece on a shopping trip to Louisville. Family legend has it that Mattie Harmon was going to marry again, although the perspective husband is not identified, and she was shopping both for Christmas and for a new dress for the wedding.

By the time Malcolm had learned of the train wreck, and made his way to Shepherdsville, his mother was already on her way to Louisville on the relief train. She died early the next morning at the hospital, and her remains were sent to a morgue, still unidentified. It was there that Malcolm finally found her.

It was a double tragedy with both Mattie Harmon and her niece, Estella Nutt, dying as a result of the wreck. Thus, in a span of perhaps a decade, Malcolm lost both his parents, his wife, and his cousin.

But life goes on. Not long after Mattie's death, her grandson, Louis, joined the navy. Then Malcolm married again, this time to Miss Addie Troll, daughter of Charles and Annie Troll. Addie taught school at Louisville Girls' High School.

Addie Harmon died in 1947; Malcolm followed ten years later. They had no children.

Malcolm's son Louis was living in Chicago when he died in 1983.

Edith Hatfield

Edith Hatfield was one of the fortunate few who sustained only relatively minor injuries in the train wreck. *The Louisville Evening Post* reported that she suffered a laceration about her left eye and forehead. There was no mention of the horror her eyes had seen. In later years, she would have little to say about the accident itself. Perhaps the memory of it was too difficult.

Edith was born in 1898 to John and Nina (Perkins) Hatfield. Her family was living in the Deatsville area in Nelson County. Almost certainly she had been to Louisville, perhaps to shop, and was heading home with her purchases. Whether she was traveling alone or with friends is not known.

We can imagine that Edith was carrying small presents for her parents, and her siblings: John, Marion, Gilbert, and little Glendolin, a four year old. But the best present of all turned out to be Edith herself, alive and safe after such a horrific experience.

In 1922, Edith married Owen Cooper Walker, son of Felix and Mary Walker. They would have three children: Richard, Harold, and Mary Glenda. Owen died in 1954; Edith followed in 1970.

Lena Hatfield

The Courier-Journal reported, "Miss Lena Hatfield, of Bardstown Junction, suffered a scalp wound and wrenched shoulders." Fortunately for her, she survived her injuries. But just exactly who was she?

Since it was common practice to identify single ladies with the title "Miss" and married ladies with "Mrs." and the given name of their husbands, we started looking for a single lady named Lena Hatfield in Bullitt County.

We found no Lena Hatfield in the 1910 census for Bullitt County. In the 1920 census, there was a Lena R. Hatfield who is married to Vesey Hatfield, but they married in March 1918, and she was Lena Evans at the time of the wreck. Vesey was a son of Wilson and Elin (Tinnell) Hatfield. Lena's parents were John Lewis and Sarah Jane (Hatfield) Evans. By 1920, Vesey and Lena had moved to Louisville where he was working as a furniture varnisher.

We also found Lennie Lee Hatfield, married to William Elias Hatfield, living at Clermont, which is next door to Bardstown Junction. William and Lennie were married in June 1915. William had a son and daughter by his first marriage; Lennie brought a daughter from her first marriage. Then the two of them had two daughters and a son. Lennie, who was a native of Green County, died in 1964. William, a native of Clermont, was a retired employee of Bernheim Distilleries when he died three years later.

Finally, we found a Lena Hatfield living in Hardin County in both 1910 and 1920. She was single, sister to Stephen D. Hatfield, and in 1910 was 38, and worked in Hardin County as a public school teacher. By 1920 she was still in Hardin County, working as a bookkeeper in a hotel. It is conceivable that in 1917 she had taken a job, teaching perhaps, in the Bardstown Junction area. However this is only conjecture.

This Lena Hatfield was born in October 1871 in Grayson County to Ben and Malinda (Hunt) Hatfield. She died in Hardin County in June 1935, age 63. She never married.

We tend to think that Miss Lena Hatfield, who was injured in the train wreck, was this latter lady; but we are uncertain.

Thomas W. Hoagland

Thomas and Bertha Hoagland were devastated when their son, John Robert was struck and killed by a locomotive along the tracks near their home in May 1917. A disagreement over what fair compensation for that loss should be led the Hoagland's to sue the railroad.

The case was set to come to trial in Shepherdsville in the August term, but was postponed. It was set again for Dec 13, but Judge McCandless was absent due to the funeral of a friend. Finally, everything was in place and the jury was selected on December 20. The trial began that afternoon. Testimony was heard, but the late hour caused the judge to carry the case over to the next day.

Hoagland was represented by Ben Chapeze; the railroad by Ernest Woodward. One of the witnesses was Jimmy Morrison who had apparently witnessed the accident that killed Hoagland's boy. Also present for the case was George Duke, the railroad agent at Bardstown Junction.

Thomas grew up in Bullitt County, a son of R. I. and Martha Hoagland. Their farm was located in central Bullitt County, and contained the site of the former Dry Lick saltworks. He married Bertha Ellwanger in Louisville in 1901, and by 1910 they had four children, a daughter and three sons. Thomas was working as a locomotive fireman at the time.

When the Accommodation arrived in Shepherdsville, many of those involved with Hoagland's case boarded the train for the short ride home. Hoagland and Chapeze shared a seat on the train.

According to a later report in *The Pioneer News*, "Hoagland received several breaks in the wreck, his left leg broken below the knee, knee cap broken, elbow crushed, face cut all to pieces, head mashed, right side hurt, with several other parts broken." It would be July 4th before he could leave the hospital and return home.

On August 8th, the trial concerning his son's death was resumed. Two days later, after hearing all the testimony, the jury determined that the railroad was not responsible for young Hoagland's death.

Hoagland also brought suit against the railroad for his own injuries. According to Woodward, the railroad offered to settle with him, but he rejected their offer. On 16 Aug 1919, the case was finally completed with the railroad being required to pay Mr. Hoagland's costs. Woodward later remembered that the railroad's earlier offer was more than what Hoagland eventually received from the court.

The family remembers that Thomas wore a permanent brace on one leg, and nearly always wore a hat to cover a steel plate inserted into his head. He always had his pipe, so he was almost certainly in the smoker car; a fact that probably saved his life.

While Hoagland was in the hospital, a 19-year-old German nurse named Dorothy personally cared for him. She later became a member of the family when she married John Ellwanger, Bertha's brother.

Thomas Hoagland continued to live on his farm for many years. His family would grow, adding two more sons, and three more daughters. His wife, Bertha died on 18 Oct 1934, but Thomas lived on until 1962. In his last years, he provided significant information to Robert McDowell in McDowell's research into the early saltworks on Bullitt County.

The Hurst Family

Joseph and Julian Hurst, sons of Gam and Molly (Finn) Hurst, were young bachelors in Bardstown in 1910. Then Joseph married Louisa Losson, daughter of John and Sarah (Wilson) Losson, and Julian married Mary Spalding, daughter of Thomas and Nellie Spalding. Joe and Louisa, affectionately pronounced Wee-sa, had a daughter, Sarah Carolyn in November 1915, and a son, Joseph Raoul Losson Hurst in April 1917, born the day his uncle, for whom he was named, was buried. Julian and Mary had two sons, Harry in July 1916, and Julian Jr. in April 1918.

Tragedy first struck when Louisa Hurst took her infant son to Louisville to see a doctor. She was accompanied by Annie Reed, the child's nanny. On the return trip to Bardstown, they boarded the train in Louisville and took seats in the rear coach. However, a friend of Louisa's later boarded the train and wished to sit with her. Louisa told Mrs. Reed that she would take care of the baby, indicating that Mrs. Reed should go sit in the other coach. Most likely this saved Mrs. Reed's life.

When the train wreck occurred at Shepherdsville, Louisa and little Joseph were killed. *The Louisville Evening Post* shared the tragic story.

"Among those who suffered deplorable loss was Joseph Hurst, a farmer of Bards-

town, who lost his wife and his seven months old boy, Joseph Raoul. With his brother, Hurst arrived at the hospital in an automobile, reaching there an hour before the relief train. He inquired anxiously of his wife and baby. Later arrivals from the scene of the wreck were unable to give him definite information. He stood by the door of the north wing and silently watched the suffering women brought in on stretchers.

"His wife was brought in. The covering was lifted from her face and neither he nor any of the onlookers could identify her at first because of terrible marks about her neck and chest. His child was almost unrecognizable.

"A half hour after his little family had been taken upstairs he was informed of their deaths, and, while suffering agony of bereavement, remained collected and offered consolation to weaker members of stricken families, even going to the depot to render what aid he could."

The bodies of Louisa and little Joseph were returned to Bardstown for burial. Left with an infant daughter, Joe Hurst turned to Louisa's sister Beatrice Losson Crume for help. Beatrice and her husband Robert had four children of their own, and agreed to give young Sarah Carolyn Hurst a home.

Later Joe Hurst bought the house next to the Crumes. Carolyn, as she was known, went back and forth between the two households. Joe Hurst never married again.

Meanwhile, Julian and Mary Hurst had their second child; but then tragedy struck this home.

In the latter part of 1918, a strain of influenza swept the country. Called Spanish Influenza because it was first reported in Spain, this especially vicious flu struck its victim down in short order. In October, Mary Spalding Hurst was infected by it, and she died before the end of the month, leaving Julian with two small sons.

Like his brother Joe, Julian was not able to care for his children and continue to work as well, so he turned to Mary's parents who agreed to take the boys.

Joe Hurst continued to live in Bardstown, and operated a whiskey store until his death in 1957. He was a great collector of things such as tools, knives, arrowheads, and unusual rocks. He kept all of this on display in his store.

Julian Hurst, who worked as an insurance agent, remarried and lived in Fayette County until his death in 1941.

Mrs. Kate Ice

Catherine "Kate" Cundiff married Thomas Robert Ice in March 1900 in Bullitt County. She was born in November 1882, a daughter of George W. and Jennie Bell (Moore) Cundiff. He was born in December 1880, a son of Joseph and Elizabeth (Barnes) Ice.

They had three children: Mamie in 1902, Eula in 1903, and Jeffie in 1905. Tom worked hard on the farm, and Kate kept house and saw to the needs of her family.

Tom, Kate, and Jeff Ice.

Then, before Mamie's fifteenth birthday, Tom contracted pulmonary tuberculosis. He went downhill rapidly and died in February 1917, leaving Kate with a family to support. She managed with the help of family and friends. This would be the first Christmas without Tom.

Kate was in Louisville, getting a wedding dress for her daughter Mamie who was planning to marry Arthur Burns. Perhaps as she returned home on the train, her mind may have been on the wedding, and on wondering if Mamie was ready to marry. No word of her injuries in the wreck have been found, but they were sufficient to take her life.

Later in life, Jeff Ice shared his memories of that night with his second wife, Clara. She related her memory of what he said for us.

"Jeff hitched up his team of horses and went to Bardstown Junction to pick up his mother. Arriving there, the station master told him the train had been detained at Shepherdsville and for him to go on home and someone would bring his mother home later when the train arrived. Jeff decided to go on to Shepherdsville and pick up his mother instead of waiting. When he arrived in Shepherdsville he saw the train wreck. It was a scene of total chaos! He stayed and tried to find his Mother but was told she was on the car that was completely demolished and there was no chance that she had survived. He said there was much confusion, screaming, people crying and searching for their loved ones. Bodies were everywhere. Finally someone took him in hand and made him go home saying they would send someone the next morning. Jeff never talked about the funeral or his pain at losing his only remaining parent."

At the time of their mother's death, Mamie was 15, Eula was 14, and Jeff was 12. With the double tragedy of losing both parents, the Ice children grew up quickly and made their way in the world.

Arthur Burns and Mamie Ice were married on Christmas Day, a solemn day with little joy for anyone. A year later, in September 1918, young Eula, just after her fifteenth birthday, married William Morrow Cundiff.

Jeff Ice went to live with his Uncle Harvey Cundiff. He later married Jenrose Carby, daughter of John and Josephine Carby. They had two children: Thomas C. Ice, born in September 1926, and Norma Jean Ice, born in January 1931. Norma Jean died in April 1935 as the result of Wilms' tumor which is a rare type of kidney cancer that affects children.

Jenrose Ice died in 1948 from melanoma cancer. Her son Tom Ice died in 1964, also from melanoma cancer. He was 38.

Jeff Ice married again in July 1955, and had two more sons. Then he developed leukemia and died in December 1970. His second bride, Clara remembers him this way:

"While reliving all these memories I am once again amazed that one man could go through so much and still be as kind, gentle, and thoughtful a man as he was. He was quick to aid anyone in need and a friend to all who came his way." Would that each of us could be remembered so well.

Charles Jenkins

Both *The Louisville Evening Post*, and *The Springfield Sun* reported that Charles Jenkins of Springfield was slightly injured, but able to leave the hospital shortly after being taken there.

In the decade from 1910 through 1920, there were quite a few men named Charles Jenkins living in Kentucky, but none of them lived in Springfield, or any other part of Washington County. This includes an examination of both census records, as well as the World War I draft registration records.

There was a Charles Thomas Jenkins living in western Anderson County, and a Charlie Parker Jenkins living in the small community of McAfee in Mercer County; but these were the only two living in counties adjacent to Washington County.

Of the many men by the name of Jenkins living in Washington County, the only one with a name even similar to Charles was James Chester Jenkins who lived in Willisburg.

Perhaps the Charles Jenkins slightly injured in the wreck is one of these; or perhaps not.

Charles Todd Jesse

Not everyone aboard the Accommodation that evening was listed by any of the Louisville newspapers as killed or injured. Perhaps Charles Jesse was one of those who escaped their notice. We know from *The Pioneer News* that he filed suit against the railroad, along with a number of others, and that the railroad settled with him out of court.

Charles Todd Jesse was born in 1877, in Shelby County to James and Eliza (Todd) Jesse. He married Elizabeth Ellen Robertson, daughter of George Washington and Abagale Mariah (Linney) Robertson, in April 1917. Charles and Elizabeth had three children: James Henry Jesse (born August 1918 in Bullitt County), Mary Todd Jesse (born April 1923 in Jefferson County), and Elizabeth Hanna Jesse (born March 1925, also Jefferson County).

Sometime in the early 1920's, the family moved to Anchorage where Charles became the manager of Dr. Jesse Cotton's estate. Dr. Cotton was a member of the faculty of the Presbyterian Seminary. They were living there when, in April 1930, Charles was discovered dead in the barn, likely following a heart attack.

Charles Todd Jesse

61

The 1930's may have been a difficult time for the family following Charles' death. We know that by 1940, the girls were boarding at the Presbyterian Orphanage, that James was living with his Aunt Hattie Jones, and that their mother Elizabeth was working as a housekeeper for William Simmons in Bullitt County.

Still, like quite a few families during the depression, they survived and even prospered.

James Henry Jesse was able to attend Centre College where he was editor of the school newspaper. After graduation, he started a weekly newspaper in Middletown until he was drafted into the army in 1941. He left the service in 1946 as a first lieutenant in the Army Air Forces.

Following his time in the service, James Henry worked for newspapers in Mississippi and Florida. He was editor and publisher of the *Charlotte Herald* in Punta Gorda, Florida, and founder of the paper, *Florida Today*. Following this he was publisher and president of the *Nashville Banner*.

James Henry married Gloria Wollank in 1943, and they had two children.

Mary Todd Jesse served in the U. S. Navy during World War II, where she met and married Andrew Fuller. Following her service in the navy, Mary had a career in retail sales, and retired from J. C. Penney. Andrew and Mary had one daughter.

Elizabeth Hanna Jesse married Sylvester Beasley in Chicago in 1953. Betsy, as she was known, was living in San Joaquin, California when she died in 1965.

Elizabeth Robertson Jesse lived until 1963, passing in Fort Walton Beach, Florida.

Charles W. Johnson

The Louisville Herald reported two days after the wreck on the identification of another victim, and said, "With the establishment of the identity of W. C. Johnson, a farmer living between Samuels and Deatsville, at 5 o'clock yesterday afternoon at Bax's undertaking establishment, all bodies brought here on the special train have been identified. Johnson's head was crushed and he was dead when found. S. R. Demaree of Bardstown identified him. The body will be sent to Samuels, Ky., tomorrow afternoon."

Two days after that, *The Kentucky Standard* in Bardstown reported that his funeral had been held at New Salem Baptist Church at Cox's Creek.

Learning more about him and his family became an adventure in research and detection. He has been variously identified as W. C., William Charles, Charles, and Charles William Johnson, but for our purposes we will refer to him as Charles W. Johnson.

Charles married Kate Whitesides in 1881 in Louisville where she was living while working as a dressmaker. Her parents were William and Patsy Whitesides of Bullitt County.

Their first child, Ada was born in Cumberland County a year after their marriage, according to her death certificate. Ada married Henry Clifford Paulley in 1899 in Nelson County. They would have seven children before she died of pneumonia in 1922.

Charles and Kate's second child, Ola was born in 1889, when Ada was already seven years old. Ola married Stanley Raymond Demaree in 1907, and it was he who identified the body of his father-in-law. Stanley would later be mayor of Bardstown twice. Ola died in Bardstown in 1960.

Charles and Kate's final child, Eva, was born in 1894. Eva first married Benjamin F. Hoffman, and they had a daughter, Margaret Geneva Hoffman in 1913. Eva would later marry Virgil Parks in Tulsa, Oklahoma, and following his death in 1933, she would marry Fred Hurd. Eva was living with her daughter Geneva in Somerset, Kentucky when she died in 1983.

Kate Johnson's life was cut short when she died in 1914 of acute articular rheumatism.

With his wife gone, and his daughters all married, Charles Johnson was living alone. We don't know why he was on the train. Perhaps he had been to Louisville on business, or to buy presents for his grandchildren, or maybe to visit his eldest daughter and her family. Whatever the reason, it was the last trip he'd ever make.

John Bernard Keyer

John Bernard Keyer was born in 1858 in Scranton, Pennsylvania, the second son of Thomas and Mary (McNaulty) Keyer, immigrants to America from Ireland and England. Like most immigrant families, they were hard workers. Thomas Keyer worked as a boiler maker; his eldest son Martin learned the telegraph skills and was working in Memphis when he contracted yellow fever and died in 1878, at the age of 22.

This was a hard blow, and left young John with the responsibility of leading his generation of the family. As soon as he was old enough, he went to work for the railroad in Louisville. By 1880, both he and his brother William were working as railroad firemen.

In 1888, John married Bridget "Bezzie" Scales in Louisville. They would have five children: Martin Joseph, Thomas Michael, Adeline Mae, Harry Charles, and Juanita Keyer.

We know that, by at least 1897, John was a railroad engineer, likely even earlier. While injuries and death were common enough in the railroad business, John had been fortunate to never have been in an accident where someone was killed. All that changed in May 1906.

John was bringing the Knoxville Express into Louisville early on a Monday morning. He was minutes from the depot, and traveling at a slow rate of speed, when, as the train rounded a slight curve at Seventh and Hill Streets, a flange broke off the wheel of the combination smoking car, the second coach behind the engine. That car's momentum carried it off the rails and into nearby boxcars on a siding.

Despite the quick action of the conductor and engineer in bringing the train to a halt, the rear end of the smoker car and the front end of the ladies' coach struck the boxcars.

Nine men were killed, four of them bridge carpenters from Brodhead, Kentucky. Twenty-one others sustained serious injuries. The newspaper reported that workers from nearby plants assisted the train crew in helping the injured.

By the time everyone had been cared for, John Keyer was exhausted and sick at the injuries and death he had witnessed. A coroner's inquest cleared the train's crew of any wrongdoing, and blamed the accident of mechanical failure; but John continued to have nightmares about the wreck, and stopped being an engineer for a time.

However, he was back at his engineer's post by 1910; and by 1917, he was working on the Springfield Accommodation run.

John Keyer was patiently waiting for the signal to proceed on his way toward Bardstown Junction, when the train porter delivered the conductor's message to back into the siding, and allow an express train to pass. To do so, he had to move the train forward in order to back in to the siding.

He had just passed the switch for the siding, and was preparing to reverse his engine, when the wreck occurred. In an instant, the old nightmares were realized again.

Later, in reading his comments to the railroad commission, one can sense the outrage in his voice that the railroad had allowed this to happen to his train and to the people whose lives had been entrusted to him; and the horror he felt at not having been able to prevent it.

It's not clear how much longer John Keyer drove the locomotives, but he continued to work for the railroad up until his death in 1927.

Silas C. "Sie" Lawrence

On January 3rd, *The Springfield Sun* reported in Silas Lawrence's death

"The toll of death from results of the fatal crash at Shepherdsville is slowly mounting. The forty-eighth victim Mr. Sie Lawrence, a well known farmer of this county, died at St. Mary and Elizabeth's Hospital Wednesday morning at three o'clock after a valiant fight against death from his injuries. It was feared that death would result from the day of the wreck, as he suffered a crushed skull and other injuries. Mr. Lawrence was sixty-eight years old, and one of the most highly respected citizens of the Texas section of the county, where he had lived during the greater portion of his long and fruitful life. He was a member of the Wesley Chapel Methodist church and a devout Christian gentleman. He was an honest, fair and square business man whose word was his bond. He numbered his friends by his acquaintances and bore the highest respect of all who knew him."

Silas C. Lawrence was born in February 1850 in Washington County, the fourth son of David and Frances (Settles) Lawrence. He married Debra Ann Brady, daughter of James and Deborah Brady, in February 1872. At his death, he left his widow and six children to mourn his passing, including sons James, Pope, and Thomas Lawrence, and daughters Fannie, Eva, and Bernice.

Of the children, James married Gertrude Leonard, Pope married Anna Lou Sparrow, Thomas married Nellie Spires, Fannie married

Robert Hays, Eva married Thomas Golden Key, and Bernice married Tyra Gibson. Debra lived until February 1927, before succumbing to tuberculosis.

Neither Sie nor Debra would live to see their youngest daughter Bernice married. Nor would they get to dote on her two sons and three daughters.

The Maramans

The Maraman family had been in Bullitt County for more than a hundred years, starting with Francis Maraman who settled on a farm on the south side of Salt River near Shepherdsville in 1813. Death struck the family hard in September 1839, taking Francis, his wife Mary, and their eldest son Charles, and leaving behind three daughters and four sons, including Henry Oldham Maraman who married Elmira Troutman in 1841. Their son, Charlie Mike Maraman, would become the father of David and Howard Maraman who were aboard the train that evening.

Charlie Mike and Susan (Henderson) Maraman had eight children before he died in 1912. Howard, born in 1874, was their third; David, born in 1880, was their fifth.

Howard Maraman

Howard Maraman married Emma Bowman, daughter of H. C. and Mary (Shepherd) Bowman. They had two daughters, Mary Catherine, born in 1903, and Susan Elder, born two years later. Mary Catherine married James Henry Pope; Sue Elder married George W. Wigginton. George and Sue Elder were the parents of George Jr., Betty Ann (Robey), Sue Charles (Jones), and Mary Catherine (Harper) Wigginton.

David and Howard were sitting near one another on the train when the crash occurred. Initially, both were thought to have been killed.

Howard was laid beside the dead until someone noticed his hand move. The back of his skull was crushed. He was sent on the relief train to the hospital in Louisville where the crushed bones were removed and a silver plate put in its place. The scalp was pulled over it, and after a month he was sent home to become a walking invalid for the rest of his life.

Howard and Emma Maraman

Before the wreck, Howard had been a tall, strong, working farmer owning several farms (some sub-let) and a home in Louisville. After the wreck, his family was told he must never be hit on his head. He could no longer farm or oversee his sub-let ones. Over the years, all properties, except his home place and a connecting farm, were sold.

Emma, who had never worked outside the home, became a corset-iere for the Spirella Corset Company. She was welcomed into the private homes of the wealthy where the ladies could be measured and fitted in the privacy of their own homes for various undergarments. She was paid well by the company, thus bringing in the much needed cash for day to day expenses.

Howard died in his 83rd year, in 1958, leaving his wife Emma, and his two daughters and their families. Emma was 85 when she died in 1965.

David Henry Maraman

David Henry Maraman was one of those killed at the wreck site. He had married Wilhelmina Josephine Saar in 1911. She was a daughter of John and Annie Catherine "Kate" (Eisenbach) Saar.

Wilhelmina Maraman took her three children to live with her brother, John Saar. Then by 1930 they were living next to her parents. By 1940, her daughter Ida had married Roy Troutman. Not long after that, Ida's sister Eva married Noah Whittle, and their brother Charles married Margaret Ellen Philpot.

Wilhelmina and her children at a Maraman reunion in 1919.

Roy and Ida Troutman had two children: Peggy (Brock) and Roy Gene Troutman; Noah and Eva Whittle were the parents of David E. Whittle; and Charles and Margaret Maraman were the parents of Donna (Davis) and Charles H. Maraman.

SALE
Postponed on account of the blizzard to
Thursday January 17th. 1918
AT 10 A. M.
I will offer for sale on the premises about 1 mile west of Shepheresville, on the Long Lick road the personal property of David Maraman Dec. as follows

1 Pr. work mules	1 Buggy
1 Pr. work horses	1 Surrey
2 Brood sows	1 Runabout and harness
1 Sow and 8 pigs	2 Sets wagon harness
16 Shoats	2 Mowers
2 Cows 1 Lot of loose hay	1 Wheat drill
1 Lot of fodder	1 Hay rake
600 Bu. of corn more or less	1 Disk harrow
2-2 horse wagons	1 Corn drill

Some Household furniture, garden tools, broken lots of harness and other articles too numerous to mention.

The above property will be sold on a credit of 9 months for all sums over $10.00 under that amount cash in hand. Purchasers must execute note with approved surety bearing interest from date before moving property.

O. W. Pearl Admr.
Jnas Roey Auct.

Sale Poster for David Maraman Property

Wilhelmina Saar Maraman lived out her life in Shepherdsville, passing at the age of 88 in 1977.

Joseph Edward Marks, Jr.

Both *The Louisville Times* and *The Springfield Sun* reported the day following the wreck that Joseph Marks of Bardstown had been killed in the accident. His name was soon removed from the lists, and we are not certain that he was even on the train that night.

A son of Joseph Edward and Texanna (Edelen) Marks, Joseph Jr. was an infant when his father died in 1892. By the 1900 census, he and his mother and siblings were living with his widowed grandmother in Bardstown. Ten years later, in 1910, the census indicated that he was working as a bookkeeper for a local distillery.

By late May in 1917, Joseph had been working for the Illinois Central Railroad as a tariff clerk for a couple of years. Still single, he was living at the Memphis, Tennessee Y.M.C.A. His World War I registration card indicates that he was "very deaf."

By November of 1918, he had secured a job as an accountant and disbursing officer in the American Embassy in London, England. His passport photo is shown here. He was still there in the 1920 census, but returned to Memphis the following year, at least long enough to marry Ermine Horrell in February. She obtained her passport in April, and they left for Rome, Italy, Joseph's new assignment.

Their first child, a daughter named Dorothy, was born in 1922 while they were in Italy.

The following year, Joseph resigned his embassy post and returned to Kentucky where he became traffic manager for the Burley Tobacco Growers' Co-operative Association in Lexington.

From 1930 to 1940 he was associated with the Lexington Chamber of Commerce, and in 1940 entered private law practice with his son James Morgan Marks.

Joseph was nearly 40 when he entered the University of Kentucky to study law. He was counsel for the Kentucky Railroad commission when he died in 1952.

He and Ermine had two other children, Joseph Edward III, and William Gutherie Marks.

Following Joseph's death, Ermine married Dr. William S. Webb, retired head of the department of physics at the University of Kentucky. Dr. Webb died in 1964, and Ermine next married Hermon C. Robinson who had been executive secretary of the Lexington Tobacco Board of Trade.

Hermon too had passed when Ermine moved to Greencastle, Indiana in 1974 to live with her daughter. She died there two weeks later, leaving her daughter, and two remaining sons, and nine grandchildren.

Ezekiel John Masden, Jr.

A week after the wreck, *The Springfield Sun* reported, "The engineer, Mr. Keyer, of this place, and his fireman, Mr. E. J. Masden, also escaped with slight injuries caused by the impact." This is the only place where the fireman of the Accommodation is mentioned with regard to the wreck.

Ezekiel John Masden, Jr. was born in August 1893 in Bullitt County Kentucky. He was described as of medium height and build with brown hair and eyes. His occupation was listed as a fireman for the L & N railroad.

Ezekiel John Masden's father, Ezekiel Sr., died before 1900, and his mother kept the family going by running a boarding house in Louisville.

It is interesting to note that in the 1900 census, John Ford and his wife and daughter were boarding with the Masdens. This is the same John Ford who was involved in the wreck.

Sometime just prior to the 1920 census, Ezekiel married a lady named Pearl Wagner. They moved to Mobile, Alabama by 1920. The census that year indicated that he was a railroad engineer, an occupation he would hold for the rest of his career.

Ezekiel's career as an engineer was not without incident. In November 1949 he was at the throttle of the outbound Pan American, when an express car was derailed over the Rigolets Trestle near New Orleans. He slammed on the brakes possibly saving the train from tumbling into the water below.

He would be at the throttle in 1958 when a man was walking parallel to the tracks with his back to the train and suddenly darted into the path of the locomotive traveling at 70 mph which dismembered his body. And then again, in 1961, an elderly woman wandered onto the tracks at night in front of his L. & N. Gulf Wind-Piedmont Limited train. He was nearly on top of her before seeing her. Such incidents were unfortunately all too common in the life of a railroad engineer.

Ezekiel and Pearl spent the rest of their lives living in Mobile, Alabama. He died there in 1971, and she followed in 1977. They had no children.

Emily Haycraft Mashburn

Emily Haycraft taught school while living with her parents, Samuel and Julia (Arthur) Haycraft. Her father was an auditor for the railroad.

Henry Hamilton Mashburn was a student at the Baptist Seminary in Louisville when the two met. After his graduation from the seminary, Henry became pastor of the Baptist Church in Louisburg, N.C., and in November 1902, Emily's parents were pleased to announce that Henry and Emily would marry in December.

Their first four children were born in North Carolina: Elizabeth Wilson Mashburn (1903), Samuel Haycraft Mashburn (1905), Henry Hamilton Mashburn, Jr. (1906) and Julia Mashburn (1908). After they moved to Bardstown, their daughter, Emily Bond Mashburn was born in 1912.

Emily's father died of acute bronchitis in 1915. Her mother continued to live in Louisville near Emily's brother, Hugh Chester Haycraft.

There is some indication that Emily had made her way to Louisville earlier in the week, perhaps to visit family and also do some shopping, and was returning to Bardstown on the evening train. According to one report, she lived for about ten minutes following the wreck before succumbing to her injuries. Her funeral was held in Bardstown, and her remains were taken to Elizabethtown for burial.

Emily Mashburn
(image from microfilm)

With five children to care for, Henry sent word to his relative Adelphia Mashburn in North Carolina, asking her to come and help with the children.

His youngest daughter Emily died in 1925 of acute nephritis and peritonitis at the age of 13. Then his daughter Elizabeth married Thomas Merlin Rodman in Bardstown in 1924, and they had a son, also named Thomas. Unfortunately, the marriage was not to last, and Elizabeth and her son were living with her brother Henry and sister Julia in 1940.

Julia Mashburn remained single, and worked as a secretary. She died in 1979. Her brother Samuel married Dorothy Elizabeth

McAdams, and they had three children: Emily, Samuel Jr., and Forest C. Mashburn. Julia's other brother, Henry Jr., married Theodosia Tebbs, and they had Henry III and Julia Rounsavall Mashburn, a daughter.

In 1929, with his children grown, Henry Mashburn married Mariam Wood, a local school teacher. They shared nearly a decade together until his death in 1937.

John McKinley McClure

James McClure and Mary Elizabeth Dunn were married in LaRue County in 1886, and over the years their family grew to include five daughters and a son, John McKinley McClure who was born in 1894 in Roanoke, which is just northwest of New Haven and south of Boston.

This McClure family moved to Bullitt County sometime before 1910, and settled near Bardstown Junction.

John McKinley McClure was aboard the Accommodation that evening, along with Charles Showalter and Will Shelton, his brothers-in-law. Showalter was married to Ada Belle McClure, and Shelton to Maude McClure.

In the days following the train wreck, several newspapers identified a McKinley McClure of Bardstown Junction as one of those who had been injured, although no mention was given of the extent of his injuries.

The Pioneer News reported in February that several Bullitt County residents had filed suits against the railroad because of the wreck. One was John McClure for $20,000. Court records show that McClure settled with the railroad in April, but no sum is given.

John was inducted into the army in February 1918, and sent to Camp Taylor for basic training. However, he was back home by the 1920 census, living with his parents.

His sister George Etta married Walter Cundiff about that time. His youngest sister,

Bertha married Elmer Cundiff in 1926, and his sister, Martha married Dudley Hatter in the same year.

He appears to have married around 1927, for he appears in the 1930 census in Cincinnati with a wife named Mary Ellen McClure. He was working as a railroad laborer at the time. Also in Cincinnati in 1930 were his sisters George Etta and Bertha with their husbands who were both working as carpenters.

John and Mary Ellen were still together when he completed his World War II draft registration card in 1942. However, they were separated and divorced in 1945. John seems to have continued living in Cincinnati for the remainder of his life. He died there in 1979.

Elizabeth McElroy

The Springfield Sun captured the pathos of the stricken McElroy home with its report on the funeral of Elizabeth McElroy.

"Miss McElroy was an only child, the life and joy of her home. She possessed many beautiful traits of character which endeared her to all who knew her, and was a social favorite among her society set. She was a bright and accomplished girl of grace and beauty, whose young life was the hope of her fond parents who were suddenly stricken with the almost unbearable grief at their loss.

"The church was filled to overflowing with sorrowing friends who gathered to pay their last respects to their young friend. The many beautiful floral designs were silent testimony of the esteem in which the departed was held. The grief stricken parents have the deepest sympathy of their many friends in their sorrow. Among those who attended the funeral from a distance were many young school friends who were horrified to learn of the tragic death of their beloved companion."

Elizabeth McElroy was born 25 Nov 1900 to Howard B. and Annie (Cunningham) McElroy of Springfield. Her grandparents were William and Sue (Calhoun) McElroy, and Andrew and Elizabeth (Bullock) Cunningham. She was a student at Science Hill Academy in Shelbyville, and was on her way home for the holidays when the wreck occurred.

Her friend, Mary Alethaire Simms arrived in Louisville from St. Mary's Female College, at Notre Dame, Indiana, along with Thomas Spalding, a Notre Dame student and athlete. Happy to see one another, Elizabeth and Alethaire shared a seat on the train.

According to *The Louisville Times,* both girls "were crushed between the telescoped seats and timbers and death was instantaneous."

When news of the wreck reached Springfield, Howard and Annie rushed to Louisville, only to find that their daughter, their only child, was dead. Annie was so distraught that she had to be taken to the Norton Infirmary for treatment.

Howard and Annie were to have no more children. Elizabeth had been their pride and joy, and it is likely that they never fully recovered from their loss.

On 25 Jun 1943, Annie McElroy was admitted to St Joseph Hospital in Louisville. Her death certificate reports that she died of a fractured skull due to jumping from the third floor of the hospital. Whatever else might have troubled her, we can't help but believe that the loss of her precious daughter must be contributed to her final action.

Howard McElroy, who had been president of the Springfield Light & Water Company, died on 10 Sep 1944 at the age of 71.

Lillian Jones Miller

Oliver and Dona (Roach) Jones lived in the small community of Cromwell in Ohio County with their three daughters, Effie, Lillian, and Ernestine. Effie married Murray Hudson, and Ernestine married Nicholas Speed Barrass, both of whom were electrical engineers working in the coal mining industry.

Lillian married Robert Howard Miller, and they moved to Bardstown where Robert opened his doctor's office. Their first child, Robert Jones Miller, was born in 1908. His brother, Charles Howard Miller, was born in 1911.

Lillian's younger sister, Ernestine had two children, Nicholas and Edward, before she became ill with meningitis and died in November 1916. Her parents could not know that they would lose yet another daughter the following year.

Lillian may have traveled to Louisville with friends to buy Christmas presents for her two sons on that fateful day. She was almost certainly in the first coach to be struck, and likely died almost immediately.

Dr. Miller claimed her body from the funeral train when it reached Bardstown. The funeral was conducted in their home, and then he took her back to Beaver Dam for burial.

Left with two sons to rear, and a medical practice to maintain, Robert remarried, this time to Lola Prall, daughter of Thomas and Ida Prall. By 1920, they were living in Louisville. They added two daughters to the family, Dorothy, born in 1920, and Hazel, born in 1925.

Robert and Lillian's sons both married in 1937. Robert Jones Miller married Edna Smock, and Charles Howard Miller married Margaret Mary Kinberger.

Charles was living in St. Louis and his brother was still in Louisville when their father died there in 1957. His remains were returned to Beaver Dam and placed next to Lillian's grave.

Mabel Brown Miller

In March 1879, Joseph Brown, son of Charles and Margaret (Kurtz) Brown, married Laura Warrall, daughter of Henry and Emma (Hall) Warrall, in Bardstown, a joining of two hard-working families. Joseph was 25, Laura was 18. Two years later their daughter Mabel was born. She would be the first of seven children born to this butcher and his bride.

Mabel was born in April 1881. It seemed in 1914 that she was destined for spinsterhood, at the age of 33, when Thomas Jefferson Miller, a cashier at the New Hope bank, asked her to be his wife. They were married in November, and began their lives together in New Hope.

On Monday, December 17, 1917, Mabel wrote a letter to her brother Joe who was living in Texas. It was a typical letter between a sister and her brother, and captured life in a close family. She would not live to write another.

According to a letter her mother wrote to Joe later, Mabel had been in Louisville for two days, and was coming to Bardstown on the evening train. Her mother wrote, "They found her with her face turned up. She was the only one you could recognize readily."

Mabel Brown Miller
(image from microfilm)

Mabel's skull had been fractured from behind, but her face was untouched. She was one of only three with funerals in Bardstown whose casket was open.

In her mother's letter, the family's grief soaks each page. Both letters are included in the Appendix B of this book.

A year and a half later, Thomas married Bernice Beatrice Kelley, a local school teacher. They would remain together until his death in 1947 at the age of 64. Bernice lived until 1966, dying at the age of 85.

At his death, Thomas was cashier and vice-president of Peoples Bank of New Hope. He left no descendants.

Walter McMakin Miller
Amelia Smith Miller

In what the newspaper described as "a social event of importance," W. Mack Miller and Amelia Smith were married at Bardstown Baptist Church in December 1902. Mack Miller was the son of Charles and Maggie (McMakin) Miller of Cox's Creek, and grandson of Isaac Miller, both of whom had been prominent farmers in Nelson County. Mack himself was an "enterprising stock trader" who seemed to specialize in mules. Amelia was a daughter of Thomas Jefferson and Elizabeth (Langsford) Smith. Mr. Smith was president of the People's Bank in Bardstown.

Tom Smith Miller 1909

Mack and Amelia's only child was a son, born in 1905, and named Tom Smith Miller after Amelia's father.

By December 1917, Mack and Amelia had recently sold their farm and moved to Bardstown where Mack entered the real estate business. They were living with Amelia's mother, Lizzie Smith. It would be Lizzie who gathered young Tom in her arms and provided him with a home.

While there was some discussion in the community that Mack and Amelia were having marital problems, they seemed to have solved them, or at least put them aside for the holidays. They were in Louisville that day, likely shopping for presents for their eleven-year-old son who had remained in Bardstown with his grandmother.

Mack and Amelia Miller
(images from microfilm)

Both Mack and Amelia died at the scene of the wreck. Their bodies were returned to Bardstown on the funeral train, and their funerals were held at the home of Lizzie Smith, Amelia's mother.

In their obituaries, Mack was described as "a loyal and true friend, no exertion was too arduous and no trouble too great when helping his friends. He was progressive in his ideas and a splendid judge of real estate values." Amelia was described as "an active and prominent member of the Baptist church and an ardent church worker. Hers was a noble Christian character and like unto her husband no undertaking was too great when she could alleviate suffering."

Young Tom Smith Miller grew up in his grandmother's home. He married Mary Smith of Bardstown, and they had six children, including three girls (Mary Amelia, Lucy, and Margaret) and three boys (Edward McMakin, Tom Smith Jr., and Walter Lee).

Tom Smith Miller was a realtor most of his life. He lived until 1971; his wife Mary died in 1996.

Garnette McKay Moore

Garnette McKay Moore was planning a special Christmas, and had invited her sisters Ophelia and Emily to join her. Emily, the widow of Effingham M. Sturgis, lived in Zanesville, Ohio, and had already arrived. Ophelia, the wife of John Edwin Robinson, lived in Fairmount, West Virginia, and was due to arrive before Christmas.

These siblings, along with their brother Harry, who lived in Texas, were children of Enoch Edwin and Ophelia (Wilson) McKay. E. E. McKay was a prominent lawyer and judge in Bardstown and Louisville.

For a time Garnette worked in the internal revenue office in Louisville. It was here that she met Lee Jouett Dudley, son of William Talbot and Mary (Jouett) Dudley. Lee and Garnette were married in 1896, and were soon the proud parents of a son they named for Lee's father.

They moved quite a bit, living in Chicago in 1900, and later with her sister Emily in 1910. During that time, they lost their son William when he died in 1906.

Lee Dudley worked as a real estate agent until he became ill. He died on January 9, 1913, and was buried in Frankfort alongside his son in the Dudley family plot.

It was an especially trying time for Garnette as her father died a week later, and then her mother passed in September.

Garnette returned to her ancestral home in Bardstown to live. Here she met and married Thomas Slevin Moore the next year. Thomas, a widower, was president of the Mattingly and Moore distillery at Bardstown.

Thomas and Garnette lived a busy social life, and this Christmas was no exception.

Garnette and Emily took the train that morning to Louisville to do some shopping, and to meet Emily's daughter who was supposed to be coming on the train from Cincinnati to met them.

When they arrived at the depot that evening, Emily's daughter had not arrived. At first both ladies boarded the

Garnette McKay

train, but then Emily decided to remain in Louisville and wait for her daughter. This decision almost certainly saved her life.

Garnette was one of those found dead at the scene of the wreck.

In her obituary, *The Kentucky Standard* of Bardstown wrote, "Mrs. Moore was a woman of great mental ability and was preeminently a leader. She was a member of the U.D.C. and also of the Bardstown Woman's Club and served two terms as President of each organization and was also Chairman of the Womans Federated Clubs of the Fifth District of Kentucky."

Also, the Zanesville correspondent to *The Newark Daily Advocate* of Newark, Ohio, wrote following her death, "Mrs. Moore had hosts of friends in Zanesville who were greatly shocked when apprised of her death. She was known to many Zanesville people as Mrs. Lee Dudley, for it was during her widowhood that she resided with Mrs. Sturges and her marriage to Thomas S. Moore of Bardstown, Ky., was solemnized at the Sturges home. ... Mrs. Moore was a dramatic reader and gave a number of private readings in this city during her residence, which covered a period of three years."

Life went on for her husband and siblings. Her brother, who had married Mary Sue Loftin in Texas, lived there until his death in 1947. Emily McKay Sturges died in Zanesville in 1955, and her sister Ophelia and Ophelia's husband both died in West Virginia in 1957.

Tom Moore married for a third time, this time to Nellie Simon Kleimeyer who brought a son, John Walter Kleimeyer to the marriage. Tom sold his distillery and later bought the Talbott Inn from T. D. Beam in 1926. It remained in the Moore family until 1964. Tom, himself, died in 1937 in the midst of the Depression.

It's hard not to imagine that the brightest years of his life might have been those few he shared with Garnette.

George Washington Moore

George Washington Moore was born in 1893 to James and Ada (Oliver) Moore. As a teenager he hired out to work on a neighbor's farm, and then traveled to Illinois where he worked for Louis Strugal on his farm in Lanesville. He was there when he completed his World War I draft registration in June 1917, and it may be that he was on his way home to Springfield for the holiday at the time of the wreck.

A week after the wreck, *The Springfield Sun* reported, "George Moore, who was reported as seriously injured, was able to leave the hospital and come to his home near Mooresville."

George was called up to serve in the army, through the Kentucky National Guard. Following the war, he was instrumental in organizing the 53d Machine Gun Squadron of the Kentucky National Guard in Springfield.

He married Mary Inez Smith, and they had six children: Reba, George Jr., Frank, Mary Inez, Thomas, and Louis.

George worked at a variety of jobs, including as caretaker for cavalry horses, as well as doing

---

some farming. However, when World War II broke out, he was ready to serve again. According to his obituary, he had two years of active duty, and took part in three invasions, Africa, Sicily, and Italy.

George W. Moore

During his time in the service, George was awarded four bronze stars, and a purple heart, and achieved the rank of master sergeant.

George died in October 1954, in Springfield.

Mary Inez married again, this time to Forrest Carrico. When she died in August 1978 in Springfield, all six children remained to honor their parents' final resting place in the Holy Rosary Cemetery in Springfield.

Lucas Moore

Lucas Moore, son of Henry and Jane (Pile) Moore of Washington County, married Mary Sue "Mamie" Brown in 1883 in Springfield. They had three children, a daughter Eloise who married George Marion Quick, a son Henry Raymond who married Grace Evelyn Whetherbee, and a daughter Frances Lucretia who first married Charles Mark Dolan.

Sadly Lucas and Mamie went their separate ways. Later Lucas married Josephine McElroy, and Mamie married first John Phelps and then John Breeding. Mamie was living in Cook County, Illinois when she died in 1941.

Eloise Moore Quick tragically died in 1909, leaving two children. One was named Roy; we have found no record of the other. Her husband later married Pearl Napier. Henry and Grace Moore had two children: Grace Eloise and John Norman Moore. And Charles and Frances Dolan had four children: Dorothy, Daniel, Jack, and Ted.

Lucas Moore was Commissioner of Agriculture under the Republican governor, William O. Bradley. By the time of the wreck he was working as a field agent for the United States Bureau of Crop Estimates. He had made a trip to Louisville on official business only a few days prior to the fatal wreck, and was on his way back to Springfield.

The Louisville Times reported the next day, "Papers in the pockets of his clothing established the identity this morning of Lucas Moore, field agent for the United States Bureau of Crop Estimation of the Custom House. Mrs. Moore received word last night of the number of dead and wounded and went immediately to Sts. Mary and Elizabeth Hospital where the injured were being brought in. No trace of Mr. Moore was found and the lists of both the dead and injured did not show his name. At Cralle's undertaking establishment early this morning T. Scott Mayes, internal revenue collector noticed a resemblance of the badly disfigured features of one of the bodies and an investigation established the identity."

Lucas Moore

A week later, *The Springfield Sun* reported that his remains had been returned to Springfield, and that burial was made in the old family grave yard at the old homestead of his grandfather, known as the Bennie Pile place, near Maud.

Josephine McElroy Moore, who had retired from the nursing profession when she married Lucas, returned to it following his death. In 1918 she became the superintendent of nurses at City Hospital in Louisville. Then in 1921, she married Samuel H. Gregory of St. Louis and made her home there.

James Hartwell "Jimmy" Morrison

Jimmy Morrison was born in 1902, and had just passed his 15th birthday at the time of the wreck. *The Pioneer News* reported, "He passed through the grades at Bardstown Junction School and graduated in the spring of 1917. He entered the Shepherdsville High School in the fall of 1917. Though small in stature, and young in years, he showed marked ability in his High School studies, especially mathematics."

His parents were Jackson and Minnie (Hovious) Morrison, and he had three siblings, Grace, Andrew, and Cornelius.

Jackson Morrison had been born a deaf-mute, and the family moved about quite a bit as he sought to find work to support them. They were in Nelson County when Cornelius was born, and in Pennsylvania at the time of the 1910 census. There Jackson found a job in a factory, but apparently it didn't last for they moved back to Kentucky and settled in Bullitt County where Jackson opened a small shoe repair business in Shepherdsville. Because of his handicap, he depended on Jimmy to communicate with customers.

Jimmy had apparently been a witness to the death of 11-year-old John Robert Hoagland the previous May in a railroad accident. When Hoagland's father sued the railroad, Jimmy was called to be a witness at the trial. It had been scheduled for earlier, but had been postponed, and was finally beginning on the day of the wreck. When the trial broke for the evening, Jimmy boarded the train to travel home to Bardstown Junction.

His family was devastated at his death. Jackson Morrison, feeling he could no longer run his shoe shop without Jimmy's help, posted an announcement in *The Pioneer News* in January: "Notice: To my many friends and customers, since the train wreck which has taken my dear son, James and the horror of it all, I find that I can no longer run my shoe shop in Shepherdsville, but will move it to my home near Bardstown Junction."

The family continued to get by. Jackson repaired what shoes and boots that came his way, and worked at farming. When the World War I draft registration was called, he dutifully registered. It was recorded that he was "deaf and dumb" which disqualified him for service. He was described as of medium height and build, with brown eyes and black hair.

Jimmy may have looked a lot like this picture of his father.

In 1920, Jackson and Minnie had another daughter they named Vera. Then tragedy struck again when she drowned in the summer of 1922. According to the coroner's inquest, the cause of her death was "by drowning in pond; supposed to have been decoyed in pond by little ducks."

Jimmy's sister Grace married Louis Schwartz in 1927, and they had a son named for his father. They were living in Ohio when Grace died in 1983. His brother Andrew married Lucille Paris, also in 1927, and they had two sons, George and James. Andrew and Lucille were living in Louisville when he died in 1977.

Jackson moved the family to Jefferson County by 1930 where he worked as a farm laborer, and his son Cornelius took up the shoe cobbler trade. By the 1940 census, Jackson and Minnie were back in Adair County, living with her mother. Minnie died there in 1943. Jackson moved to Ohio to live with his son, Cornelius. He died there in 1953.

The Muir Family

We can only speculate on the life George Shadburne Muir might have led, given the chance. At sixteen, he was already a student at St. Joseph's College and was preparing himself to attend Yale University. From all indications, he was a very popular and energetic young man with considerable promise.

But George never got the chance to fulfill his promise, as he and his parents were all killed in the train wreck.

The Kentucky Standard, Nelson County's newspaper, ran extensive obituaries on the family. Concerning George's father, the paper wrote the following:

"Nathaniel Wickliffe Muir was born in Bardstown sixty-five years ago. He was the eldest son of the late Honorable Jasper W. Muir, one of the most prominent attorneys and business men of Kentucky. When but sixteen years of age N. W. Muir entered the banking establishment of Wilson & Muir, as a clerk. To that institution he devoted his entire life. Owing almost entirely to his efforts the business expanded from the small bank of Wilson & Muir to the large and flourishing institution of Muir, Wilson & Muir of Bardstown and Bloomfield. N. W. Muir was recognized as one of the best posted and most reliable banking authorities in Kentucky. And at any time he chose to accept he would have been made president of a large Banking Co. of Louisville, but he steadfastly refused, preferring to devote his energies and talents to the bank with which he had been associated all his life."

"N. W. Muir was broad minded and one of the most charitable men of Nelson county, and a number of indigent families of this clip were supported almost entirely by him. He was a member and treasurer of the Pres-byterian church and a Democrat in politics. He was widely known and of a social disposition. He had gone to Louisville with his wife and only son Thursday morning for the purpose of making some Christmas purchases."

About George's mother, it said this:

"Mrs. N. W. Muir was before her marriage Miss Cora May Shadburne of San Francisco, a daughter of an old personal friend of Honorable Jasper W. Muir. When but a young girl she visited her father's friend and at his home she met her future husband. Mrs. Muir was fifty years of age. She was one of the most widely known and popular women of the entire south.

"She was an enthusiastic member of the Daughters of the Confederacy, and attended all the State and National meetings of that body. She was State President of the Jefferson Davis Monument Association, and had but a few weeks previous to her death returned from Chattanooga, Tennessee where she attended the National Convention, U.D.C. She was also County Chairman of the Kentucky Branch National League for Defense. Mrs. Muir was a great social favorite, and was one of the most generally beloved women of this city. She was a Catholic by birth and education."

Nathaniel and Cora Muir

Cora May Muir was a daughter of George D. and Ada (Maher) Shadburne. George D. Shadburne served with distinction during the Civil War. Following the war, he married Ada Maher, and they moved to San Francisco, where he became a lawyer, and they became important members of San Francisco society.

George was a son of William Henry and Eliza Ann Shadburne. Originally from Bardstown, Kentucky, the Shadburnes moved from Texas to Madison Parish, Louisiana before 1860. George's uncle, for whom he was named, Dr. George D. Shadburne, also a native of Bardstown, Kentucky, was well known in Madison Parish and apparently settled there between 1843 and 1850.

Ada Maher Shadburne was an adopted daughter of Philip and Caroline Maher. Following her death, George Shadburne married again, this time to Florence McKay, a woman 35 years his junior whom he had met while visiting his daughter in Bardstown. George D. Shadburne passed away in May 1921 in Alameda, California.

Frank Linnis Nunn

Frank Linnis Nunn's death in the train wreck was a blow for his mother, sister, wife, and daughter.

Frank's parents were John W. and Jennie (Privett) Nunn. His father had been dead since 1898, and he had lived in Louisville with his mother and sister, Anna, until he married Mary Martha Malone, a school teacher, in August 1910. She was a daughter of James and Kathryn (Sinclair) Malone. Five years later, they were blessed with a daughter they named Elizabeth, but called Betty.

Meanwhile his sister had married William Doolan, an attorney, in 1911.

A telephone message in Louisville informed Mary Nunn of the disaster before seven o'clock, and she hurried to the depot, leaving her young daughter, Elizabeth, in the care of her mother. No one there could tell her anything about the fate of her husband.

"Maybe Frank escaped injury and is trying to lend what aid he can to the less fortunate." she said to a reporter.

Mary made her way to the hospital where she learned that her husband was not on the first relief train, so she returned to the depot to sit through the long wait for the second train, bearing the dead. When she could bear the wait no longer, she introduced herself to an employee in the information window who phoned to Shepherdsville and received word that Nunn was dead.

Hearing this news, she fainted and had to be carried to a table in the lobby, where military physicians had difficulty in reviving her. A taxi was called and she was taken home in a hysterical state.

The body of Frank Nunn was mangled beyond recognition. Identification was made by his clothing and the contents of his wallet.

Frank Nunn
(Photo provided by Joyce Toth. Additional photos on page 178.)

Frank Linnis Nunn was a ticket accountant of the L & N and was going to Nazareth to assume charge of the business anticipated in connection with the holiday travel by the students at the college there. He was expected to return to Louisville the next day.

The entire family was devastated at their loss. Jennie Nunn turned to her daughter and son-in-law for comfort; she would live with their family until her death in 1946. Mary turned to her parents for help. Little Betty Nunn was too young to understand what was happening, but would surely miss her father.

Somehow, each dealt with Frank's lose, and life moved on. It is likely that Mary received compensation from the railroad, probably with the help of her brother-in-law. She returned to teaching, and saw to it that her daughter received a good education. Following high school graduation, Betty attended the University of Kentucky where she met Fred Fugazzi. They would marry and spend the rest of their lives together.

Mary Malone Nunn married Hugh Barclay Hammond in 1945, and they enjoyed five years of happiness before his death in 1950. Mary died just before Christmas 1961, in Lexington with her daughter at her side.

The Nutt Family

Claud Leon Nutt was but seven years old when he awoke at Sts. Mary and Elizabeth Hospital in Louisville where his father gave him the sad news that his mother and aunt had been killed. His father had lost an eye, and suffered broken ribs that required him to remain in the hospital for several weeks.

His great aunt, Mattie Harmon was engaged to be married, and wanted to go shopping in Louisville to purchase her wedding clothes and get some Christmas gifts. At day break Claud, his mother, Estella, his father, Daniel, and his Aunt Mattie drove a surrey two hours to reach a livery stable at Salt River Station before boarding the train to Louisville. They would be minutes from disembarking from the return train when disaster struck.

After the crash, Claud was found in a snow bank by a friend of the family. His elbow was crushed and he later learned that one doctor wanted to amputate his arm. Although he was able to use it later in life, and it functioned well, he couldn't completely straighten it out.

His mother, Estella Harris Nutt, was born in 1884 to William Simeon and Sarah Elizabeth "Bettie" (Jones) Harris. Her grandparents were James R. and Amanda Harris, and Patrick Henry and Elizabeth (Roby) Jones. She married Daniel Nutt in 1906, and they had three boys, James Ray, Claud, and Robert. Ray Nutt was born in 1908 and died in 1991 in Shelby County. Robert, the youngest, was born in 1912 and died in 1965.

His father, Daniel Nutt, was born in 1877 to Robert and Susan (Lutes) Nutt. His grandparents were James and Nancy Nutt, and Charles and Lucinda (Miller) Lutes. He later married Zilpah Crist, daughter of John and Irene (Conley) Crist, and they had a son, John in 1920. Unfortunately, he died less than a month later. Then in 1922 they had a daughter they named Susan. Susan Nutt married Albert Johnson.

At the time of the wreck, the family was living on a large farm in the Cedar Grove area. They later moved to Mt. Washington, and it was there that Claud met Ruby Dickey at a party in the home of Henry Lutes on Stringer Lane. They later bought the home and raised their eight children there. The children included three girls, Darlene, Fonda, and Mabel, and five boys, Glen, Donnie, Dannie, Lyndol, and Van Nutt.

Daniel Nutt died in October 1957, and Claud's step-mother Zilpah followed in 1970.

Claud was occasionally interviewed concerning the wreck. In 1988, Byron Crawford wrote a piece for *The Courier-Journal* on Claud's experience. Then in 1996, Missy Baxter interviewed him for another *Courier-Journal* piece printed two days before the wreck's anniversary.

In it, Claud was quoted saying that his family brought joy to his holiday season despite sad memories. He said, "In my lifetime, I have been through an awful lot of stuff, but the wreck,

I tend to think about it, especially this time of the year."

Claud died in 2000.

Maggie Mae Overall
Forrest Overall

Following the wreck, *The Kentucky Standard* wrote brief obituaries for Maggie Mae and Forrest Overall. Concerning Maggie Mae, it wrote, "Miss Maggie Mae Overall was a daughter of Mr. Asa Overall, a well known citizen of this county. She was a cousin of Forest Overall who met death in this same wreck. Miss Overall was a splendid Christian young woman and was greatly beloved by a large circle of friends. She had spent the day in Louisville shopping. The funeral was held at New Salem church Sunday morning."

It also wrote that "Forrest Overall was the son of Dr. J. B. Overall of High Grove. He was a young man of great promise. He was popular with both old and young and was highly esteemed in the community in which he resided. He has a brother, James Overall, who is now a member of the United States Army. He is survived by his father. His mother is dead."

When word of the train wreck reached Asa Overall, grief was no stranger to him. At 79, he had already buried three wives and two children. Now he would have to bury his youngest child, his grandson, and also his step-son, Emory Samuels.

Asa was born in 1838 to Jack and Lydia (Brown) Overall. He married Julia Thurman, daughter of Nicholas and Sarah (Stallings) Thurman, in 1867. They had four children including two that died as infants. One of the others was John Breckinridge Overall, born in 1869. John would become a well-known physician.

After Julie died in 1872, Asa married her sister, Malinda Thurman three years later. They had four children before she died in 1883.

Then in 1885 he married Mrs. Mary Frances (Stoner) Samuels, daughter of R. J. and Isabel (Newbolt) Stoner, and widow of Robert B. Samuels. Mary Frances brought two sons to the marriage, Emory and Charles Samuels. Then Asa and Mary Frances had two daughters: Fannie Belle in 1887, and Maggie Mae in 1893.

Meanwhile, his son, John Breckinridge Overall, married Mattie Lee Harris, daughter of James and Ann (Deacon) Harris, and they had several children including a son, Forrest, in 1901.

In November 1911, Asa lost his last wife when Mary Frances died; and then in February 1914, John lost his wife, Mattie. John married again in 1916, this time to Annie McClure, a daughter of William and Lillie (Crume) McClure.

Maggie Mae Overall was 24, and Forrest Overall was 16 when the wreck occurred and cut short their promising lives.

Asa Overall died in 1922. His son Dr. John B. Overall served as a doctor in the military during the war. He later moved his family to Springfield where he spent his last 25 years, including his last seven years as the town's mayor. He died in 1943.

Carl Herbert Perkins

The Perkins and Pinkston farms were close by one another near Willisburg in Washington County, so it was no surprise when Carl Herbert Perkins and Elizabeth Pinkston married in 1897.

Carl was Sydney and Mary Elizabeth (Derringer) Perkins' son; Elizabeth was the daughter of Cavanaugh and Armatha (Curtsinger) Pinkston. Carl and Mary Elizabeth had two sons, Paul and Russell, before she died in 1904.

Carl married again, this time to Sallie Boone in 1907. They would have eight children: Herbert, Joseph, Carl Jr., Mary, Nellie, Charles, Gertrude, and Thomas.

The day following the wreck, *The Louisville Evening Post* reported that C. H. Perkins of Washington County was seriously injured. Then on January 3rd, The Springfield Sun reported, "We learn that pneumonia has developed and that Mr. C. H. Perkins, a victim of the Shepherdsville wreck, is in a precarious condition at St. Mary & Elizabeth Hospital in Louisville. Besides other injuries and bruises, Mr. Perkins' left arm was torn off."

But survive he did. He was back in Willisburg on his farm when he completed his World War I draft card in September 1918. An interesting note: the card makes no mention of the loss of an arm, and there is a place for such a notation on the card. Perhaps the earlier report was mistaken.

Then tragedy struck the family in October when his son Russell became one of the many who died of the influenza that swept the nation.

His eldest son Paul married Gillie Farris and moved to DeKalb County, Illinois sometime in the mid-twenties. They too would have a large family.

Carl and Sarah were still living on the farm in Willisburg in the 1940 census, along with their six youngest children.

However, they were in DeKalb County, Illinois when Carl died in 1967. Sarah was also there a decade later when she died as well. Both were returned home to be buried in the Willisburg Cemetery.

David Phillips

David Phillips was born in December 1866 at Bald Knob, a rural area of Franklin County dotted with hills and some fertile bottom land.

He was the eldest of seven children born to Francis Marion and Ellen Ann (Harrod) Phillips.

In October 1889, David married James Nolia McCarty in Nelson County at her mother's home. Nolia's father, John Stapleton McCarty was deceased; her mother's name was Elizabeth (Hall) McCarty. The McCarty's lived in the Fairfield area.

By 1900, David's family was living in Jeffersonville, Indiana, and he was working as a watchman on a bridge. By then, they had three children, two daughters named Elizabeth Elton and Nannie Mildred, and a son they named Isaac Clifford Phillips. In the next decade they would add three more children: Geneva Betrix and Jesse Morris, both born in Indiana, and Lula Yager Phillips, born in Shelbyville, Kentucky in 1908.

The family managed to elude the census taker in 1910, at least as far as we have been able to determine, but their eldest daughter Elizabeth married Jesse Shain in Bardstown in November 1914. Then her sister, Nannie Mildred married Alford Churchill Shain a month later.

We are uncertain where the family was located in December 1917, when David Phillips lost his life in the train wreck. *The Kentucky Standard* described him this way: "About 50 years old and resided between Balltown and New Haven. The body was taken to the home of Griffin Shehan from where the funeral took place Sunday afternoon."

It is unclear if Mr. Shehan was a neighbor, a friend, or simply someone assigned to attend to the funeral. David's death certificate was completed in Shepherdsville where he was perhaps unknown, and it erroneously identified him as single.

It was Sherry Lee of the Bullitt County Genealogical Society who tracked down his family for us.

According to one newspaper report, Mrs. David Phillips received $10,000 from the railroad for the death of her husband.

Nolia and her four unmarried children were living in Nelson County in the Botland area along the Springfield Pike in 1920. Next door were Jesse and Elizabeth Shain and their three children.

Geneva Betrix Phillips married Joseph Alton Miles in 1924, and her mother was living with them in Louisville in the 1930 census.

In 1940, both Shain families were living in Louisville along the Preston Street Road, along with their mother-in-law, Nolia. Jesse Shain was a woodcutter in a lumber mill; Alford Shain worked in maintenance in a creamery.

Then when Nolia Phillips died in 1946, she was living in rural Bullitt County. Her daughter Elizabeth Shain was the informant for her death certificate.

Of the children, Elizabeth Shain was living in Sellersburg, Indiana at her death in 1949. Nannie Mildred Shain was 83 when she died in Louisville in 1978. Isaac Clifford Phillips was visiting a daughter in Louisiana when he died in 1987. He was a retired employee of the old Standard Oil Company of Kentucky. Geneva Betrix Miles was 84 and living in Bardstown when she died in 1987. Jessie Morris Phillips was 65 when he died in Louisville in 1973. He was a retired carpenter. And Lula Yeger Hall Canty was 91 when she passed in 1999 in Bardstown.

There were numerous children and grand-children to mourn their passings; none of whom would ever enjoy the companionship of their ancestor, David Phillips.

John & Bettie Phillips Family

John Phillips was the youngest child of Thomas and Elizabeth (Beall) Phillips of Washington County. The family lived in Fredericktown, about halfway between Bardstown and Springfield. John married Elizabeth "Bettie" Wright in 1883. She was a daughter of Morgan and Elizabeth (Hickerson) Wright, also of Washington County. John and Bettie would have three daughters and a son.

After venturing to Texas for a time, where their last daughter Ella was born, the family moved to Bardstown around 1897. The 1900 census showed John as a saloon-keeper, but he soon joined the local police force. At the time of the wreck, John was the Town Marshall of Bardstown.

Their son Thomas Ray Phillips married Nell Hooge in 1910, and they soon moved to Oklahoma City where he went to work for the Continental Insurance Company. The three daughters, Maggie May, Phoebe Elizabeth, and Ruby Ella were still living at home when the wreck occurred.

John and Bettie Phillips
(image from microfilm)

May Phillips was in a Louisville hospital following surgery. Her parents and her sister, Ella, were on their way back home to Bardstown when the wreck occurred. Ella received bruises about her face and body and an abrasion on her left ankle. Her parents did not survive the wreck.

Life would go on for the children. In a double wedding in October 1918, Ella married

Charles Leland Taylor, and May married Lovell Edelen Marks. Then the following July, Phoebe married Patrick H. Haley.

Charles Taylor was a county agent for ten years before joining the faculty at Western Kentucky State College. He was head of the agriculture department from 1942-1958 until his retirement. He and Ella had two sons, John and William, and a daughter Dorothy. Charles died in 1965, and Ella in 1980.

Lovell Marks, who was a brother to Joseph E. Marks mentioned elsewhere, had opened a

automobile garage in Bardstown in 1911, and later became a road contractor. He and May lived in Bardstown where they had three daughters, Elizabeth, Anne, and Edna Marks. Lovell died in 1952, May in 1978. The picture shown on this page of John Phillips as a policeman was provided by a great-grand-daughter of Lovell and May Marks.

Patrick and Phoebe Haley were in Wabash County, Illinois in the 1920 census where he worked as a manager for the telephone company. A decade later they were in Madisonville, Kentucky with their two sons, Phillips and Bert Haley. Phoebe died in Owensboro in 1958. Patrick lived another three years, dying at his home at Morton's Gap in Hopkins County.

Thomas Ray and Nell Phillips remained in Oklahoma City the rest of their lives. They had two sons, Ray Jr. and Proctor, and a daughter also named Nell. A 50 year employee of Continental Insurance Co, Ray retired in 1958 as state agent for Oklahoma. He died in 1965, his wife Nell in 1970.

John and Bettie Phillips did not survive to enjoy their many grandchildren, but they are not forgotten.

Alice May Pulliam

Mary Alice May was the first child born to John S. and Annie (Wakefield) May of Spencer County; but she had two older step-brothers, Hurbert and William Hinkle, children of her mother by an earlier marriage. She would later be joined by two sisters, Sallie and Bessie.

Two days before Christmas in 1899, Alice was aboard the local train on a return trip from visiting relatives in Louisville. The crowded train stopped at the tiny Gap in Knob station just north of Shepherdsville to let T. C. Coleman and a few others disembark when a heavy freight train appeared in the fog, and before the local train's engineer could do more than set his train in motion, the freight rolled into the trailing coach.

It's possible that the 17-year-old Alice had never seen death close-up before, and the memory of the crushed body of Mrs. Cora Carothers would remain with her. Eighteen years later, as the Accommodation train pulled away from the Gap in Knob station, we can imagine Alice May, now Mrs. Arch Pulliam, breathing a sigh of relief.

She had been to Louisville to visit her uncle and aunt, Ernest and Lydia May, and she was bringing presents from them back to Bardstown. At the Shepherdsville depot she waited, perhaps impatiently, for the train to be on its way. Then the crash occurred, and this time it would be Alice May Pulliam who lost her life.

Ernest and Lydia were the first to arrive at the hospital. According to *The Louisville Times*, "Relatives of Mrs. Pulliam had telephoned them asking if Mrs. Pulliam had taken the Bardstown train and apprising them of the wreck. Mr. and Mrs. May at once hurried to the hospital, hoping that their niece might have been as fortunate as in the previous wreck. Both hoped for the best until the mangled form of Mrs. Pulliam was found in the local morgue yesterday morning."

Alice and Arch Pulliam had married in Bloomfield in December 1905. They would not have any children. Nearly two years after her death, Arch Pulliam married her sister Sallie in August 1919. They adopted a son who would take his adopted father's name.

Arch Pulliam, Sr. would serve in many capacities. For eight years he was Nelson County Circuit Court Clerk. He was later Deputy State Insurance Commissioner, and then chief field deputy of the Department of Internal Revenue in Kentucky at the time of his death in 1936.

Following Arch's death, Sallie May Pulliam moved to Danville where she managed the

Centre College book store for more than 30 years. She died in 1977, and joined her husband, parents, and siblings in the Bardstown City Cemetery.

Frank Ratliff

According to *The Louisville Evening Post*, Jesse Francis "Frank" Ratliff suffers a fractured left leg, a deep scalp wound, and burns on his hip. His condition was deemed serious. By the middle of February, *The Pioneer News* was pleased to report that he was back home after several weeks in the hospital.

Frank Ratliff was born in 1883 to Charles and Nancy (Murphy) Ratliff, sometimes spelled Ratcliff. He married Nancy Evelyn Lutes in 1906. Evelyn was born in 1881 to Asa and Rebecca (Deacon) Lutes.

Frank and Evelyn's first child, a son they named Rath, was born in 1907. Two more children were born to the couple, Ophelia in 1911, and Edwin Lutes Ratliff in 1913.

Following his recovery, Frank and Evelyn continued to live on their farm in Lotus, and rear their three children. Unlike so many others affected by the train wreck, they lived long lives, as did their children.

However, the consequences of the wreck were ever with Frank Ratliff, as his granddaughter reported that he walked with a bad limp the rest of his life.

Evelyn died in 1967, and Frank followed a little more than a year later.

Their daughter Ophelia married Sidney Satterly, and they had one daughter, Sharon. Sidney, a former Staff Sergeant in World War II, died in 1968. Ophelia lived until 2000.

Rath Ratliff married Hazel Hall. They had two sons (Leason, Gale) and two daughters (Freda, Glecia). Rath died in 1985 in Shepherdsville. Hazel lived three years longer, passing in 1988.

Edwin Lutes Ratliff died in 1988. He was the retired owner of the old Ratliff Flower Shop, and a veteran of the second world war. He was survived by his wife, the former Erma Meier, a son Rodger Ratliff, and two grandchilden.

It's unlikely that Frank Ratliff's children and grandchildren ever really knew of the horror he had lived through that cold December evening.

Annie Mitchell Reed

Annie Reed came to Louisville that day in the employ of the Joseph Hurst family of Bardstown. According to Annie's daughter, Catherine, Mrs. Hurst had a doctor's appointment in Louisville, and Annie went along to take care of the Hurst baby. On the return trip they boarded the train and took seats in the rear car, the one farthest from the noise, soot and ashes

Annie Mitchell Reed

cast off by the locomotive. Then a friend of Mrs. Hurst boarded the train and wished to sit with Mrs. Hurst. Since the car was rapidly filling up, Mrs. Hurst said she would hold the baby, and Annie could go sit in the next car, the one designated as the combination smoker and colored car.

While the accommodations were less pleasant in that car, Annie may have been satisfied to be relieved of the responsibility of caring for the baby. Little did she know that this would also save her life.

When the wreck occurred, and the rear car was demolished, Mrs. Hurst and her baby, and presumably the lady who took Annie's seat, were all killed. Although the smoker car was partially destroyed, and Annie was buried under some wreckage, she escaped by breaking a window and crawling out. Miraculously, she was uninjured.

Annie's parents were Nelson and Addie (Downs) Mitchell. We believe Nelson's parents were George and Evaline (Lee) Mitchell. Addie Downs' parents were John and Catherine "Kitty" (Maddox) Downs. Annie's parents divorced when she was ten, and she went to live with her father.

She married Lem Reed in 1901, and her first child, a daughter they named Frances, was born the next year.

Annie and Lem Reed moved their family to Bardstown from Washington County in 1911. They supported their family by doing the kinds of work open to them in a segregated society. Lem worked most often as a farm laborer; Annie took in laundry, and worked as a nanny and a cook.

By 1917, Annie had given birth to eight children, six of whom still lived. Although she probably didn't know it at the time of the wreck, she was carrying her ninth child, a son who would be born the following August. Together with that son whom they named Earnest, Lem and Annie had five children after the wreck - five families that would not have existed had Annie lost her life that day.

Lem and Annie went back to Springfield in 1926, because her father was sick and they helped run the 40-acre farm. He died that same year. They lived there until Annie's death in May 1936.

A year before her death, Annie suffered her first stroke with only minor damage. She had difficulty with one of her legs and tended to drag it. Her daughter, Catherine remembers the day her Mom died. "She had a terrible headache and she had sent one of kids up the street to borrow some aspirins. Lem was across the river at the stockyard to sell a cow at the time of Annie's death and one of his neighbors hollered out to Lem that he needed to hurry home because his wife was dead."

Catherine said that Annie was a wonderful seamstress and made all of their clothes. She was of the Methodist faith and attended a small church at Beechland which had services twice a month. On Sunday, Annie, her children and some neighbors would walk to Pleasant Grove Cemetery which was approximately 3-4 miles from their house.

Catherine also remembered that some of her brothers built a baseball diamond on the property, and they and neighborhood kids would play baseball.

After Annie's death, Lem and the younger children remained in Springfield to run the farm. During the school year however, the younger children, Catherine, Louise, and Joe moved back to Bardstown and stayed with their older sister, Frances and her husband, James Edward Simms, to attend school. When school was out for the summer, they returned to Springfield to help run the farm. Catherine remembers that she had to do a lot of the work to keep the household running smoothly.

Lem married Hillary McElroy in 1943, and the family moved back to Bardstown in 1944 for good. The children continued to stay with their sister, Frances, but saw their father on a daily basis. James and Frances Simms had no children of their own, but they loved having all the little ones around.

It was at this time that Lem started playing the banjo at My Old Kentucky Home. In 1999 Lem Reed was posthumously honored by being inducted into the Nelson County Hall of Fame. At the ceremony, he was described this way:

"The legendary Lem Reed, known affectionately as 'Uncle Lem Reed,' made a tremendous contribution to tourism in Bardstown with his self-taught musical talent. Lem played

the banjo and greeted visitors with a musical welcome to My Old Kentucky Home from the mid 1940's until his death in October 1955. His banjo plucking and singing attracted the attention of thousands of tourists at the park each year. The visitors loved him and made repeated trips bringing friends back to the park to see and hear Uncle Lem.

"His notoriety spread when his picture appeared in national travel magazines. Tourists would send back pictures and one of the earliest post cards of the Home has Uncle Lem sitting on the steps to the mansion, strumming his banjo.

"His passing was sad news to many visitors who came asking for 'Uncle Lem.' But his humble contribution does not go unnoticed and appreciated by those who remember the soft strumming sounds of 'My Old Kentucky Home,' or some other Foster favorite."

Despite the hardships of living in a segregated society with limited opportunities, Lem and Annie Reed did well by their family, and they are remembered fondly by their descendants, many of whom continue to live in the Bardstown area.

Felix Leonard Riney

Several Louisville newspaper reports indicated that a Leonard Riley was injured in the train wreck. However, *The Springfield Sun*, where he lived, gave his name as Leonard Riney. He received a cut on his head and multiple bruises, and was taken to the hospital in

Louisville where he stayed at least until the new year. By the middle of February, he was home. The newspaper reported that he was suing the railroad for $12,500 for compensation for his injuries. After that, he seems to disappear.

Felix Leonard Riney was born in February 1894 to William and Annie (Smith) Riney in Springfield. His father, William, was the second son by that name born to Joseph and Isabel (Cambron) Riney. The first William died in 1853 of lockjaw, and the couple named their next son William also. Helen Anastasia "Annie" Smith was born in February 1865 in Marion County to Benedict Joseph and Harriet (Rhodes) Smith.

Leonard's father, William Riney died in 1906. He and Annie parented eight children: six boys and two girls. When Annie Riney died in 1948, she was survived by "one daughter, Mrs. O.B. Robinson, Louisville; five sons, Joseph, William, and Leo Riney, Detroit, Michigan, Robert and David Riney, Springfield; two sisters, Mrs. E.K. Enders, Denver, Colorado, and Mrs. Ralph Longnecker, Los Angeles, California; twenty-three grandchildren and seventeen great-grandchildren" according to her obituary in *The Springfield Sun*.

We have found no death certificate, or report of his death, but there is a gravestone for Leonard F. Riney in the Saint Rose Cemetery in Springfield with a death date of November 12, 1918. Perhaps he was a victim of the influenza sweeping the nation at that time. We don't know.

Augustine Leon "Lee" Roby

Lee Roby was tall and slender, with brown eyes and black hair. A man who worked with his hands, he was used to getting dirty, but nothing like the appearance he presented following the train wreck.

The next day, *The Louisville Times* reported that "Lee Roby, a produce man of Bardstown,

presents a terrible appearance at Sts. Mary and Elizabeth Hospital. His face is black where it was ground into the earth. His shoulder is crushed and while he was lying on the ground after the wreck a woman bound his injuries with string torn from her underskirt. Mr. Roby did not get the name of his benefactress. The man who sat with Mr. Roby was killed. Mr. Roby did not know his name."

A son of Daniel Martin and Harriet Ann (Bean) Roby, Lee was born in 1889. He married Anna Mae Lutes in 1911. She was a daughter of Thomas Jefferson and Anna Elizabeth (Flaherty) Lutes.

At the time of the wreck, records show that Lee Roby was a half-owner of a truck farm, which accounts for his being called a "produce man" by the newspaper.

At the time of the wreck, Lee and Anna Mae had two children: Leo Augustine and Hilary Lutes Roby. They would add six more in succeeding years.

In the years following, Lee would drive a truck for the state highway department before going to work at Flaget Hospital in Bardstown.

Lee and Anna Mae lived long and productive lives. She passed in 1972 at the age of 77, and he died the next year, age 83.

Of their children, a daughter Stella May was born in 1927, but died when she was but five years old. One other child, Hilary Lutes Roby died before his parents when he passed in 1964 at the age of 49. He had been an electrician for the L. & N. Railroad for ten years, and was married to Margaret Sullivan.

Anna Mae had been carrying their third child when the wreck occurred. He was born the following May, and was named Marion. He would marry Rosemary Robinson, and they would have several children including Sandra, Linda, Ronald, and Robert Roby. Marion died in his 60th year in 1978.

Another son was Felix Pitt Roby, born to Anna Mae in 1921. Felix was a Coast Guard veteran of World War II, and an employee of the Pennsylvania Railroad Company. He married Irene McGovern, and they had a son named Michael. Felix was living in Alameda, California when he died in 1984.

Leo Roby was 79 when he died in 1992. He was a retired machinist for the old International Harvester Company. He was married to Ethel Pottinger.

William Pius Roby was born in 1930. We know that he worked in one of the distilleries, and that he married Clara Lois Adams in 1976. He died in 2007.

Ann Eleanora Roby was born in 1924. She married Raymond Gill, and they had two daughters, Shaun Marie and Leann. Eleanora was 86 when she died in 2010.

Helen Roby was the last of Lee and Anna's children. She was born in 1931 and lived until 2013. She was an employee of Brown-Forman Distillers for 35 years before retiring. Helen never married.

The Roby's were among the fortunate that terrible evening in Shepherdsville. Lee survived, and eight children were blessed with a father.

Samuels

Both Emory Samuels and Harry Mack Samuels traced their ancestry back to Robert and Mary (Wakefield) Samuels who moved from Pennsylvania to Nelson County, Kentucky prior to the birth of their youngest son, John Samuels in 1786. They brought with them an older son, William who was born about 1780. Emory Samuels was a great-grandson of William Samuels; Harry Mack Samuels was a great-grandson of John Samuels, William's brother.

The Samuels family gave its name to the Nelson County community in which it lived. William married Sarah Hoagland, and one of

their sons was Taylor W. Samuels who opened a distillery just east of Deatsville on the Bardstown branch of the L. & N. Railroad in 1844. Taylor married Lavinia Osborne and one of their children was Robert B. Samuels, Emory Samuels' father.

Emory Beamis Samuels

Robert Samuels married Mary Francis Stoner, daughter of R. J. and Isabel (Newbolt) Stoner, and they had two sons: Emory B. and Charles F. Samuels. After Robert's death, Mary Francis married Asa B. Overall in 1885. They had two daughters: Fannie Belle in 1887, and Maggie Mae in 1893. Both Emory Samuels and Maggie Mae Overall would die in the train wreck.

Emory Samuels married Edna May Magruder, daughter of William and Delilah (Harris) Magruder. They had two sons. Maurice William Samuels was born in 1913, but died less than three years later in 1916 of pneumonia. The second son, Emory Beamis Samuels, Jr., was born in 1916. Known throughout his life as Beamis Samuels, he attended the University of Kentucky, and was a staff sergeant in the army during World War II. He married Gladys Mae Burkhardt. Beamis lived until 1986; Gladys died in 2003.

Beamis Samuels, Jr.
(college photo)

At Emory's death in the train wreck, *The Kentucky Standard* newspaper of Nelson County wrote "He was the most prominent man of the north end of this county. He was a [grand]son of T. P. Samuels of Deatsville and proprietor of the large mercantile establishment at that place. He also had farming interests."

After Emory Samuels' death in the train wreck, Edna moved close to her parents where she was living in 1920. She married Gus Hardin sometime after the 1930 census. They lived in Cox's Creek. Edna died in 1970. Gus lived until 1999.

Harry Mack Samuels

John Samuels, son of Robert and Mary (Wakefield) Samuels, married Rachel Kurtz in 1814. Their first son was Wilson Samuels, and he married Martha Stoner. Their first son was William B. Samuels, born in 1842, who married Mary Jane "Mamie" Barclay. Henry Mack Samuels was their son, born in 1875.

Mamie Barclay Samuels was born in 1844 to J. H. and Elizabeth (Thompson) Barclay. Sometime following William B. Samuels' death in 1902, Mamie married a Mr. Hess according to her death certificate. She died in 1923.

Harry Mack Samuels married Katie Carlisle in 1899. Their daughter, Lydia, was born in March 1900 according to the 1900 census that also shows Harry's family living next door to his parents. Harry was working as a grocer.

A decade later, their son William had been born, and Harry had joined his cousins in the distillery business. He is listed in that census as the secretary/treasurer for the distillery. By September 1918 he was the superintendent of the distillery farm.

The advent of prohibition is seen in the 1920 census record where Harry is listed as a farmer; no mention of the distillery. However, Harry seems to have done well for his growing family. Katie had given birth to two more daughters, Dorothy and Martha. In 1930, at the beginning of the Great Depression, the census lists Harry as a "capitalist."

Katie Carlisle Samuels died in 1945. Sometime after that, Harry moved to Louisville, where he died in 1952.

Of their children, Lydia Samuels married James G. Bullock, an accountant for the L. & N. Railroad. They had a daughter Joan, and two sons, James and Phillip. James died in 1993, and Lydia followed in 1998.

William Harry Samuels was born in 1902. He married Virginia McGinnis, and they had two daughters, Dorothy and Alice, and two sons, Harry and Johnny. Virginia died in 1976, Harry in 1988.

Dorothy Miriam Samuels married Henry Caleb Bell, and they had two daughters, Kathryn and Dorothy, and two sons, Donald and Henry. Henry Caleb Bell died in 1960. Dorthy lived until 1989.

We know little of Martha Samuels, except that she was born in 1913 and died in 2003.

A final Samuels note: Taylor William Samuels, the founder of the Makers Mark Distillery was a first-cousin to Emory Samuels, and a third-cousin to Harry Mack Samuels.

Thomas William Schaefer

Thomas William Schaefer was the ninth child born to Christian and Lula (Moss) Schaefer, but only five had survived to that point. Christian Schaefer was born in 1856 in Germany to Andrew and Susan (Hosselbach) Schaefer. He arrived in America in 1880, and married Lula Moss some eight years later. Lula's parents were John Calvin and Delilah (Whitaker) Moss. She was born in 1868 in Louisville.

By 1917 their sons were growing into young men. Thomas, who was born in 1900, was finishing his schooling at St. Xavier in Louisville. He may have traveled by train each morning to Louisville and returned home to Clermont on the evening train. As he boarded the train that fateful evening, his thoughts may have been more on the holiday and his mamma's cooking than his school work. She would wait in vain to ever feed him again.

His death would not be the last the family suffered. Their son Oscar Paul Schaefer joined the army, and rose rapidly in rank, reaching sergeant in 1918. As a member of the 9th Infantry Regiment, 2nd Infantry Division, he was fighting in France where he was wounded. He died of his wounds in September 1918, and was buried in the St. Mihiel American Cemetery in Thiaucourt, France.

Then Lula lost her mother in 1920, and her husband when Christian died in November 1924. He was 68. Lula lived almost ten years after his death, dying in July 1931.

Neither of their remaining sons ever married; leaving a promising family barren of a new generation.

Frances (Susie) Sheckles

At 18, Susie Sheckles went to work as a live-in maid and nanny for the William Simmons family. In the segregated society in which she lived, it was actually a decent job. At the time the two Simmons daughters were quite young; Susan Simmons was four, and Evalina (later known as Willie Maye) was two.

We are uncertain who Susie Sheckle's parents were, but in 1900 she was living in the household of George and Isabelle Sheckles, and was identified as their granddaughter.

When Mrs. Simmons decided to take Susan with her to Christmas shop that fateful morning, Susie Sheckles went along as well. By now Susan was twelve, and had grown very attached to her nanny.

When the wreck occurred, we think Mrs. Simmons was in the passenger car, the first one to be struck by the express train. It is likely that her daughter, Susan, was in the next car sitting

with Miss Sheckles. Miss Simmons was killed; Susan and her nanny survived.

The censuses in 1920 and 1930 show Susie Sheckles living with her uncle and aunt, Dee and Susan (Sheckles) Weathers on a farm off Cedar Grove road, quite near the Simmons farm. She continued to live with her aunt after her uncle died.

Over the years, Miss Sheckles continued to work for the Simmons. She never married.

In 1972 she made out her will, leaving her entire estate, minus her sewing machine, to the Mount Zion Baptist Church in Shepherdsville. The sewing machine was to go to Willie Maye. When Susie Sheckles died on 4 Jul 1977, her remains were buried in the Simmons Family Cemetery on what had become the Hackett farm.

According to the funeral home records, in addition to her friends, Miss Sheckles was survived by several cousins including Carrie Hoagland, Birdie Rose, Mary Jane Butler, Clarence Carson, and Samuel Weathers.

The church used the proceeds from her estate to help finance the construction of their fellowship hall, a place Susie would almost certainly have enjoyed. The picture of her shown above hangs prominently in the hall.

Charles William Shelton

Charles William Shelton was born in 1885 in Bullitt County to James Henry and Eliza E. (Cundiff) Shelton. His father was born in 1855, a son of William and Elizabeth (Cundiff) Shelton.

His mother, Eliza, was born in 1859 to James B. and Gillie (Boots) Cundiff.

Charles married Maude H. McClure in 1909 in Bullitt County. Maude was born in 1892, a daughter of James F. and Mary E. (Dunn) McClure. Her younger brother, John McKinley McClure, would be on the train with her husband that fateful evening. Also aboard would be Charlie Showalter, the husband of their sister, Ada Belle McClure.

Charles and Maude Shelton had five children; Escor in October 1910, Edward Mitchell in August 1912, Eliza in April 1916 who died a year later in October 1917, Calvin in August 1918, and Edna in December 1922, all while living in Bullitt County. During that time Charles farmed to support the family.

It is not clear what injuries Charles suffered in the wreck, but at least one newspaper described his injuries as serious. Like many others, he sued the railroad, and like most he settled out of court.

Sometime in the 1920's, Charles and his family moved to the Madisonville neighborhood of Cincinnati. There he and his two oldest sons were in the business of building hardwood floors. His brother Paul was living with them, and working as an automobile salesman. His brother-in-law, John McKinley McClure and his family were also in Cincinnati at this time.

Charles William Shelton was nearly 90 when he died in 1975, after years of working in the hardwood flooring industry. Maude was 90 when she died in 1982.

Of their children, Mitchell married Viola Levitz, and they had a son named David. Mitchell died in 1976. Calvin Shelton died in January 1989. He had married Marie Lewis, and they had a son named Ronald. In October of that year, his brother Escor Shelton died. Escor had married Kathryn Haney and they had two children, Robert and Elaine. And Edna Shelton married J. L. McCord and they had a son named James. Edna was the last of these siblings to die when she passed in 2011.

Each of these children and their families were grateful that Charles had survived the train wreck.

John and Charlie Showalters

Perhaps John and Charlie Showalters had been in Shepherdsville and boarded the Accommodation there to return home to Bardstown Junction, or perhaps they were in Louisville, we're not certain; but they were aboard when the wreck occurred, most likely in the smoker car. John suffered a fracture over his left eye, and severe lacerations on his body. Charlie Showalters had bruises and abrasions on his face and body, and possible internal injuries; but they would survive this tragedy.

The Showalters family (often spelled without the final s) had been in Bullitt County at least as early as 1870 when Jacob Hite Showalters married Sarah Hall there in July 1870. Among their many children were John William Showalters who was born in November 1875, and Charlie Showalters born in May 1882.

John married May Roach, and at the time of the wreck they had four children, Arthur, Anna, Lillian, and Ethel. May (aka "Anna Mae" or "Susie Mae") Roach Showalter was born in 1884 in Louisville to William and Julia Ann (Philpot) Roach.

Of John and May's children, Anna Mae Showalters died of meningitis in September 1910. Sarah Ethel first married Richard Noe, and they had a daughter Virginia. She later married Dewey Gill. Lillian married Clyde Crigler and they had five boys, David, Bill, Arthur, John, and Walter. And Arthur Showalters married Sara Lee Phillips and they had three children, Mary Jane, Arthur Jr., and Richard Thomas Showalters.

Charlie married Ada Belle McClure, and they had four children at the time of the wreck, Gertrude, Ethel, Charles, and Sarah. Their son Earl was born in 1920, and then they had twin daughters, Della and Stella a few years later. Ada Belle McClure Showalter was born in 1887 to James and Elizabeth (Dunn) McClure who lived at Belmont. Her sister, Maude had married Charles William Shelton who was on the train that evening. Also, her brother, John McKinley McClure, would ride it as well.

Of Charlie and Ada's daughters, Gertrude married Roy Franklin Walker and they had four children, Billy Jo, Roy, Helen, and Verna Ray Walker. After Roy's death in 1980, Gertrude married Hamlet E. Croan. Ethel first married Jerome Humphreys and they had a son, also named Jerome. Following her husband's death in 1951, Ethel married Clarance J. Sharp. Sarah Elizabeth married Clyde McCubbins and they had three children, Sara Jo, Clyde Jr., and Russell. Della married Roy Kulmer and they had seven children including Dorothy, Linda, Delia, David, James, Norman, and Paul. And Stella married Bill Goodin and they had four children, Judy, Garry, Larry, and Terry.

Of their sons, Charles was killed in an automobile accident south of Shepherdsville in 1940. He never married.

Earl Showalter was a decorated World War II army veteran serving as a 1st Scout in the Asiatic-Pacific Theater. He received 2 purple hearts and 5 Bronze stars, earning one of those in the Philippine Liberation. Earl first married Helen Deats and they had two daughters, Sheila and Debra. He later married Anna Blanton. He retired from Brown-Foreman after 40 plus years.

John Showalters was 89 when he died in 1964. His younger brother Charlie was 84 when he passed in 1966. They had both survived the terrible train crash and had gone on to head large families of children and grandchildren.

The Simmons Family

Susan and Willie Maye Simmons lost their father William Simmons a week before Christmas in 1914. Susan was nine, Willie Mae was seven. Their mother, Carrie May Simmons was 36, a daughter of William and Evelyne (Forsythe) Brown. She would rely on the support of her family, and the constant presence of the girls' nanny Susie Sheckles, in rearing her two daughters.

In the words of a friend, J. R. Zimmerman, "If you never knew Mr. William Simmons you missed a great deal." Zimmerman went on to describe Simmons this way: "He was one of those princely fellows, brim-full of good humor and it just radiated from him to all who were fortunate enough to be around him. His long experience as a stock buyer and seller, made him a fine judge of credit. He was President of the Peoples Bank, and his business sense helped that institution immensely, while personal popularity added hundreds of depositors to its list of customers."

While his death was a shock to the family, he left them well-provided, and his wife was described as one of the wealthiest women in Bullitt County.

That December morning, Carrie left her younger daughter with her mother, and set out with Susan and her nanny for Louisville, intending to do some serious Christmas shopping. On the return journey they surely must have had many gifts to share. We speculate that Carrie and her daughter rode in the car farthest from the locomotive, and that Miss Sheckles was riding in the next car forward. Perhaps at Shepherdsville, knowing that they would be disembarking as soon as the train crossed the river, Carrie may have sent Susan to help Miss Sheckles with packages.

Miss Sheckles and Susan were slightly injured in the crash, but for hours no one could find Carrie Simmons. Finally, Coroner Masden sent two men to search the rubble for her. She was found beneath a mass of wreckage near the train's engine, and they had great difficulty removing her body from beneath it.

Following her death, the girls lived with Carrie's mother as they grew up.

Susan married Charles Ewell Craik, Jr., an Episcopal minister, in June 1924. He was the son and grandson of Episcopal ministers. He served at numerous churches in Kentucky, including ones in Lexington, Hopkinsville, and Louisville. Willie Maye Simmons lived with her sister until a family visit to Maine introduced her to John Everett Hackett. They were married in South Harpswell along the southern coast of Maine in August 1935.

John and Willie Maye lived in Maine for several years before moving to Kentucky where he took over the management of the Simmons farm.

They had a son, William Everett Hackett in 1943.

Charles and Susan had no children of their own, but Susan doted on her nephew, teaching him games and buying him a lot of books. He would be the fifth generation to live in the old farm house.

Charles Criak died in 1967. Besides being an Episcopal pastor, he had been an avid swimmer and a water safety examiner for the Red Cross for many years. He was also an avid newspaper reader and frequently wrote interesting letters to the editor.

During his lifetime, William Hackett served in the army in Vietnam. He married Mary Lou Streble in 1971, and was later a loan officer for

the First Federal Savings Bank in Shepherdsville. He died in 1998.

Both Susan and Willie Maye passed in 2001, Susan in April, Willie Maye in June. And John Everett Hackett followed in 2005.

Susan was a genealogist, and in her will she donated money to the Ridgeway Memorial Library to establish the genealogical room that was added when the library was remodeled; a room that sits but a short distance from where her mother was found so long ago.

Mary Alethaire Simms

Mary Charlotte "Lottie" Wall married Benedict Simms in Springfield in 1876, and by the 1900 census they had a family of eleven children including their youngest, Mary Alethaire.

They added another daughter in 1901, Mary Isabelle Simms, amid hopeful plans for the future successes of each of their children.

The first blow came in March 1909. Their son Leo Godfrey Simms, who had attended Centre College in Danville, was working in Hendersonville, North Carolina as a school principal when he became gravely ill. His later obituary in the Springfield paper, *The News-Leader*, said, "His mother left at once for his bedside and shortly thereafter his father and brothers. The boy's time was limited, however, as he was suffering from paralysis of the brain, which neither the skill of science nor the devotion of loved ones could thwart."

Then their son, Benedict Francis Simms, Jr., contracted tuberculous in his lungs and died in September 1916. He was 26 and single.

Next came the terrible blow when Alethaire was killed in the train wreck.

She was nineteen, and had been attending St. Mary's School for Girls at Notre Dame near South Bend, Indiana. She was a gifted musician and was always a popular favorite in the cast of vocal plays and school entertainments and it is reported that she was preparing to enroll in the Institute of Musical Art in New York City, the school that would later become the Juilliard School of Music.

Alethaire Simms

She was returning home for the holidays, together with her cousin, Tom Spalding. They had a two-hour lay-over in Louisville before making connections on the morning train to Springfield which left Louisville at 9:00 a.m., but they failed to get to the depot in time and missed it, forcing them to wait in Louisville for the evening train.

Lottie Wall Simms

Both perished in the train wreck. Their bodies were returned to Springfield where the families joined together in funeral services held at St. Dominic's Church. They were buried in St. Dominic's Cemetery.

With the household in deep mourning, Ben Sr. was stricken with a stroke and paralysis near the end of January. He lasted less than three weeks, dying on February 16.

Lottie Simms endured yet one more loss in 1921 when her son, John Manning Simms, died of tuberculosis at the age of twenty-four.

Lottie died in August 1927 at the age of sixty-nine, leaving a heartbroken family to mourn her passing.

James Everett Smith

James Everett Smith was a farmer and stock dealer in the Bardstown area at the time of the wreck, and was living there with his wife Sarah Fletcher, daughter of William and Annie (Combs) Henderson of Bullitt County.

Everett suffered a scalp wound, a cut on his cheek, and some bruises, but nothing worse in the destruction of the passenger coaches. He was apparently on the way back to Bardstown when the wreck occurred. Ironically, his mother, Mrs. Noah Smith was in Shepherdsville from her home in Louisville, visiting with her daughter Ophelia Patterson when the wreck occurred. *The Louisville Times* reported that she rode back to Louisville with him on the relief train.

Everett was born on a farm west of Belmont in Bullitt County in 1881. After attending the local schools, he attended Lynnland College and studied under W. B. Gwynn who had earlier been the head of the Pitts Point school.

He married Miss Fletcher Henderson in October 1903, and by the 1910 census they were living in Nelson County. Meanwhile his parents, Noah and Lena (Howlett) Smith were living in Louisville; however Noah was involved in business pursuits in Shepherdsville.

Following the wreck, Everett moved back to Shepherdsville and went into retail business with his father.

Although he had survived the train wreck, he couldn't overcome the pneumonia that took his life in January 1925. He was well-liked in the community and, despite the deep snow and biting winds then blowing, the church was filled with mourners, and many braved the cold to follow his remains to Hebron Cemetery.

Noah Smith was already in his early seventies by this time, and with his son gone, chose Ralph Henderson, brother of his daughter-in-law, to take Everett's place in the business.

Noah died in 1932, and by that time Ralph Henderson had joined with Samuel Hardy to form the business known for years as Henderson-Hardy in Shepherdsville.

Sarah Fletcher Smith continued to live in Bullitt County until her death in 1970. They had no children.

Mike Smith

The day following the wreck, *The Louisville Evening Post* reported that Michael Smith, a 37 year old living at Salt River Station, had a fracture of his left hip and bruises.

Also that day, *The Springfield Sun*, in its list of injured, listed "Mike Smith, Louisville, in dying condition." That same evening *The Louisville Times* reported that Mike Smith of Louisville had his arm "torn out," and was in serious condition. In its list of injured and dying, he was listed among the dying. Then, the next day, *The Louisville Herald* wrote, "Mr. Smith's left arm is torn from his shoulder." *The Courier-Journal* also reported the next day, "Mike Smith of Louisville, left arm torn off at the shoulder." That information was repeated in the *Kentucky Standard* of Bardstown in their Christmas Eve edition.

Then, in its 11 Jan 1918 issue, *The Pioneer News* of Shepherdsville reported, "Mike Smith, who was hurt in the wreck Dec. 20, has about recovered and is out again."

From these reports, it appears obvious that there were two Mike or Michael Smiths involved in the wreck, one from Louisville and one from near Shepherdsville.

But then it gets complicated. In trying to learn more about these two men, we've discovered seemingly conflicting records.

The first record we find is for Mike Smith, born 10 Sep 1878 in Nelson County, whose occupation is painter. In this record from Clark County, Indiana, dated 8 Jul 1911, Mike is

marrying Belle Tomlinson, a divorcee, whose maiden name is Miller. On this record, Mike's father is identified as Henry Smith, and his mother as Mary Prothers or Crothers; the initial letter of her maiden name is difficult to decipher. Mike indicates that his father is dead, and that his mother lives in Louisville.

The second record we have located is a marriage between Mikle Smith and Mrs. Clara Carpenter in Bullitt County on 29 Nov 1917. This record gives Mikle's age as 37, and indicates that he is single, not widowed or divorced. It also says that he was born in Nelson County; that his father was Perry Smith, and his mother Mary Overhawster nee Smith.

This Mary "Overhawster" is found on a marriage record in Farmersburg, Indiana, dated 18 Apr 1898, in which she is marrying Joel F. Overholser. Her "bride name" is given as Mary E. Carrithers, and her parents are named as James Carrithers and Cora Hite. Joel and Mary appear in the 1910 census in Farmersburg, but may have been in Louisville by 1911.

We know that this Mary is the mother of the Mike Smith of Shepherdsville, because, on the occasion of her death in 1923, *The Pioneer News* reported, "Mrs. Mary Overholser, aged 69 years, died at her home in Louisville Friday night of pneumonia. She was laid to rest Sunday evening in Cave Hill. She leaves a husband, Joe F. Overholser of Louisville, and one son, Mike Smith of this County by her first husband."

Regarding Clara Carpenter, we know that she was born in 1886 to Sam and Amanda (Nall) Stovall in Elizabethtown; that she married Charles Vivian Carpenter in 1909, and gave birth to a son Roy Carpenter the next year; and that Vivian Carpenter died in late 1910. After giving birth to two sons, Edward Clifford Smith in 1918, and Mitchell Smith in 1924, Clara and Mike lived in Shepherdsville until his death in 1944. She died there in 1953.

The next Smith record we have is dated 12 Sep 1918. It is the World War I registration card for Mikle S. Smith. On it we find that he lived on Route 3, Shepherdsville, that he was born 10 Sep 1878, that his occupation was painting, that his wife was named Clara, and that his left hand was "off."

Then we find a World War II registration card for Mike Smith who lives in Shepherdsville. It indicates that he was born in Nelson County on 4 Sep 1880.

The final record we have found is a death certificate for Mike Smith, a resident of Shepherdsville, who died on 20 Jan 1944. The informant for this record was Roy Carpenter, Mike's step-son. On it he indicates that Mike was born 4 Sep 1880 to Perry L. Smith and Mary Jane Carrithers. He is listed as a house painter.

On the occasion of his death, *The Pioneer News* wrote the following:

"Mr. Mike Smith of this place, well known citizen of our town for many years, died at his home here Thursday, and was buried Sunday at Hebron after funeral services at The Baptist Church by Rev. Sodeman. Mr. Smith came to this county from Nelson some thirty years ago and a few years later was married to Mrs. Clara Carpenter, and have long made their home in Shepherdsville where he held a responsible position with and for Mr. and Mrs. G. S. Patterson. He served as their agent and had active charge of all their property here and in Bullitt County, and seemed at all times to be a most loyal and energetic agent.

"Mr. Smith has no near relatives, only his widow who survives him and two sons, Edward C. of this place and Mitchell K., who is in The United States Navy, and one step-son, Roy Carpenter of this place."

So there you have it. We think most of these records refer to Mike Smith of Shepherdsville. However, the confusion about when he was born, 1878 or 1880, about what exactly were each man's injuries in the wreck, about who their parents were, and about what really became of the one from Louisville, are all things for which we have no answers. Do you?

William Thomas Simms Spalding

Tommy Spalding was a fine athlete. After completing his studies in the Springfield schools, and attending St. Joseph in Bardstown, he enrolled at Notre Dame where he excelled in both football and baseball. He was also a good student, and was studying electrical engineering at Notre Dame.

With Christmas fast approaching, he and his cousin Alethaire Simms were eager to return home to Springfield for the holiday. Alethaire was studying at St. Mary's College nearby. They took the train to Louisville where they planned to make connection with the train to Springfield. However, they missed their connection on Thursday morning at Louisville, and had to wait for the evening Accommodation train; a wait that would prove fatal.

The Springfield Sun would describe him this way: "Thomas Spalding, aged twenty-four years, was the son of Mr. and Mrs. B. A. Spalding, and a young man of sterling character, who had a lot of friends here and at Notre Dame, where he was attending school. Tommy, as he was familiarly known, was a famous athlete, a splendid baseball player and a football star. He

was one of the brightest boys who have gone out from the Springfield High School to enter college elsewhere, and had a brilliant career before him. He was just completing a course in Electric Engineering and expected to enlist in the service of this country in the capacity of an Electrical Engineer during the coming year."

Thomas Spalding was born in 1893, a son of Benedict and Alethaire (Simms) Spalding of Springfield. Theirs was a large farm family, and all deeply felt the pain of his death.

The *Notre Dame Scholastic*, the school newspaper, described him this way: "Tom was very popular among the students at the University. His cheery disposition and quiet humor won him many friends, and the expressions of sorrow and regret on the lips of students returning to the University after the holidays showed how warmly they loved him and how keenly they feel his loss."

Tom's brother, 22 year old George Spalding, came to make the identification of Tom's body. He could only recognize his brother by his shoes, so mangled was his body.

As terrible as Tom's loss was to the family, life had to continue. Ben and Alethaire had many other children, all grown or nearly so, and their company, and that of grandchildren, would help ease, but never remove the pain of their loss.

James W. Stansbury

Ella Stansbury was 18, her brother Clarence was 14, their sister Jennie was 7, and the baby Lounetta was just barely 3 years old when they saw their daddy off to Louisville that morning. Their mother, Mary Jane expected him home that evening with the presents he'd agreed to get for everyone. He would not make it.

J. W. Stansbury may have been sitting with his wife's sister, Kate Cundiff Ice, on the train. Both were killed at the scene.

J. W. was born in 1871 to James M. and Nancy Jane (Carpenter) Stansbury. He married Mary Jane Cundiff in March 1896, and Ella was born three years later. They had a farm near Bardstown Junction.

The Pioneer News described him as "a kind and loving husband and father and one of the best neighbors we have ever known, and will be greatly missed by all. He was loved by all who knew him and he was always ready and willing to help in every thing he could that would be of any good to his fellow men."

After the wreck, Mary Jane Stansbury received a settlement from the railroad, and used it to help support her children. By 1930 the family was living near Shepherdsville. Her son Clarence and her son-in-law, John Boxley who had married Jennie Stansbury, were both general store merchants. Her daughter Ella had married Samuel Hardy who was operating a hardware business in Shepherdsville.

Samuel and Ella had two children, Eloise and Jimmy. Samuel died of pneumonia in 1932. His hardware business with Ralph Henderson continued under the direction of Henderson until Ella's son Jimmy came of age. After Ralph Henderson died in 1957, Jimmy Hardy led the business until it closed in 1996. Ella lived until 1976.

Clarence Stansbury married Eugenia Masden. They had no children before Clarence was fatally injured in a car crash in 1948. Eugenia later married Cecil Cash.

Jennie Stansbury married Jack Boxley and they had a daughter Charlotte Ann before he died of pneumonia in 1942. She later married Paul Carney. She died in 1968.

Lounetta Stansbury married Bill Williams in 1935. He was a highway engineer. They had a long and happy marriage until his death in 1992.

Mary Jane Cundiff Stansbury never remarried. She died on 1 Apr 1968, age 87.

Ben Talbott

Ben Talbott had been summoned to Louisville to participate in sessions of the income tax school held annually for deputy revenue agents. After attending sessions on Wednesday and Thursday, he was on his way home to Bardstown when the wreck happened.

Ben was born and reared near Bardstown, a son of John Cotton and Naomi (McManus) Talbott. His grandparents were Daniel and Sarah (Cotton) Talbott, and Charles and Mary Ann (Robey) McManus.

He married Mamie Newman, a daughter of John E. and Marian (Olive) Newman. Her father was a successful lawyer in Louisville until his death in 1973. Her mother was said to be an exceptionally fine poetess. She moved her family to Bardstown after his death where her son, William who had been a freight agent in Louisville, entered the livery stable business.

Ben Talbott
(image from microfilm)

Ben and Mamie had four daughters: Marian Olive, Susan Evelyn, Aimee, and Florida; and a son, Ben Johnson Talbott. Aimee Talbott married Lewis Guthrie; the other children were still living at home as Christmas approached in 1917.

After engaging in the hotel and livery business Ben Talbott sold his interests to his brother George, and entered the revenue service, under the last administration of President Cleveland. He was appointed deputy collector for the Nelson County district.

Ben Talbott was one of those killed at the scene. His remains were returned to Bardstown where services were held in St. Joseph's Catholic church with burial in St. Joseph's cemetery.

Mamie Talbott moved her family to Louisville prior to the 1920 census, where she bought a home located at 1119 South Second Street, just south of St. Catherine Street. Her daughter, Aimee Guthrie's family remained at Bardstown where her husband Lewis was a bookkeeper at one of the local banks.

Lewis and Aimee Guthrie would have at least six children, including three born before the death of their grandfather. Their children were Newman, Nancy, John, Benjamin, Lewis Jr., and James.

Mamie Talbott died in May 1920 as she approached her sixty-first birthday. She bequeathed the Second Street property to her daughters Florida, Evelyn and Olive. Her personal estate, valued at $13,000, was to be distributed among her five children. This likely included what remained of the railroad settlement.

The children, all now adults, continued to live at their home on Second Street until 1928 when Ben Johnson Talbott married Mary Francis Nash, and moved about two blocks away to 122 Ormsby Ave.

The 1930 census found the remaining Talbott sisters still on Second Street. Over on Ormsby Avenue, Ben's family was growing with a son, Ben Johnson Talbott, Jr., and a daughter Martha Ann Talbott.

Ben and Mamie's son Ben took a job as a toll collector on a state highway bridge in Pulaski County at Burnside. There he became infected with Vincent's Angina, an acute communicable infection of the respiratory tract and mouth. He died there in October 1934, leaving his wife and children in the midst of the Great Depression.

Of his sisters, Florida Talbott married Gardner K. Byers in 1932, but the marriage lasted only two years. She was living in

Bardstown when she died in 1975 at the age of 80.

Evelyn Talbott joined her sisters in Bardstown where she worked as a bottler in a local distillery. She never married, and died there in 1967.

Her sister Olive was there as well. She retired from the old Fairfield Distillery, and spent her remaining years in Bardstown where she died in 1977.

Aimee and Lewis Guthrie's children presented them with 25 grandchildren before Aimee died in 1962. Lewis had been a distillery executive before his retirement. He joined Aimee again in 1967.

Their sister-in-law, Mary Frances (Nash) Talbott, Ben's widow, married John Dutton in 1944, but the marriage ended four years later. She later married Elwood B. Willingham who worked for the Louisville Truck Terminal, and was a Navy veteran. He died in 1983.

Mary Frances died in 1994, leaving her son Ben who was then in Minnesota, and her daughter Martha Ann, six grandchildren and 10 great-grandchildren; thus ending the generation of Ben and Mamie's offspring and their spouses.

James W. Thompson

James W. Thompson was deputy revenue agent of the Narcotic Department with offices in Louisville. His uncle, T. Scott Mayes, was Internal Revenue Collector for the region.

He was in Louisville Wednesday and Thursday to participate in sessions of the income tax school held annually for deputy revenue agents. He and Ben Talbott were taking the Accommodation to their homes in Bardstown that evening, and planned to return to Louisville the next morning.

We're not quite certain of the nature of his affliction, but it was severe enough that the 1880 census described him as paralyzed, and in a note written by A. M. Warren, Chief Law Agent for the railroad following the wreck, he was described as a cripple who walked with crutches.

James was born in Springfield to James Nelson and Virginia Kitura (Mayes) Thompson. Nelson and Virginia were married in February 1867, and James was born about two years later.

His sister Margaret was born in 1874. She married John Henry "Jack" Beam in 1896, the second of his three wives. Beam was the founder of the Early Times Distillery, and one of the organizers of the Farmer's Bank and Trust Company of Bardstown. His first wife was Maria Nall who died in 1891, leaving one son, Edward Beam.

Margaret died of peritonitis in June 1903. She had no children.

When J. H. Beam died in 1915, his will contained the following bequest. "I hereby give and devise the portrait of my former wife, Margaret Thompson Beam, to her mother, Virginia K. Thompson if she is living at the time of my death and if she is not living at said time, I then devise said portrait to James W. Thompson the brother of my said wife."

James lost his life in the train wreck. His body was sent to Springfield for burial. In Warren's note, mentioned above, he wrote that Thompson left a wife and mother. We have been unable to determine with certainty the name of his wife.

His mother was grief-stricken. Her husband was dead, having died in 1899. Her daughter was dead. Now her son was dead, and she had no grandchildren.

The following April, Virginia had her will written. Her daughter Margaret had given her three small diamond rings prior to her death, and Virginia specified to whom they should go, with her earnest desire that they remain in the family of her father's descendants "in memory of my beloved daughter Margaret Thompson

Beam." With no family of her own to bequeath, she devised the remainder of her estate to her brothers and their families.

She died a month later in May.

N. H. Thompson

The day after the wreck, *The Louisville Times* reported the following: "Deputy Coroner Kammerer discovered today that the man who died on the relief train last night was ... probably N. H. Thompson, of New Hope. ... On the body was found a silver railroad watch with a locomotive engraved on one side. On the face was the legend, 'Train Dispatcher,' and on the works was engraved 'Missouri Pacific.' The man had two pair of glasses in his pocket, both purchased from Dr. A. M. Phar, of Bardstown, one pair new. The name 'W. H. Johnson' had been scratched with a knife on the case of the watch."

In the days that followed, A. M. Warren, working for the railroad, tried unsuccessfully to locate someone connected with Mr. Thompson in New Hope, Loretta, and New Haven. He also talked with Judge John Kelley in Bardstown who declared that he had never heard of Thompson at Bardstown. Warren reported this to James J. Donahue, attorney for the railroad, on December 26.

Who was N. H. Thompson? Someone had identified him by name either at the scene in Shepherdsville or after his body reached Louisville; but a week later the trail was turning cold. It has remained cold for us as well.

The name N. H. Thompson appears occasionally in various places such as newspapers, but we have been unable to definitively connect any of them with the one listed as the train wreck victim. For now, and perhaps forever, he will remain just a name on a list.

Ethel Thornton

It's not clear how 16-year-old Ethel Thornton was involved in the train wreck since she was not mentioned in the Louisville papers as being injured; however, *The Pioneer News* listed her as one of those who were suing the railroad as a result of it. The paper reported that she was suing for $10,000, but later reported that the case had been settled out of court.

Ethel was born in March 1901 in Bullitt County, a daughter of Judson Thornton by his second wife, Lottie (Garrett) Thornton.

Judson had lost a son by his first marriage, when John Willie Thornton died of tuberculous on 4 Apr 1916. He was only 27, but already in business as a merchant before his death. Judson would lose another son, Ballard Thornton, a year after the train wreck to influenza.

But, Ethel came home, safe and apparently sound, from the death and destruction at Shepherdsville on that fatal evening. For this the Thornton's could be grateful.

Judson was a storekeeper in the Clermont area at the time of the wreck. Later, in 1921, he sold that business and bought a farm in the Zoneton area. From there he moved to the Highland Park area and engaged in the real estate business. But by late 1925, he was back in Clermont where he had purchased a large property and would engage in the grocery business.

From a variety of items printed in *The Pioneer News*, we know that Ethel Thornton was a popular young lady who attended many social functions.

Ethel lost her mother in March 1928. A bit more than a year later, in July 1929, she married Charles C. Garrett, a cousin living in Nelson County.

Charles and Ethel had a daughter, Rebecca Joan Garrett in 1933 in Bullitt County. Then in

1934, Ethel gave birth to Marvin Leo Garrett in Nelson County. Following this birth, Ethel suffered from postpartum hemorrhaging, and she died two weeks later.

Charles Garrett was left with two infants in the midst of the Great Depression, and he turned to his sister Rebecca for help. Rebecca and her husband, Charles Fields took the children in and reared them.

Their father, Charles C. Garrett died in 1965 at his home at Clermont.

Joan Garrett married Thomas Vincent Pike in Louisville in 1949. Together they would have ten children, and 22 grandchildren before she died in 2008. Her obituary in *The Kentucky Standard* said, "She was a lifelong homemaker, a charter board member of Hospice of Nelson County, a Sister of Charity of Nazareth Associate, and a member of St. Joseph Parish for 54 years where she served as a Eucharistic minister, an usher, a member of the Altar Society and a team member for RCIA and the Ministry Formation. She had previously served as a CCD teacher with the parish and was a former member of the parish council."

Leo Garrett married Barbara Ann Miles in 1956 in Louisville. He worked for 25 years for the Kroger Company, and was head dairyman at their Southland Terrace store when he died in 1977. Leo and Barbara had one son. When Barbara died in 2005, she left her son, four grandchildren, and five great-grandchildren.

Ethel missed the joy of watching her children and grandchildren grow up.

Joseph Roscoe Tucker

Two days after the wreck, *The Courier-Journal* reported, "Several of the injured were not removed to Louisville, but remained under the care of physicians at Shepherdsville. Roscoe Tucker, 17 years old, was selling newspapers in the smoker of the Accommodation train when the No. 7 plowed through. He suffered cuts on the head and injuries to the back."

Roscoe was actually 16, born in March 1901 to Joseph Thomas and Maggie (McCue) Tucker. Maggie was Thomas' second wife. He had married Amelia Bell in 1870, and they had two daughters, Blanche and Georgia, before Amelia died in 1875. The girls were reared by their mother's parents.

Thomas and Maggie Tucker

Thomas was already 50 years old when he married Maggie McCue, then 27. They had Roscoe first, and then his brother Urey two years later. When Thomas died in 1921, the newspaper described him as "a model husband, an affectionate, indulgent father, a kind and accommodating neighbor and splendid citizen." As time would tell, he was perhaps a too indulgent father, for Roscoe would find himself in different kinds of trouble throughout his life.

Following the wreck, Roscoe and Urey worked together in a repair shop in Shepherdsville, but following his father's death, the family moved to Louisville. By 1932, Roscoe was married to Anna Bailey. The two of them had apparently built an elaborate alcohol still operation in a three-story house on East Broadway between Barrett and Baxter Avenue that was discovered by the police and Federal agents in July.

Roscoe had been arrested a year earlier for manufacturing moonshine along with his brother Urey. When Urey said it was his operation, Roscoe was released; but family tradition indicates that Urey accepted the blame to save his brother.

Roscoe and Anna were indicted by the Grand Jury in October, but we find no record of a conviction; and with prohibition coming to an end the next year, it is possible that their case never came to trial.

Apparently Roscoe and Anna were divorced in 1942, and he married Aline May (Thompson) Kinslow in 1945. This marriage last two years. They divorced in 1947.

Meanwhile, Maggie Tucker, who had been living in Louisville, first with Urey, and then by herself after he married, came to the end of her life in October 1946, in her seventy-eighth year.

It seems from numerous newspaper reports that Roscoe Tucker was too fond of his product, as he was too frequently charged with offenses related to drinking. The last job he held was that of an air conditioning salesman before his death in November 1967.

His brother Urey was more fortunate. He married Irene (Hubbuch) Lell in 1931. She brought two children to the marriage, James and Jeanette. Together Urey and Irene had two sons, Urey Jr. and Charles.

Together Urey and Irene had eight grandchildren and six great-grandchildren to enjoy up until their deaths. Urey died in January 1977; Irene followed him in December.

Sarah Elizabeth Ward

William C. Ward was 28 and Sarah Elizabeth Morrison was almost 17 when they married in LaRue County in November 1897. He was a son of John L. and Nancy (Chancy) Ward; she was a daughter of James M. and Mary (Poteet) Morrison, and sister to Jackson Morrison.

W. C. and Sarah had their first child in July 1899 when Roy Ward was born. Next born was

Harry J. Ward, born in 1901, followed by Morrison C. Ward a year or so later, and Clara Ward in 1908.

We know the family was living at Bardstown Junction by 1910. W. C. was the proprietor of a general store and the postmaster there when tragedy struck in July 1911.

The Bullitt Pioneer reported on 14 Jul 1911 that "during the severe electric storm Wednesday, Mr. W. C. Ward, well known merchant and postmaster at Bardstown Junction, was struck by lightning and instantly killed while standing on the ground stacking hay in the field. ... Mr. Ward's remains were taken to his old home in Greensburg, Ky for interment."

Sarah was left with a farm, a store, and four children, ages three to twelve. They managed to continue with the help of family and neighbors; and Sarah's brother Jackson Morrision and his family soon lived nearby.

On April 2, 1917, President Wilson went before a joint session of Congress to request a declaration of war against Germany. A month later, soon-to-be 18-year-old Roy Ward joined the army. A year later he would be in England, writing a letter to his mother that was shared in the local paper.

One of his requests from home was a copy of the *Everyday Engineering Magazine* which indicated the kinds of things he was interested in learning.

Five months after Sarah shared his letter with the newspaper, Christmas was fast approaching. We speculate that Sarah was in Shepherdsville that afternoon, and planned to board the Accommodation for the short ride to her Bardstown Junction home. Perhaps she found the ladies' coach already full, and stepped into the smoker car for the trip home.

Newspaper reports later said that she suffered injuries about her head and back, but she was one of the fortunate ones who survived the wreck.

Her nephew was not so fortunate. She would have the task of consoling Jackson Morrison on the death of his son Jimmy.

Most of the family continued in Bullitt County until about 1924 when Sarah moved to Winchester, Ohio.

From his obituary in 1970, we know that Roy Ward spent most of the rest of his life in the military, and was a 30-year Air Force veteran. In the army and air force combined he had served in both World Wars, Korea, and Vietnam. We know that he married Ethel Bitner, and they had two children, Joan and John Ward.

Harry Jackson Ward spent much of his life in Baltimore, Maryland. He died there in February 1968, leaving his widow, the former Ruth Von Schricker, a son Harry Jr., and two step-children, Ruth and Earl.

Morrison C. Ward was a Louisville & Nashville Railroad conductor for 30 years before retiring in 1949. He died in Louisville in August 1955, leaving his widow the former Lillie Lee Miller, and a son Tom Ward.

Clara Ward married Mason Edwards in 1927 in Ohio. They had five children: John William, Mary Lou, Virginia Carolyn, Ruth, and Mary Lee Edwards. Clara died "of complications" in September 1940, shortly after the birth of her last child.

Sarah Elizabeth Morrison Ward was 83 in 1964, when she died in Hillsboro, Ohio at the Happy Hours Nursing Home. Whatever the extent of her estate, she made certain it was shared equally by her four children or their children. Roy and Harry each got a fourth; grandson Thomas Ward (son of Morrison) got his father's fourth; and Clara's five children each got a fifth of her fourth. She was careful to name each one: John William Edwards, Mary Lou McCoppin, Virginia Caroline Strain, Ruth

Edwards Shoemaker, and Mary Lee Edwards Batchelor.

Although she was a widow for 53 years, it appears that her family still prospered in her hands.

Jesse Weatherford

Jesse Weatherford was born 29 Sep 1879 in Marion County, Kentucky, and died 24 Sep 1973 in Chattahoochee, Florida in his 94th year. During his life he sold jewelry, operated a telegraph for the railroad at Shepherdsville at the time of the train wreck, and married perhaps as many as eight times.

He was the last of at least seven sons born to George and Elizabeth (Coppage) Weatherford. After the 1880 census record, the next time we discover Jesse is when he married Mary L. Vandyke in April 1899. He was 19, she was 41 with four sons from a previous marriage. They were together in Marion County in 1900, where he was listed as a watch repairer. We believe she died in 1904 in Moreland, Lincoln County, Kentucky.

We think we find Jesse in Marion County in 1910 married to a lady named Dovie. According to the census record, they had been married six years. The one inconsistency is that he was listed as a farmer.

Now it gets a bit confusing. We're not sure what became of Dovie, but a Jesse Weatherford married Ora Qualls in Lincoln County in April 1914, and she died of complications from measles in June. They were living at Yuma in Taylor County at the time of her death.

We next find Jesse in Bullitt County in 1917 with a wife whose parents lived in Hart County. Her name (or nickname) may have been Pampie, for that was the name he listed as his nearest relative on his World War I draft registration card.

Jesse was working as the telegraph operator at the Shepherdsville depot at the time of the wreck. His part in this disaster is described elsewhere in this book. He was also repairing watches and selling jewelry as well.

The Pioneer News contains frequent mentions of Jesse and his wife, including telling of her trips to visit her folks (but never naming her), as well as frequent advertisements by Jesse for his jewelry shop.

Then mentions of his wife stopped in late May 1919, and by July he was being described alone. We do not know what became of her, but suspect there may have been a divorce.

Then Jesse married Mollie Gilbert Cosby in October 1921. This marriage lasted until October 1925 when she divorced him.

We're not sure where he was from that time until 1940, but in that year's census he was living in Casey County, running a jewelry shop in Columbia, and married to Emma Jean who was 17.

Emma Jean may have divorced him as well for he was next located in Hardee County, Florida in March 1945 where he married Annie Whiteside. That marriage lasted one year. He then married Addie Painter in April 1949 and they were divorced the same year.

And that's the last we see of Jesse Weatherford until his death in 1973. An interesting life, to say the least.

Henry Wilhite

The day following the train wreck, both *The Louisville Herald* and *The Springfield Sun* listed Henry Wilhite of Bardstown Junction as one of those injured in the wreck. He was not so identified in *The Courier-Journal* or *The Louisville Times* in any edition.

Also, there is no Henry Wilhite (any spelling of the name) identified in the Bardstown Junction area in either the 1910 or 1920 census.

Nor did such a man register with the World War I draft in 1917-1918. Henry is not found in Nelson County, Marion County, or Washington County either.

Three adult male Wilhites did register with the draft in Bullitt County. One was Hugh Berkley Wilhoyte, a Baptist minister in Mt. Washington. A search of contemporary *Pioneer News* issues make no mention of him with regard to the train wreck, although he is mentioned several times with regard to his occupation.

The two others were James Manrow Willhite who worked on the farm of James Davis in far western Bullitt County near West Point, and Guy Willhite, a tenant farmer working near Cupio, a small community in western Bullitt County on Knob Creek just south of present day highway 44W.

It is just possible that one of these two men may have been misidentified as Henry Wilhite. It is also possible that there was a Henry Wilhite near Bardstown Junction for a short time who failed to be recorded in other records. Perhaps we will never know.

James Marvin Williams

James Marvin Williams is one of only a handful of victims of the train wreck for whom we have detailed information as to his injuries. When he and the railroad were unable to come to an agreement on a settlement, the case was tried in Washington County Circuit Court where he was awarded $6,000. The railroad appealed the verdict to Court of Appeals, and his testimony was read into the record.

The record stated that "the car in which plaintiff [Mr. Williams] was riding was split open, and plaintiff was thrown upon the track, where he lay bleeding and unconscious, with his clothes practically torn from his body. He was then carried to a hospital, Where he remained for about a week, when he was placed on a stretcher and taken in an ambulance to the train which carried him to Springfield. For two months he lay in bed, being unable to rise or sit up except with the support of his hands. He was taken to Louisville, where he had braces fitted for his back, and he was then able to walk on crutches. He received several cuts and bruises about his body, two of the bones in his foot grew together, and any weight on his foot caused him great pain. There was a loss of motion in his back, and he could not move his back without great pain. There was also a semiparalysis of his lower limbs. During all this time his suffering was intense, and still continues."

The company's physicians testified that his injuries were only temporary, and that he would soon recover. However, the court judged that "there is evidence tending to show that the injury to plaintiff's foot is permanent, and that the injury to his back is probably permanent, that plaintiff's nervous system has been greatly shocked and impaired, that his suffering has been intense and will probably continue for some time to come."

The Court of Appeals sided with Williams and affirmed the $6,000 judgment.

Marvin Williams was born in November 1889 to John and Katherine (Marshall) Williams in Springfield. He married Mary Amelia Bittenback in November 1908, and they were living in Washington County with his widowed mother in the 1910 census. Their daughter Lorraine was born the previous July. Then their son, James Douglas was born in April 1914.

In June 1917, Marvin indicated on his World War I draft registration card that he was a self-employed grocery man, of medium height and weight, with blue eyes and light brown hair. A bit more than six months later Marvin found himself in the midst of a horrific train wreck.

He apparently sold his grocery business in Springfield, for we found his family in Jeffersontown in Jefferson County in the 1920 census where he was working as a salesman in a retail feed store.

We think that he and Mary were divorced sometime before 1925, for by October of that year, when her mother died, Mary identified herself as Mrs. H. L. Sanders on the death certificate. Then she and her son Douglas were listed in Omaha, Nebraska in the 1930 census with her second husband, Hercules Sanders who was a printing lithographer.

Her daughter Loraine had married William Frederick Burke of Shelbyville in December 1926. This marriage apparently didn't last for she later married Charles Robinson Evans in 1932 in Nebraska. By 1935 they were in California. Charles and Lorraine had two daughters. He was an interior decorator by profession. Charles died in 1985; Lorraine lived until 2007.

James Douglas Williams was living in San Mateo County, California in 1940, still single, and working as a tire salesman. We're not certain what became of him later.

Hercules and Mary were living in California when he died in 1957. We are not yet certain when Mary died, although there was a Mary A. Sanders, born in December 1887 in Kentucky, who died in Monterey, California in October 1977.

Meanwhile, a James Marvin Williams married a lady named Anna Louise in Louisville in June 1922; and they moved to Akron, Ohio where they divorced a year later.

He then married Margaret Clay, and their first son, Edgar Milton Williams was born in March 1926, in Cleveland. Next were twin sons, one named for his father and the other named Clifford Marshall Williams, who were born in 1928 in Cincinnati.

They moved around quite a bit, for in the 1930 census they were living in Mendon, a small community in Mercer County, Ohio. Marvin was identified as an insurance salesman. Margaret's father Edgar W. Clay was living with them.

A decade later they were back in Cincinnati with three more children, two daughters, Mary Faith and Martha, and another son they named Glenn Morris Williams. Marvin was still selling insurance.

It appears that this James Marvin Williams died in Portsmouth, Ohio in December 1973.

Although there are numerous consistencies that tie this James Marvin Williams to the one who survived the train wreck, we can't say with absolute certainty that they are one and the same. Only additional research may answer that question.

William H. Wolfenberger

William Wolfenberger was beside himself with grief following the train wreck. As the engineer for the express train, he saw the collision develop before his eyes, saw the bodies tossed about and smashed beneath his train, leaving a memory that would haunt him for the rest of his life.

William was born in Gallia County, Ohio in 1858 to Michael and Mary (Eakle) Wolfenberger who had moved there from Virginia not long before he was born. A decade later the family was living in Bowling Green, Kentucky. By 1882 William had two brothers, Birdie and John, and a sister Ida. Two years later, he went to work for the railroad as a locomotive fireman. Within four years, he was an engineer, working his way up through experience to operate the largest of the company's locomotives.

William married Mary A. Bardmaker in Clarksville, Tennessee in November 1882. He was 24 and she was 17. Their daughter Nora was born in 1887; Byrd Mae followed in 1890, and Anna Margaret joined her sisters in 1895.

The family was living in Louisville in 1917. The girls were still at home. Nora was working as a bookkeeper in a dry goods store, and Byrd split her time between teaching and being a stenographer. By now, William had been operating locomotives for nearly thirty years, and there was little about them that he didn't know.

William Wolfenberger retirement photo

Following the wreck, and his subsequent trial and acquittal in Bullitt County, William went back to doing the only thing he really knew how to do; pilot locomotives. The railroad had no desire to lose a man with his experience, and by 1920 he had been given the job of "traveling engineer." A traveling engineer was essentially a leader and teacher of the best methods for handling and operating locomotives.

He worked in this capacity for another dozen years, finally retiring at the end of 1931.

His daughter Nora had married William J. Hanley in 1920. By 1930 they had four children: William, Mary, John, and James. Her husband worked as an insurance agent, first in New Albany, Indiana, and later as an agency manager in Columbus, Ohio. During the war, he served as a sergeant in the Army 21st Engineers.

Byrd Mae Wolfenberger married Frank Jellison, and they lived in several places including Chicago, Salt Lake City, and Los Angeles. Frank had served in the Air Force during both World Wars, reaching the rank of master sergeant. They had no children.

William Wolfenberger died in 1937. His widow Mary lived until 1960.

Their daughter Margaret never married. She worked as a secretary for the Harlan Coal Company until her retirement. She died in Louisville in 1970.

William Hanley died in Columbus in 1958. His widow Nora died there in 1973.

Frank Jellison died in 1943 during his last tour of duty. His widow Byrd Mae lived until 1983. They are all buried in the Saint Joseph Catholic Cemetery in Bowling Green.

Appendices

Appendix H - Page 137

Report of the

Kentucky Railroad Commission

Read the report of the Kentucky Railroad Commission, published at the end of January 1918; one of the most detailed accounts of the Shepherdsville wreck.

Appendix I - Page 157

Interstate Commerce Commission

The ICC also issued a report on the wreck near the end of January. Their conclusions were somewhat different from those of the Kentucky Commission.

Appendix J - Page 165

Muir v. Louisville & N. R. Co.

This case before the federal district court was an attempt by the railroad to end the various suits for compensation against it in the state courts in Nelson County. Their arguments were interesting, but flawed according to the court.

Appendix K - Page 175

Louisville & Nashville Railroad Company

v. Commonwealth.

When the Bullitt County courts found the railroad guilty of operating a public nuisance, the railroad appealed the case to the Court of Appeals. This is the report on that appeal.

Appendix L - Page 179

Signaling and Manual Block System

Read excerpts from *The Elements of Railroad Engineering* by William G. Raymond, written in 1914, that describe how the manual block system works.

Appendix M - Page 183

Early Correspondence

Gary Gibson of Shepherdsville discovered a collection of papers and correspondence at an auction that date back to the time of the 1917 Shepherdsville train wreck. Some are included here.

Appendix A

L&N

TIME
TABLES

LOUISVILLE
AND
NASHVILLE
RAILROAD

No. 277

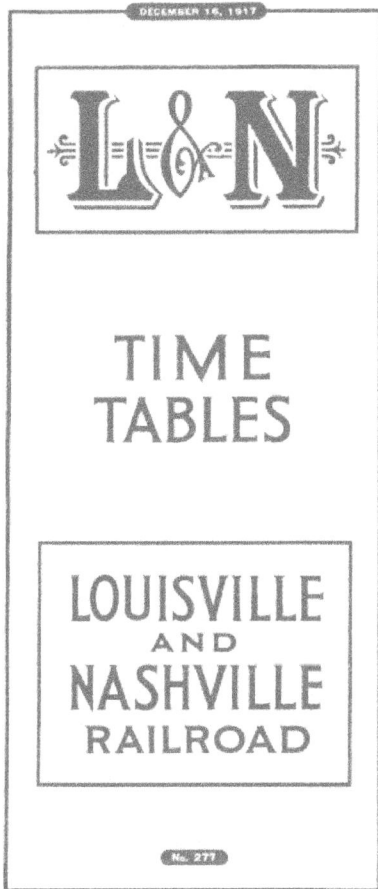

This time table chart was published just four days before the train wreck. The chart to the right gives the time schedule that the Flyer (#7) should have been following. As noted elsewhere, it did not leave Louisville until 4:53 p.m. on the day of the wreck.

On the next page is the chart for the Accommodation (#41).

7 Daily	Dis-tance	Trains do not stop at stations where no time is shown.
AM 11 15	.0	Lv . . . . Cincinnati . . . . Ar
	.0	" . . Penna.-L. & N. Station . . . "
. . △ . .	.0	" . . . Central Union Station . . . Ar
. . △ . .	2.4	" . . . . Covington Lv
11 25	1.8	" . . . . Newport . . . . "
11 35	4.8	" . . . . Latonia . . . . "
. . . . . .	7.9	" . . . . Maurice . . . . "
. . . . . .	12.5	" . . . . Independence . . . . . "
. . . . . .	17.4	" . . . . Bank Lick . . . . . . "
. . . . . .	21.1	" . . . . Walton . . . . "
. . . . . .	26.1	" . . . . Verona . . . . "
. . . . . .	32.4	" . . . . Zion . . . . "
. . . . . .	34.9	" . . . . Elliston . . . . "
. . . . . .	39.9	" . . . . Glencoe . . . . . . "
. . . . . .	45.4	" . . . . Sparta . . . . "
. . . . . .	48.1	" . . . . Sanders . . . . "
. . . . . .	51.8	" . . . . Eagle . . . . . . "
f12 55	55.9	" . . . . Worthville . . . . "
. . . . . .	59.9	" . . . . English . . . . "
. . . . . .	66.4	" . . . . Turner . . . . "
. . . . . .	69.6	" . . . . . Campbellsburg . . . . . "
. . . . . .	74.3	" . . . . Sulphur . . . . "
. . . . . .	77.6	" . . . . Pendleton . . . . "
(21-30)	84.4	" . . . . Lagrange . . . . "
. . . . . .	87.3	" . . . . Buckner . . . . "
. . . . . .	92.4	" . . . . Crestwood . . . . "
. . . . . .	94.0	" . . . . . . Pewee Valley . . . . . "
. . . . . .	96.0	" . . . . O'Bannon . . . . "
. . (30) . .	98.4	" . . . . Anchorage . . . . "
. . . . . .	99.2	" . . . . Lakeland . . . . "
. . . . . .	102.1	" . . . . Lyndon . . . . . . "
. . . . . .	104.9	" . . . . . . St. Matthews . . . . . . "
. . . . . .	106.6	" . . . . . . Crescent Hill . . . . . . "
2 28	109.2	" . . . . Baxter Avenue . . . . . . "
2 36	. . . . . .	Lv . . . . . . Fourth Street . . . . . . "
2 45	113.7	Ar . . . . **Louisville** Lv
3 00	113.7	Lv . . . . **Louisville** . . . . Ar
. . . . . .	. . . . .	" . . . . Fourth and G Lv
. . . . . .	117.0	" . . . . . South Louisville . . . . . . "
. . . . . .	123.3	" . . . . South Park . . . . "
. . . . . .	127.0	" . . . . Brooks . . . . "
. . . . . .	128.9	" . . . . Hubers . . . . "
. . . . . .	132.1	" . . . . Shepherdsville . . . . . . "
. . . . . .	135.9	" . . . Bardstown Junction . . . . "
. . . . . .	138.9	" . . . . Belmont . . . . "
3 44	143.4	" . . . . Lebanon Junction . . . . . "
. . . . . .	145.7	" . . . . Booths . . . . "
. . . . . .	147.7	" . . . . Colesburg . . . . "
. . . . . .	152.8	" . . . . Tunnel Hill . . . . . . "
4 12	156.1	" . . . . Elizabethtown . . . . . . "

LOUISVILLE & NASHVILLE

Table
12

LOUISVILLE AND SPRINGFIELD

		43 Ex.Su.	41 Daily	Dis- tance	Trains do not stop at stations where no time is shown.	42 Ex.Su.	44 Ex.Su.	90 Sun.	
		AM	PM			AM	PM	AM	
.....	.....	9 00	4 35	.0	Lv.... **Louisville** ....Ar	8 20	3 40	9 30	.....
.....	.....	9 05	4 40	.....	" ...Fourth and G. ...Ar	..B..	..B..	9 25	.....
.....	.....	9 12	4 47	3.3	" ..South Louisville..Lv	8 05	3 25	9 15	.....
.....	.....	f.	f...	4.1	" ...Highland Park... "	f	f	f	.....
.....	.....	f 9 22	f 4 59	9.6	" ....South Park. ... "	f 7 52	f 3 12	f 9 02	.....
.....	.....	f 9 28	f 5 06	13.3	" ......Brooks...... "	f 7 44	f 3 05	f 8 55	.....
.....	.....	f.9 32	f 5 10	15.2	" ......Hubers...... "	f 7 39	f 3 00	f 8 51	.....
.....	.....	9 40	5 18	18.4	" ...Shepherdsville... "	7 33	2 53	8 45	.....
.....	.....	9 50	5 29	22.2	" ...Bardstown Jct... "	7 25	2 45	8 37	.....
.....	.....	9 55	5 34	24.1	" .....Chapeze...... "	7 19	2 39	8 29	.....
.....	.....	9 58	5 37	25.0	" ....Clermont..... "	7 16	2 36	8 26	.....
.....	.....	f10 04	f 5 43	26.7	" ......Hobbs...... "	f 7 12	f 2 32	f 8 22	.....
.....	.....	10 11	5 50	28.8	" .....Lotus...... "	7 07	2 27	8 17	.....
.....	.....	10 16	5 56	31.4	" ....Deatsville...... "	7 01	2 21	8 11	.....
.....	.....	10 20	6 01	33.2	" .....Samuels...... "	6 55	2 15	8 05	.....
.....	.....	f10 30	f 6 12	37.3	" .....Nazareth...... "	f 6 46	f 2 06	f 7 56	.....
.....	.....	10 37	6 19	39.4	" ....Bardstown..... "	6 40	2 00	7 50	.....
.....	.....	f10 45	f 6 29	42.5	" ...Early Times.... "	f 6 33	f 1 53	f 7 43	.....
.....	.....	f.	f.	44.7	" ....Greenbrier..... "	f	f	f	.....
.....	.....	10 55	6 37	45.2	" ....Woodlawn..... "	6 25	1 45	7 35	.....
.....	.....	f11 05	6 47	48.8	" ......Croakes...... "	f 6 15	f 1 35	f 7 25	.....
.....	.....	f11 10	f 6 53	50.7	" ......Booker...... "	f 6 11	f 1 31	f 7 21	.....
.....	.....	f11 17	f 7 00	53.9	Lv....Valley Hill..... "	f 6 05	f 1 25	f 7 15	.....
.....	.....	11 30	7 15	59.3	Ar.....**Springfield** ..Lv	5 55	1 15	7 05	.....
		AM	PM			AM	PM	AM	

B—Stops to discharge passengers at Fifth and A Streets.

This chart shows the time schedules for each of the Accommodation trains between Louisville and Springfield. As noted in the chart, the Accommodation train #41 was scheduled to leave Louisville at 4:35 p.m., arrive at Shepherdsville at 5:18, and then at Bardstown Junction at 5:29 where it took the line toward Bardstown.

However, on the day of the wreck, #41 did not keep its schedule, and made several unscheduled stops along the way, causing it to arrive at Shepherdsville at about 5:25 or about seven minutes late.

Appendix B
Mabel Brown Miller Letters

Three days before she died in the train wreck, Mabel Brown Miller wrote a letter to her younger brother Joe, who was in Texas at the time.

We include it here as an example of the lives that all of the train wreck victims were experiencing leading up to the day of the wreck. In it we find a loving sister taking time out of a busy holiday season to write some personal thoughts and general gossip to her brother who was far away.

None of the victims expected to die or be maimed that Christmas season. None of the families expected to have their lives shattered by this tragedy. Like Mabel, they were looking forward to a happy holiday.

Included on these pages is a facsimile of Mabel's letter, together with our transcription of it. Within the transcription we have included additional information provided by a descendant.

Monday -

My dear Joe:

Enclosed find check for $5.00 which is your Christmas gift. I wanted to give you a subscription to some magazine but couldn't decide on what I thought you would like so just decided to leave it with you.

Has it been cold out there, we are having such cold weather, snow on the ground, don't look like it will ever go off. Tom [her husband] said it was 8 degrees below zero this morning. Ethel [Mabel's younger sister] went over home to have her teeth fixed about a week ago, couldn't get home until this morning. S. B. [Shirley Brown Troutman, Ethel's son] has been with me.

I had a letter from Alma [Alma Brown White, her sister] last week, she is up to Lexington, said she told Garrard [Alma's husband] she was coming home, he said, "Why you have just been home" so I don't know wither she is coming home Christmas or not. Said Helen Brown [Alma's daughter] was afraid of the snow. She can't walk yet, but stands alone and can say a few words such as kitty, George, light. I guess I will go home about Wednesday, may just go into L-ville & go home from there. I know everybody will be so busy & such a jam I dread going. Humphrey [Humphrey Miller, Tom's brother] went Friday afternoon, hasn't come back yet, are looking for him home tonight, said he might enlist while he was there. Don't know whether he meant it or was joking.

Margaret & Jesse, Lucile & Paul were here yesterday. Charlie has gotten his papers. They ask about you often. Jesse has been looking for a farm, has about decided on one near New Castle, it is 8 miles from the railroad. I bet they don't go. Rose Buckner married a boy that lives near here. He used to live in Lebanon. Geo. Wilson, you may have met him. He is about 22 yrs old. She & her sister-in-law were going to Lebanon the other night, they stopped in here & ate supper with us. Rose seems to be tickled to death about being married.

I sure do miss little Sou-boy [nickname for Shirley Brown Troutman]. We worked examples all the time. He said he wished he had his percheser board here. Remember how he made us play with him last winter.

Monday—

My dear Joe:

Enclosed find check for $5.00 which is your Chris gift. I wanted to give you a subscription to some magazine but couldn't decide on what I thought you would like so just decided to leave it with you. Has it been cold out there, we are having such cold weather, snow on the ground don't look like it will ever go off. Tom said it was 8 degrees below zero this morning. Ethel went over home to have her teeth fixed about a week ago. couldn't get home until this morning. B. B. has been with me. I had a letter from Alma last week she is up to Lexington said she told Garrard she was coming home he said, "Why you have just been home" so I don't know wither she is coming home Chris or not. Said Helen Brown was afraid of the snow. she can't walk yet, but stands alone & can say a few words such as (2.)

Did I tell you Mack Miller & his wife had separated. They say she is going to sue for divorce. Geo. M. Able & his wife separated, but they have gone together again.

Rose said she went to the Thanksgiving dance in B., everybody had a good time, the music was grand. Muff [Cecelia, Mabel's youngest sister] said the same thing.

Well Sou-boy [nickname for Joe] hope you will have a Merry Christmas I will write again after I come back from Bardstown. Hope you will have a good dinner Christmas day.

Just lots of love.

Mabel

December 17th.

kitty, George, light. I guess I will go home about Wednesday may just go into L-ville & go home from there I know every body will be so busy, & such a jam I dread going. Humphrey went Fri. afternoon hasn't come back yet am looking for him home tonight. said he might enlist while he was there. don't know wether he meant it or was joking.

Margaret & Jesse, Lucile & Paul were here yesterday. Charlie has gotten his papers they ask about you often, Jesse has been looking for a farm has about decided on one near New Castle it is 8 miles from the rail-road. I bet they dont go. Rose Buckner

married a boy that lives near here, he used to live in Lebanon Geo. Wilson, you may have met him he is about 22 yrs old. She & her sister-in-law were going to Lebanon the other night they stoped in here & ate supper with us. Ross seems to be tickled to death about being married.

I sure do miss little Son-ny, we worked examples all the time he said he wished he had his purcheser board here. remember how he made us play with him last winter.

Did I tell you Mack Miller & his wife had separated they say she is going to sue for divorce, Geo. M. able & his wife separated but they have gone together again. 5.

Rose said she went to the Thanksgiven dance in B- every body had a good time the music was grand Muff said the same thing.

Well Son-boy hope you will have a merry Chris. I will write again after I come back from Bardstown hope you will have a good dinner Chris day. Just lots of love
December 19th Mabel

The next letter was written by Mabel's mother, Laura Brown, to her son Joe on Christmas Eve following the wreck.

The grief that permeates this letter is typical of the sorrow that gripped whole towns.

Our transcription of her letter follows, interspersed with the facsimile of it.

Bardstown, Ky

Dec 24th, 1917

My Dear Dear Boy

I don't know how to write to you, my heart is so full of sorrow & trouble. It seems that God has taken the flower of the family, she was the best friend of all of us, that we had.

I don't know what Bro Murrell has written you but it was the most horrible thing that ever happened in the history of the State.

Every woman on the train was killed out right, but Natelie, she is still in the hospital;

there are conflicting reports from her. Mr. Richards told me the Dr. told him her neck was broken, the Spinal cord is not broken but the vertebra has slipped, guess you will understand.

> *Bardstown Ky*
> *Dec 24th /1917*
>
> *My Dear Dear Boy*
> *I dont know how to write to you my heart is so full of sorrow trouble. It seems that God has taken the flower of the family she was the best friend of all of us, that we had. I don't know what Bro Murrell has written you but it was the most horrible thing that ever happened in the history of the State*

Mabel's skull was fractured, the Dr's said she died instantly. We have much to be thankful for that she did not suffer any. She was the only one who was not mutilated. The skin was not broken any where on her body.

So many of them was only recognized by something they had on. Mabel & Mrs Arch Pulliam & a baby was the only ones whose caskets was opened when they reached Bardstown.

Mabel had been in Louisville two days; was coming out that night to spend Christmas with us. I was waiting supper for her when Humphry telephoned me there had been a bad wreck of the Bardstown train. I felt as soon as he told me that she was hurt. Tom said he felt that she was dead.

Tom, Humphry, Grover, Mr. Cloyde, & Dr. Williams caught the fast train, got there about two hours after it happened. They found her with her face turned up. She was the only one

that you could recognize readily. Tom said her face was clean as when she left home.

They took all of them to Louisville. They were brought to Bardstown Friday night. All day Saturday & Sunday there were funerals. Mabel was taken to the church. Her funeral was at 10:30 Sunday morning. Bro Clotfeller prayed. Bro Murrell made an excellent talk from Revelations. Blessed are the Dead that die in the Lord. They sang that grand old hymn "How Firm a Foundation" that they sang at Papa's funeral. (I want it sung at mine.) Mrs. Sayer sang a solo that was very sweet.

Mabel looked so natural, she looked like she was asleep. She had so many flowers sent her, enough to cover all three graves. Mabel had as many friends, even the old men thought much of her as many said to me, everybody loved Mabel Brown. It is hard to give her up but whatever happens I know that God does it for the best. We don't know what she has been spared. There may have been a purpose in her death.

Tom is just broken hearted. I felt so sorry for him & Humphry was grieved so much, but I believe that it is all well with her. When I heard of the wreck I prayed for her & something came into my mind that it was alright with her. God gives us the assurance of these things.

Joe, I thought of you so much so far from home & loved ones amongst strangers but I knew God would help you bear it.

Joe we appreciated those checks but we are not going to cash them. You will need all the money you have. Alma sent me five dollars to send you but have been so upset - will send it right away.

Alma and Garrard are here now. Ethel did not come to the funeral. She was so nervous that Dr said it was such a shock to hear these things that it would be better for her not to come. Henry had to have ... for her poor little Shirley

Brown is so grieved Henry said the little fellow had hardly stopped crying.

The news in the Standard is so awful. I hardly know that it right to be sent to you. It is a sad Christmas. The whole town seems to be in mourning. They say that Louisville is the same way. God bless you & help you to bear your trouble as he has helped me. They all send love.

Mama

Write to Dr Miller, his wife was killed.

Muff says return these pictures.

every woman on the train was killed out right but Natalie she is still in the hospital there are conflicting reports from her — Mr Richards told me the Dr Told him her neck was broken the Spinal cord is not broken but the vertebra had sliped. guess you will understand. Mabels skull was fractured the Drs said she died instan[t]ly We have much to be Thankfull for that — she did not suffer any. she was the only one who was not mutilated the skin was not broken any where on her body. so many of them was only recognised by something they had on. Mabel & Miss ? ch Pulliam & a baby was the only ones Whose Caskets was opened when they reached Bardstown Mabel had been in Louisville two days, was coming out that night to spend Christmas with us I was waiting supper for her — when Humphry Telephoned me there had been a bad wreck of the Bardstown train I felt as soon as he told me that she was hurt Tom said he felt that she was dead. Tom Humphry Grover Mr Clyde

+ Dr Williams caught the last
train get there about two hours
after it happened. They found
her with her face turned up
she was the only one that you
could recognize readily Tom
said her face was as clean
as when she left home they
took all of them to Louisville
They were brought to Bardstown
Friday night all day Saturday
+ Sunday there were funerals
Mabel was taken to the church
her funeral was at 10-30 Sunday
morning Bro Clotfelter prayed
Bro Murrell made ~~some~~ an excelent
talk from Revelations. Blessed

are the dead that die in the
Lord. They sang that grand old
hymn "How Firm a Foundation"
that they sung at Papa's funeral
(I want it sung at mine) Mrs
Seeger sang a solo that was
very sweet Mabel looked so
natural she looked like she was
asleep. she had so many flowers
sent her enough to cover all
three graves Mabel had so
many friends even the old
men thought much of her so
many said to me, everybody
loved Mabel Brown. It is
hard to give her up but

but whatever happens I know that God does it for the best. we dont know what she has been spared there may have been a purpose in her death Tom is just broken hearted I felt so sorry for him & Humphrey had grieved so much. but I believe that it is all well with her when I heard of the wreck I prayed for her & something came into my mind that it was alright with her, God gives us the assurance of these things Joe I thought of you so much so far from home & loved ones amongst strangers but I knew God would help you bear it. Joe we appreciate these cheques but we are no use to cash them you will need all the money you have Alma sent me five dollars to send you but have been so upset will send it right away. Alma & Saward are here now Ethel did not come to the funeral she was to nervous the Dr said

it was such a shock to hear
of these things that it would
be better for her not to come
Henry had to have ...
for her poor little Shirly Brown
is so grieved Henry said the
little fellow had hardly
stopped crying The news in the
Standard is so awful I hardly
know that it ought to be sent to you
it is a sad Christmas the whole
town seems to be in mourning they say
that Louisville is the same way

God bless you & help you to
bear your trouble as he has
helped me They all send Love
                    Mama

Mr Joseph H Brown.
243 Tremont St
El Passo
              Texas

Appendix C
Eyewitness Account

While a great number of folks contributed to the rescue efforts following the collision, including most of those living in Shepherdsville, we do have one eyewitness account of the efforts of two of the passengers aboard the express train.

The day after the wreck, *The Courier-Journal* printed the account of a Miss Mary Dorcey, of Cave City, who described the efforts of Edwin Russell and "a young woman with brilliant red hair from Cincinnati."

Below is a transcription of Miss Dorcey's account, following by additional information about Mr. Russell and Miss Margaret Woods, the lady with bright red hair.

CAVE CITY GIRL TELLS OF CRASH
Miss Dorcey On Fast Train That Hit Local.
Says Screams of Dying Persons Were Horrible.
SAW BABIES AMONG DEAD

Miss Mary Dorcey, of Cave City, who was a passenger on the L. & N. train No. 7, on her way to Columbia, Tenn., said last night that when the shock of the collision came she was in a rear coach with Edwin Russell, a member of the law department of the L. & N., with offices at Louisville; a young woman with brilliant red hair from Cincinnati, and who she found later was a trained nurse, and several men. That her impression when the shock came was that they, meaning their train, had run over a log, which seemed to be the impression of others in the coach with her. That the men in the coach ran to the doors, and upon finding them locked broke them down and gained the ground to find that there was a great deal of excitement. She said when Mr. Russell, who seemed to sense the trouble at once, alighted from the car, that he began the work of rescue in the most heroic manner.

Miss Dorcey said that the accident happened about 5:30 [Thursday] afternoon about fifty feet from the Shepherdsville station. She believed there must have been about forty or fifty dead, among them several little children about one and two years old. Miss Dorcey said medical aid was summoned and that within a short time many doctors from the country around began to arrive.

Injured Carried.

The injured were carried into a church near the tracks, the hotel, the "stationhouse" and into the home of a Mr. Patterson. Here she found Miss Natalie Halstead, of Bardstown, who was unconscious and with whom Mr. Russell was working, several who were dead and many badly injured.

Miss Dorcey talked to *The Courier-Journal* about 11:30 o'clock from the Victoria Hotel, where she had gone to get a bite to eat after being brought to the city a half hour before. She intended to spend the night with friends on Sixth Street.

Miss Dorcey was unstinting in her praise of Mr. Russell and the "red-headed trained nurse from Cincinnati," as she repeatedly called her. She said she never saw anyone work like Mr. Russell worked and that he was everywhere administering to the comfort of the victims, giving them whisky to sustain them and assisting the doctors where possible.

Horrible Cries of Dying.

When asked if the train was on fire, Miss Dorcey said that she did not believe it was, but that the engine was making a "lot of noise as if from steam." She said that the air was full of horrible noises from the dying and injured. Some of the faces of the victims she said were so discolored that one could not tell whether they were black or white.

The relief train with doctors and nurses arrived, Miss Dorcey said, about two or three hours after the collision.

Miss Dorcey appeared to be quite calm, though she admitted that the shock has unnerved her considerably. It was her first idea on getting to town she said to call *The Courier-Journal*, feeling sure it would want first-hand information.

Mr. Russell was William Edwin Russell, who worked in the legal department of the Louisville & Nashville Railroad Company in Louisville. Following the accident, and during the war, he served as legal interpreter at the American Embassy in Paris.

Edwin married Clara Louise Rowell in 1912 in Washington, D.C., and they had one daughter, Jane. He died in Washington, D.C. in 1932. Shown here is his passport photo from his time in Paris.

Miss Margaret Woods was a trained nurse whose efforts at the scene may well have saved lives, or at the least eased the pain and suffering of those she helped. Miss Woods was born in Tennessee in 1867, so she was 50 years old at the time of the wreck. She would later live and work in Lexington where she died in 1960 at the age of 92.

CAVE CITY GIRL TELLS OF CRASH

Miss Dorcey On Fast Train That Hit Local.

Says Screams of Dying Persons Were Horrible.

The Courier-Journal, Friday, Dec. 21, 1917

L. & N. Wreck Inquiry Ends; Blame Fixed

The Courier-Journal, December 25, 1917, page 10.

Summary of Probe.

We, the undersigned, the duly appointed examining board of the Louisville & Nashville Railroad Company, make this brief summary of the facts in connection with the collision between train No. 7 and train No. 41 at Shepherdsville, Ky., on December 20, 1917:

Train No. 41, which is the local passenger train running from Louisville to Springfield, Ky., left Louisville on time at 4:35 p.m. Train No. 7, which is the through passenger train operating between Cincinnati and Nashville, due to leave at 3 p.m., was late and did not depart from Louisville until 4:53 p.m. No. 41 made its usual local stops and arrived at Shepherdsville six minutes late. It consumed about two minutes in discharging its passengers. It then moved forward, that is southward until the rear coach was about 360 feet south of the station building. It here came to a stop for the purpose of backing in upon the siding to permit No. 7 to pass, and almost at that instant No. 7 swept by the station and into the rear of train No. 41. No. 7 plowed through the rear coach and half way through the second coach of No. 41 and shoved the wreckage forward a distance of about 800 feet. The flagman and conductor of No. 41 were in one of the coaches and both were killed. The engineer and fireman of No. 7 were unhurt.

Informed of No. 7.

When No. 41 arrived at Brooks, which is a station five miles north of Shepherdsville, the conductor, M.S. Campbell, received information from Dispatcher Sams through telegraph operator Sanders that No. 7 had passed F.X. tower at 5:08 p.m. and that if he could not get to Bardstown Junction on time he had better let No. 7 pass at Shepherdsville. As he was leaving Brooks, Conductor Campbell said to his train porter, Earnest Chase, "we are to let No. 7 by at Shepherdsville." At Gap in the Knobs, a station between Brooks and Shepherdsville, the train porter asked Conductor Campbell if the engineer understood that he was to head in at Shepherdsville, to which the conductor replied that he had not informed the engineer, but that they would go on down to Shepherdsville station and find out there from the dispatcher about No. 7, and they could then, if necessary, back in. When the train reached Shepherdsville Conductor Campbell went into the telegraph office and himself telephoned to the train dispatcher at Louisville and was informed by that dispatcher that No. 7 was close and that he had better get into the siding. Campbell came out of the office and told the train porter to inform the engineer to back into the siding for No. 7.

Porter Throws Switch.

The porter ran forward and delivered this message to the engineer while the train was slowly moving off, and jumping upon the engine he rode it until he reached the south switch, where he alighted and threw the switch. The effect of this was to display an additional red light to the north as soon as the train had passed. The rear of No. 41 was not protected in any way by its crew as required by the rules in that no fusee was put out or torpedoes placed between Gap in the Knobs and Shepherdsville, though 41 was failing to maintain schedule time and in that no flagman with a red lantern was sent back at Shepherdsville.

After leaving Louisville train No. 7 was stopped one minute at Oak street and one minute at the Southern railway crossing, Fourth and G, and after that proceeded without any further stops until the collision. The line from Louisville to a point beyond Shepherdsville is double tracked, and trains move under standard American Railway Association rules.

In approaching Shepherdsville the track is straight for a mile and a half, except for one slight curve about half a mile north of the station, which, however does not affect the view of the signals at the station.

Duty To Await Signal.

Under the rules, it was the duty of the engineer of train No. 7 to approach the station with his train under control and not to pass it unless he received a signal from the operator to do so, which is called a "proceed" signal. This signal is made by the movement of a semaphore arm. In the night this signal is the changing of a red light to a green, and the approaching engineer must stop unless he actually sees this movement: that is, the change from red to green. Upon this occasion the engineer, Wolfenberger, states that he saw the green signal in its then position when he was about 2,100 feet from the station, and that when he was about 1,800 feet from the station he sounded four short blasts, which was a request to the operator to indicate whether he must stop or proceed. That engineer states that he saw no change in the signal and admits that he knew that not being moved in his presence, it was his duty to stop, but he thought that the signal to proceed would be given later, so he went ahead without taking any steps toward slackening the speed of his train except that he applied the air brakes lightly. When he

was within about 400 yards of the station, still observing that the signal had not been changed, he called again by sounding the four short blasts.

Applied Emergency Brakes.

He says that at that time he saw the signal drop to red, and that he then applied his emergency brakes and thought that he closed or almost closed the throttle. The fact is, however, that the train not only did not stop before it got to the station, but that it went four hundred feet beyond to the point where it struck No. 41, and then went eight hundred feet still further in spite of the obstruction afforded by train No. 41.

Upon the arrival of No. 41 at Shepherdsville, Operator Jesse Weatherford, as is customary, assisted the agent in handling the baggage, mail and express. He was working at this at about a distance of fifty-five feet from his office, and upon completing it started to return to his office when he met Conductor Campbell coming from his office and was told by him of his conversation with the train dispatcher, and informed him that he, Campbell, was going to move up and back in on the side track to let No. 7 pass. Then Weatherford proceeded to his office and when he had gotten within ten or twelve feet of it he heard the noise of No. 7 approaching, looked up and saw them at a point about 800 feet north of the office. He at once rushed into the office and turned the signal to red, grabbed his red lantern and ran out swinging it on the platform, No. 7 being at that time about 150 feet away, and almost immediately afterward it rushed past the station and onward upon train No. 41.

Trainmen Broke Rules.

From the facts elicited at our examination of which the foregoing is only a brief summary, we have reached the conclusion –

First–That Conductor Campbell and Flagman Greenwell of No. 41, disobeying the rules in falling to protect their train by the use of proper signals between Brooks and Shepherdsville where the schedule of the train was not being maintained, and at Shepherdsville while endeavoring to get on the sidetrack out of the way of No. 7.

Second–That William Wolfenberger, engineer of train No. 7, violated the rules in not approaching Shepherdsville prepared to stop before passing the semaphore signal unless he got a signal to proceed. In approaching a station it is the duty of an engineer to absolutely stop his train before reaching the semaphore unless he receives an affirmative and positive signal that he may proceed. This signal to proceed is made in only one way–that is, there must be displayed a red light, which changed into a green light, and this change must be made in view of the engineer. Upon this occasion the green light (which was the proper signal to be displayed in view of No. 41, standing at the station as it was) constituted a stop signal for Engineer Wolfenberger, as shown by Rule 221-F, the pertinent part of which is as follows:

"A fixed train order signal must never be passed if kept stationary, regardless of its position or the color it displays, without the cause being first investigated."

Must Not Take Chance.

His duty not to have taken any chances on the stop signal being subsequently changed is thus set out in Rule 221-D:

"Conductors and enginemen, when approaching train-order offices, must have their trains under control and must not assume that the signal will be changed from 'stop' indication when within the distance prescribed, as, if any portion of a train runs beyond the signal before it is so changed, an infraction of these rules will have been committed."

Another rule which required the engineer to have stopped his train before passing the station is Rule 221-E, the pertinent part of which reads as follows:

"If the proper signal is not displayed at an open train-order office, or if it is not changed from 'stop' indication in full view of the engineman, as prescribed by Rule 221-A, train must be brought to a stop and must not proceed without a clearance card, Form 156, or movement order."

Engineer's Duty to Stop.

Therefore it is the duty of Engineer Wolfenberger to have brought his train to a stop upon failing to get the signal to proceed. Instead of that, he testified that while he realized it was for him a stop signal, he supposed that it would be changed, and kept running, expecting that change, but never receiving it until just before he reached the station, when the operator, in his effort to stop him, dropped the red light. It must, however, be borne in mind that the red light, under the rules, was no more of a stop signal than was the green light displayed as this one was when seen by Mr. Wolfenberger. There was ample time and space, according to his own statement, for him to have stopped his train, not only from the time he first saw the signal, but also from the time when he called for a change and did not get it. He stated that his train was moving at the rate of forty-five or fifty miles per hour when he called for a change in the signal, and that he had slowed down to about twenty-five miles per hour when he struck No. 41; but there was ample space for him to have entirely stopped his train before he reached the station.

Three–In view of certain criticism of Operator Jesse Weatherford, based on the earlier and incomplete reports of this accident, we deem it proper in justice to him to say that there was not a particle of evidence of any violation of duty upon his part.

Weatherford Is Commended.

On the contrary he is to be commended for making every possible effort to avert the accident after he discovered that No. 7 was coming into the station at high speed.

It was perfectly proper for him to assist with the baggage, mail, etc.; in fact, it was a part of his duty. Shepherdsville is an intermediate and relatively unimportant train order station, the orders taken by this operator averaging only about one a day. It was, therefore, unnecessary that he should remain at the instrument all of the time. When this train, No. 41 came in to Shepherdsville it was proper under the rules for the operator to place the signal at green, and it would have been equally improper for him to change that signal back to red until train No. 41 had passed out from the station 200 feet or more. In the meantime the green signal maintained in that position constituted for Engineer Wolfenberger just as positive a duty to stop as if it had been red. Even if Operator Weatherford had been in the station at the time No. 41 was standing there he could not have manipulated his semaphore signals to furnish more protection to No. 41 than was furnished by the maintenance of the green light in its then position.

We cannot close this report without referring to the fact that Engineer Wolfenberger, Conductor Campbell and Flagman Greenwell were old men in the service and fully experienced, and that in 1914 they passed satisfactory re-examinations on the operating rules.

Mr. Wolfenberger has been an engineer for seventeen years and stood high in the estimation of the officers of the company.

Respectfully submitted,

W. F. Sheridan, Superintendent

F. J. Fishback, Master of Trains

J. G. Clifford, Master Mechanic

J. D. Haydon, Roadmaster

L. & N. WRECK INQUIRY ENDS; BLAME FIXED

Engineer of No. 7 and Two Trainmen On Local Are Held Responsible.

Appendix E
WRECK BLAME PLACED ON FOUR BY JURY'S FINDING

The Evening Post, December 29, 1917

Result of the Inquest Held Here Into the Death of Shepherdsville Victims.

WEATHERFORD INCLUDED

Collision Would Not Have Happened If No. 41 Had "Headed" Into the Siding.

The jury at the Coroner's inquest held here today into the deaths in the wreck at Shepherdsville returned the following verdict:

"That the said Henry Z. Hardaway, Raymond Thomas Cravens, Mrs. R. C. Cherry, Mrs. Mattie Harmon, Mrs. Mabel B. Miller, Joseph Raoul Hurst and William C. Johnson came to their deaths at Sts. Mary and Elizabeth Hospital from injuries sustained Thursday, December 20, 1917, in a rear-end collision of trains No. 7 and 41, of the L. & N. railroad, said collision resulting primarily from the carelessness of Conductor Campbell and Flagman Greenwell, of train No. 41, with contributing carelessness on the part of Engineer Wolfenberger and Operator Weatherford at Shepherdsville."

The verdict of the Coroner's jury differs from the finding of the official inquiry conducted by the L. & N. earlier in the week behind closed doors, in which Operator Jesse Weatherford was held to be free from any blame and was commended for what he had done.

Could Have Been Prevented

Testimony developed at the investigation conducted by Deputy Coroner Kammerer into the wreck at Shepherdsville indicated very clearly that if the verbal order to "head in" at Shepherdsville given to Conductor M. W. Campbell had been observed the wreck would not have occurred.

Instead he took the chance of "backing in" and this caused the wreck and loss of forty-seven lives, including his own.

Several witnesses testified the verbal order given had been to "head in" at Shepherdsville, and Conductor Campbell, according to one witness, received instructions at Shepherdsville to take the siding, as No. 7 was very close behind him.

The inquest into the deaths of those who died in Louisville as the result of the wreck at Shepherdsville on the evening of December 20 began Friday morning at the Courthouse with Acting Coroner W. T. Kammerer in charge.

Because of the great number who attended it the inquest was held in the County Court room.

The jury summoned was composed of: James Clark, Jr, Col. Fred Levy, J. J. Schulten, Fred W. Keisker, Isaac Harcourt, and W. J. Baird.

Col. Fred Levy was delayed in coming to court and this kept the hearing from being called as scheduled.

The first witnesses sworn in were: J. W. Sams, train dispatcher at Louisville; W. E. Sanders, train dispatcher at Brooks Station; Ernest Chase, colored porter of train No. 41; Jesse Weatherford, operator at Shepherdsville; Edward Ogle, conductor of No. 7; William Wolfenberger, engineer of No. 7; and W. S. Bowman, flagman of No. 7.

The wreck victims whose deaths are the subject of this inquest are: William C. Johnson, Samuels, Ky.; Mattie E. Harmon, Shepherdsville; Raymond Thomas Cravens, Taylor Boulevard; Mabel B. Miller, New Hope; Mrs. Joseph Hurst, Bardstown; Henry Hardaway, Shepherdsville; and Mrs. R. C. Cherry, Bardstown.

Coroner Kammerer asked the jurors if any of them were related to persons killed or injured in the wreck and if they were owners of stock in the L. & N.

Sams First Witness

J. W. Sams was the first witness. He was the train operator at Brooks Station [likely Tenth Street Station]. Sams testified that No. 41 did not get any orders from him. He said it was customary for No. 41 to get its orders through Tenth Street.

He said that No. 41 left Tenth street at 4:36 and No. 7 left at 4:53.

He signaled the F.X. tower that the fast train was coming.

In response to a question by Mr. Keisker, the witness said that Brooks Station is 13.9 miles from Louisville. The F.X. tower is 3.7 miles from Louisville, making a practical difference of ten miles between the two points. Shepherdsville is eighteen miles from Louisville and therefore five miles from Brooks. He said that the operating rules of the L. & N. provide that trains shall keep ten minutes apart. When the trains left Louisville they were eighteen minutes apart.

Operator at Brooks Testifies

W. E. Sanders, telegraph operator at Brooks Station, was the next witness. He testified that Operator Sams in the F.X. tower had called him and told him that No. 7, the fast train, had passed the tower and to inform Conductor Campbell of No. 41 of that fact, and to suggest to him that he "head in" at Shepherdsville if he did not think he could reach Bardstown Junction.

He testified that it was a verbal order and that he had given it to Conductor Campbell. He said he had not given the order to the engineer as it is the practice to transmit verbal orders to the conductor only. In the case of written orders they are to be given to both conductor and engineer.

He said that No. 41 had arrived at Brooks Station, discharged a few passengers, and gotten off by 5:13, one minute later. It was six minutes late when it left Brooks. No. 7 passed there at 5:24. It did not stop, but blew the right of way, four short blasts. The right of way was given him by the usual signal of changing a red to a green light, and he blew two short blasts in acknowledgment and went on his way toward the scene of what proved to be the most disastrous wreck in the history of the L. & N.

The witness testified there is no block system on the road in the evening. The trains at Brooks were running eleven minutes apart.

He was asked if No. 41 would have had time to have gotten to the siding at Shepherdsville in eleven minutes. He answered in the affirmative. He was asked if a written order would have prevented the accident. He said it would not. He was asked if it is customary to give verbal orders. He said it was. He said No. 41 could have "headed in" as well as "backed in."

Train Porter's Testimony

Ernest Chase, colored porter on the ill-fated No. 41, was the next witness. He said that Conductor Campbell had told him at Brooks Station that No. 7 was following them and that they were to "head in" at Shepherdsville if he did not think they had time to go to Bardstown Junction. He said they made three stops between Brooks and Shepherdsville, a distance of five miles. He asked Conductor Campbell if the engineer knew they were to stop at Shepherdsville, and Conductor Campbell told him that he did not, but that they would go on to Shepherdsville and find out there where No. 7 was.

They went on to Shepherdsville and un-loaded between fifteen and twenty passengers and six or seven sacks of mail. This is about the usual number of passengers and mail, and the stop took no longer than usual. After the train had been unloaded he met Conductor Campbell coming from the office of the operator, and the conductor told him to tell the engineer to "back in" at the switch. He went up to the engine, told the engineer, and rode on the front end of the engine until they reached the switch. He dropped off of the train at that point and threw the switch. He did not see either the conductor or the brakeman, who also was killed. When he had thrown the switch he looked up suddenly and saw No. 7 bearing down upon him about 50 feet away.

"What did you do then?" he was asked.

"I leaped to the side and jumped the fence."

He said he had received no intimation of the approach of No. 7 before he saw it close to him; that he had heard no warning blasts of the whistle and that he was unconscious of danger until he saw the great monster locomotive upon him.

Could Have Prevented Wreck

He said the "head in" switch is north of the station, and that, had the train "headed in" there, the passengers and baggage could have been discharged in perfect safety, and that No. 7 would have had a clear track and the accident would have been averted.

He was asked if it was the duty of the flagman to go behind and use torpedoes or fusees when the train is in danger. He said it was, but that the flagman took no such steps and was not visible about the train. He described the duties of the flagman when a train stops, saying he should have been at the switch.

He said verbal orders were frequently given in the morning when the local train is operating over the same line with No. 4, the fast train coming north.

He was asked what the proper conduct for the conductor would have been in the light of his verbal orders. He answered, "He should have headed in at the Shepherdsville station."

Conductor Ogle's Testimony

Edward Ogle, conductor on No. 7, testified that he had orders to leave Louisville at 4:30 o'clock and left twenty-three minutes late; and that No. 7 was seventeen minutes behind the schedule of No. 41. He said he had no orders with reference to No. 41; that he heard the engineer of No. 7 blow one blast signalling that he was approaching the Shepherdsville station; that he heard four more blasts for the "board" (the signal).

Ogle said on cross-examination that the engineer of No. 7 did not give the two blasts that are required in answering when the engineer sees the light change from red to green, giving him the order to proceed.

The flagman of No. 41 had time to drop torpedoes and fusees as signals to No. 7, said Ogle.

Operater Weatherford

Considerable interest was attracted by the testimony of Jesse Weatherford, the operator at Shepherdsville for the past six years. Weatherford said that the first information of No. 41 which he had was a message from Operator Sanders, at Brooks Station, asking him whether 41 was in the clear. He said he first saw the train a mile and a half away. When it arrived Conductor Campbell asked him what to do about No. 7. At that time no orders for No. 7 had been received by Weatherford, and the train crew, he said, agreed that the best thing to do was to take the siding. He accordingly put up the board, indicating that No. 41 was on the track, and helped with the unloading of the baggage. When he finished he saw the headlight of No. 7, seized a red lantern and tried to flag it, but it was too late.

No. 7, he testified was going "tolerably" fast, but would venture no estimate of the speed. He said that the engineer of No. 7 should not have passed the station until the red signal light changed to green in his presence. He didn't see the flagman of No. 41 in the rear of his train protecting it. He said he heard no whistle from No. 7, but said he might have been so preoccupied with his duties that he failed to notice the blasts.

Chief interest centered about the testimony of Engineer Wolfenberger of No. 7. He appeared careworn, saying: "Although I am under a terrible strain, and have been since the wreck, I will try to give you the facts as near as I can recall.

"We left Louisville twenty-three minutes later than ordered, and No. 41 left eighteen minutes earlier than we did." he began.

"We stopped at the Southern crossing and got a clear board at Highland Park, Drawbridge and Brooks. Just after we passed Gap in the Knobs, it was a few seconds past 5:27 o'clock, as near as I can recall.

"I sounded the station signal, one blast from my whistle, when we were about a half mile from Shepherdsville. Then I blew four blasts for orders. I could see the signal only dimly, and it was green, our signal to proceed if we had seen it change from red to green. I did not see it change, as it appeared green when I first saw it.

"There was a haze in the air, which I believe now to have been caused by the smoke from the engine of 41, but at the time I could not account for it. [words missing] natural in the atmosphere as I have found it along my route."

Tried to Stop Too Late.

Continuing, he said, "Oftentimes an operator gives us the signal before we call for it, and I believed it had already changed from red to green, meaning for me to proceed. I thought we had been given the board and blew four more shrill blasts to make certain. Then I saw the signal change to red and I applied the emergency brakes. Had the signal been given by Weatherford when I blew for the board, I believe I could have come to a stop."

When asked by Mr. Kammerer as to what rate of speed he was going at that time, he thought it was between forty and forty-five miles per hour, and about between twenty and twenty-five miles per hour when the crash came.

Interrogated by a member of the jury as to the control of his train, Wolfenberger replied, "We can't have a train under control and make up time. We expect to be protected."

In answer to a question by Mr. Kammerer as to being positive of seeing the signal, he admitted not having seen the signal change.

"Leaving Louisville," Wolfenberger continued, "we had nine cars. The engine kept slipping. There seemed to be a sweat on the rails."

Asked what he did after the wreck, he replied that he lit his torch and climbed out of his cab which was housed in with wreckage and hurried to the station where he made a report of the wreck after ordering his fireman to do what he could for the victims.

No Signal From 41.

With considerable emotion he exclaimed in answer to questions concerning the flagman of 41. "It never would have happened if he had put out his signals."

If Weatherford had known that No. 7 was following 41, and was going to pass 41, he should have put out the red signal, Wolfenberger said.

Asked about the length of his service in the capacity of an engineer, he replied that he had been driving fast passenger trains for seventeen years, and had been an engineer for almost twenty-eight years, both freight and passenger.

Fireman Testifies

The last witness was Charles E. Gossem, Wolfenberger's fireman. He told of putting his last shovel of coal in the fire as they passed Gap in the Knobs. Then he took his seat in the window as is his custom.

"The signal was on Wolfenberger's side of the cab, and I had nothing to say about it. Usually though if a station is on my side, I call it to him.

"I could see the signal clearly when we were about a half mile from the Shepherdsville station. it was green and it didn't change to red until we were right on the depot." he said.

"When the crash came," Gossem continued, "I was thrown back in the tender. The engine and tender were crushed in, and Wolfenberger had to light his torch to get out. I lit mine too, and with difficulty we made our way out of the wreckage."

In answer to questions by Mr. Kammerer as to what he did after the crash, he replied that he helped extricate victims from the wreckage. "Wolfenberger cried to me, 'For god's sake do what you can for these people while I run to the station and summon all the doctors in Louisville.'"

Wolfenberger remained on the scene until 1 o'clock and did what he could for the injured, according to the fireman.

JUROR EXPLAINS WRECK VERDICT

Should Have Shown Red Signal At Shepherdsville.

—•—

Weatherford Held To Have Been Partly Responsible.

—•—

BLAME OTHERS PRIMARILY

The Courier-Journal, Saturday, Dec. 29, 1917

SOME OF THOSE WHO MET DEATH IN
CRASH OF TRAINS AT SHEPHERDSVILLE

W. MACK MILLER — R. C. CHERRY — JOHN T. PHILLIPS — BEN TALBOTT

Mrs. N. M. MUIR — Mrs. W. MACK MILLER — Mrs. TOM MILLER — Mrs. H. H. MASHBURN

N. M. MUIR — Mrs. R. C. CHERRY — FRANK L. NUNN — Mrs. JOHN PHILLIPS

R. C. CHERRY Jr. — GEORGE S. MUIR

The Courier-Journal, Sunday, Dec. 23, 1917

Appendix F

INDICTED FOR L. & N. WRECK

The Courier-Journal, January 3, 1918

**True Bills Against Company,
Officers and Engineer**

Bullitt Grand Jury Acts After Investigation

EARLY TRIAL EXPECTED

THE INDICTED.

Louisville & Nashville Railroad Company.

B. M. STARKS, general manager.

W. F. SHERIDAN, division superintendent, who following the destruction of forty-seven lives, said: "We have not yet reached the point where we regard the newspapers as interested in our accidents."

F. J. FISHBACK, master of trains.

THE WITNESSES.

Judge A. E. Funk, W. J. Monroe, Frank Maraman, J. D. Buckman, Prof. J. H. Sanders, W. B. Cash, Muir Funk, N. W. Troll, B. B. Ball, Oscar Kulmer, C. R. Gardner, W. C. Morrison, James Maraman, Colgan Rouse, H. H. Glenn, W. S. Bowman, J. B. Keyer, H. J. Johnson, E. J. Masden.

Indictments against the Louisville & Nashville Railroad Company; B. M. Starks, general manager of the road, W. F. Sheridan, division superintendent, and F. J. Fishback, master of trains, charging "creating and maintaining a common nuisance," and against William Wolfenberger, engineer, charging involuntary manslaughter, were returned yesterday att noon by the special Bullitt county grand jury, which for the last five days has been conducting an investigation into the circumstances surrounding the fatal crash at Shepherdsville on the evening of December 20, resulting in forty-eight deaths and injuries to scores of others.

Along with the officials named in the special report, the Bullitt county grand jury mentioned Milton H. Smith, president of the L. & N., as being in a measure largely responsible for the collision, but stated that "we do not indict Milton H. Smith because it did not appear he was connected with the movement of trains."

Regarding Wolfenberger, the engineer of the fast train which plowed through the ill-fated Bardstown accommodation, the grand jury found him "guilty of gross, wanton and willful negligence in approaching Shepherdsville at such a great and excessive speed." The report refers to his long service, states that he knew local travel was always heavy just before the holidays, and holds that "therefore the great loss of life was in a great measure due to his fault, as well as the others mentioned."

Recommend New Law.

Explaining the indictments, the grand jury in their report expressed regret to learn that Kentucky has no statute making it voluntary manslaughter for causing the death a person by the gross and willful negligence of those handling an engine, and directing and being responsible for the movement of same, and recommends that such a law be enacted at the next session of the General Assembly.

Exonerating Jess Weatherford, the operator at Shepherdsville the report indicates, though, that his absence from his station was an indication of negligence, but not attributable to him individually.

The report delves into the circumstances leading up to and following the crash.

The true bill against the road and the three officials is a minutely detailed indictment in which it is set forth how the railroad has for years constituted a menace to public safety, because of a lack of safety measures for public crossings and streets, and because of the excessive speed under which trains pass through the town of Shepherdsville. The indictment states that this negligence has on numerous occasions almost caused other collisions.

On Two Counts.

The involuntary manslaughter indictment against Engineer Wolfenberger is based on two counts, specifically because of the deaths of Nat Muir, of Bardstown, and Henry Hardaway, of Shepherdsville.

Under the Kentucky statutes, Engineer Wolfenberger is liable to punishment in the form of a fine or imprisonment, or both, at the discretion of the jury. The L. & N., as a corporation, is liable only to a fine, for creating and maintaining a common nuisance, but General Manager Starks, Division Superintendent Sheridan and Master of Trains Fishback are liable to a fine or imprisonment, or both, at the discretion of the jury.

The fact that those held responsible for the Shepherdsville wreck may be tried early has been indicated by Judge D. A. McCandless, of the Tenth Judicial district, in which Bullitt county is included. In calling the special grand jury Judge McCandless also hinted at a probable special session of the Bullitt Circuit Court. Otherwise, the cases will come up at the next session of the Bullitt Circuit Court, which under the statutes begins the first Monday in April, coming this year on April 1. The case will not be called to trial, though, before April 2.

J. Lewis Williams, Commonwealth's Attorney in the Tenth Judicial district, and Tarlton C. Carroll, County Attorney of Bullitt county, will direct the prosecution. Both have established reputations of being efficient and fearless.

Stoney Weller was foreman of the special grand jury, the roster of which included prominent residents of Shepherdsville and Bullitt county.

The witnesses before the grand jury were: Judge A. E. Funk, W. J. Monroe, Frank Maraman, J. D. Buckman, Prof. J. H. Sanders, W. B. Cash, Muir Funk, Will Troll, B. B. Ball, Oscar Kulmer, C. R. Gardner, W. C. Morrison, James Maraman, Colgan Rouse, H. H. Glenn, W. S. Bowman, J. B. Keyer, H. J. Johnson, E. J. Masden.

The special grand jury's report, and the indictments against the L. & N. and three officials follow.

Tell of Investigations

Bullitt Circuit Court. Honorable D. A. McCandless, Judge Tenth Judicial District.

The Grand Jury of Bullitt County, Ky., after being in session five days for the special purpose of investigating and inquiring into the cause of the collision of two passenger trains on the Louisville and Nashville railroad inside the corporate limits of Shepherdsville, December 20, 1917, whereby forty-eight passengers were killed and many seriously injured, desire to make the following report:

We have examined about thirty-five witnesses and according to their testimony, find that the wreck was caused by a failure on the part of many of the officers, agents and employees of the Louisville & Nashville Railroad Company, to promulgate such rules and perform such service in the operations of the trains of said company as would make them safe to the traveling public.

The train known as No. 41, carrying passengers between Louisville and Springfield, and conmmonly known as the Bardstown train, was made up of old-style wooden passenger coaches and pulled by an engine of the old type. Both passenger coaches and engine were unfit and unsafe, especially when used on a trunk line, where many heavy trains of steel coaches, pulled by the largest and heaviest type of passenger engines, are operated at a rapid and dangerous speed. The further use of such old wooden passenger coaches and old type engine, should not be tolerated by the public.

Aver System Is Dangerous

We further find the system of operating trains in use by the L & N, especially between Louisville and Bardstown Junction and through Shepherdsville, to be unsafe and dangerous when an acconmmodation train doing local work and making many stops, is followed so closely by a fast through train making no stops and for the use of this system, it would seem under the testimony before us, that the officers of the company, whose duty it was to promulgate such rules and regulations as would insure safety to the traveling public, are to blame.

We find the Bardstown train left Louisville at 4:35 p.m., which was its scheduled time to leave. The fast train No. 7 was due to leave Louisville at 3 p.m., but did not leave until 4:53 p.m. At 4:38, orders were issued for it to run from Louisville to Bowling Green, one hour and thirty minutes later than its scheduled time. Under the train order, this fast train was required to make up twenty-three minutes between Louisville and Bowling Green, running part of the time behind a slow passenger local.

It seems that Conductor Campbell on the Bardstown train knew nothing about the order on which No. 7 was to run. The first information he received concerning the time and movement of the fast train was at Brooks. J. W. Sams, train dispatcher called the operator at Brooks by telephone at 5:10 and asked about the Bardstown train, and was told it had not arrived. Sams then told him by phone to tell Conductor Campbell when No. 41 arrived that No.7 passed FX Tower at 5:08 and if he, (Campbell) could not reach Bardstown Junction on time to stay at Shepherdsville.

This verbal message or order was delivered verbally to Campbell at about 5:13 at Brooks. No. 41 reached Shepherdsville a little late. The operator at Shepherdsville had no orders for that train, and while the passengers, mail and express were being unloaded, Conductor Campbell went in the office and called up Sams, the dispatcher, and asked about No. 7 and if he had time to go to Bardstown Junction.

Say Orders Not Given

It is said the dispatcher told him if he could not reach Bardstown Junction on time, he had better take the siding at once. He then pulled the train southward 200 feet from the station and stopped for the purpose of backing it on the siding, but before he had time to do so, and just as his train stopped for that purpose, it was struck by No. 7. Some blame is charged to Conductor Campbell for not heading in at Shepherdsville, but we find that he had no such orders.

We find that his orders only consisted of a telephone message delivered to him verbally at Brooks to the effect that if he could not reach Bardstown Junction on time, to stay at Shepherdsville until No. 7 passed. We find that the Bardstown train stood at Shepherdsville station about three minutes and then pulled about 200 feet southward and stopped at the switch. As to whether it was the duty of his flagman to protect the rear end of his train at that particular time by going back a reasonable distance with a red light, or whether he had the right to rely on the protection of the semaphore signal at the station to protect his train, we are in doubt and are unable to agree. We do, however, condemn the rule promulgated by the officials of the company to have the operator leave his post of duty for the purpose of assisting in handling the baggage and express, and for that reason, not being in his office to signal these fast trains when approaching or passing a station.

Weatherford Exonerated

We find that Jesse Weatherford, the operator at Shepherdsville, had been directed by his superior officer to leave his post of duty for the purpose of assisting the agent to handle the mail, baggage and express, and for that reason, we charge no negligence to him personally. We do, however, believe that his presence in the office was absolutely necessary at the moment No. 7 was approaching Shepherdsville, and believe that if he had been in the office and had displayed the red light, which is a stop signal, at the time it was called for, or should have been called for by the engineer of No. 7, the wreck, if not entirely avoided, would not have been so fearful and as it is admitted by the highest officials, to wit: Milton H. Smith, President; B. M. Starks, General Manager; W. F. Sheridan, Superintendent; and F. J. Fishback, master of Trains, and each of them are in a measure largely responsible for the collision resulting in the death and injury of so many of the citizens of this and other counties. We do not indict Milton H. Smith because it does not appear that he had anything to do with the movement of trains.

Gross Negligence Alleged.

We find that William Wolfenberger, the engineer on No. 7 was guilty of gross, wanton and willful negligence in approaching Shepherdsville at such a great and excessive speed. He knew that the No. 41, even if running on the scheduled time, could only be a short distance ahead of his train. He was an old railroad man and knew that the local travel was always heavy just before the holidays. Therefore, the great loss of life was in a measure due to his fault as well as the others hereinbefore mentioned.

We are unable to say that Jesse Weatherford, operator at Shepherdsville, or J. W. Sams, train dispatcher on duty at Louisville, or either of them, contributed to the collision by a failure to observe the rules of the company, and yet we desire to report that we believe either of them could have prevented it. Sams could have prevented it by conducting the time movements of the two trains by taking into consideration the local work of No. 41 would have to do between Brooks and Shepherdsville, and by not allowing No. 7, the fast train, to pass Brooks until he knew No. 41 was in the clear at Shepherdsville, as the two stations are only about five miles apart. We believe Weatherford could possibly have prevented the collision by being at his post of duty and then and there blocking No. 7 by displaying a red signal. While we believe each of them guilty of negligence, we are advised that they having complied with the rules of the company, it would be useless to indict them.

L. & N. System Rapped.

We, therefore, desire to report the terrible loss of life suffered by the citizens of our Commonwealth, who were unfortunate enough to be passengers on No. 41, on December 20, 1917, was due to the inefficient, inadequate, and dangerous rules and system of operating the trains of the Louisville & Nashville Railroad as well as the negligence of employees before mentioned.

We take this opportunity to call the attention of the next General Assembly to the enormous loss of life that has just occurred in our State on one of the oldest trunk line railroads, and where it was doubletracked, and recommend that a law be passed compelling all trunk line railroads to install the block system, use steel coaches and keep an operator at his post of duty at all times, to also compel the speed limit of all trains, while passing through all incorporated towns to be reduced until reasonably safe and stop for passengers at all county seats.

We regret to learn that our State has no statute making it voluntary manslaughter for causing the death of a patron by the gross and willful negligence of those handling an engine or train of cars, and those directing same, and reconmmend that such a law be enacted at the next General Assembly.

Respectfully submitted,

Stoney Weller, Foreman of the Grand Jury;

J. Lewis Williams, Commonwealth Attorney, Tenth Judicial District.

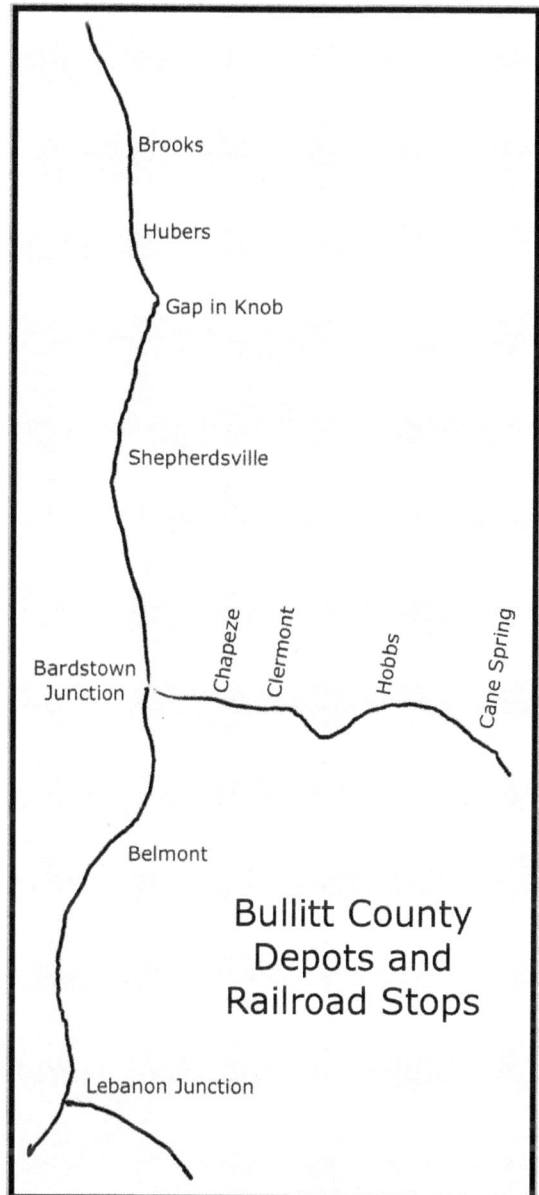

Bullitt County Depots and Railroad Stops

KENTUCKY ADVOCATE

DANVILLE, KY., FRIDAY MORNING, DEC. 21, 1917.

EXTRA

47 KILLED IN L. & N. WRECK

WORST WRECK IN THE HISTORY OF THE LOUISVILLE & NASHVILLE RAILROAD OCCURS AT SHEPHERDSVILLE

CINCINNATI EXPRESS CRASHES INTO THE REAR OF THE SPRINGFIELD-BARDSTOWN ACCOMMODATION TRAIN

TWO COACHES TORN INTO KINDLING WOOD AND FORTY-SEVEN KILLED AND FORTY BADLY HURT

The Kentucky Advocate
Danville, Kentucky
Friday, Dec. 21, 1917

Appendix G
The Shepherdsville Collision
by Jason Kelley

LOCOMOTIVE ENGINEERS JOURNAL
PUBLISHED BY THE BROTHERHOOD OF
LOCOMOTIVE BROTHERS
C. H. SALMONS, EDITOR AND MANAGER
CLEVELAND, OHIO
Volume 52, January, 1918,
Number 1, pages 414-416

The rear end collision between two passenger trains on the Louisville & Nashville Railroad at Shepherdsville, Ky., recently, furnished a striking illustration of some conditions the locomotive engineer must contend with day in and day out on the average railroad, in his efforts to render the service demanded, and how, when the inevitable wreck happens, as it must when circumstances combine in a certain way, he is made to suffer the penalty of dismissal, although he is but following out a rule of practice that is general on the road that employs him, a practice that is not only general, but one that is known to the operating officials and practically conceded, by their tolerance of it, as being necessary to the desired train movement.

The report of the Kentucky State Railroad Commission on this wreck, and all the contributing causes to it, disclosed a state of affairs that was amazing to some, but to a great many engineers in this country it was nothing unusual. We will not go into a detailed summing up of the several factors bearing on the Shepherdsville collision, where a fast passenger train behind time overtook a slow passenger train also running late, losing time, and backing in where the accident happened, excepting to say that the usual elements were present that are to be found on many other slipshod railroads. The trains were not spaced; the leading train, though losing time, was not protected either by fuses, torpedoes or flag, and the fixed order signal, the only signal that entered into the unfortunate affair worthy of consideration, was the two positions — red and green — order signal, which was green at the time, thus indicating "all right," and even if the tail lights on the preceding train were burning, and burning brightly, as the operator said, which may or may not be true, the order signal was the guiding one at that point for the engineer of the flyer, and his eyes were no doubt fixed on that signal from the moment he first came within seeing distance of it, and would have remained fixed on it until he had passed it. So the question as to the condition of the tail lights of the train ahead is immaterial, as was also the caution rule of the company, which says that, "conductors and engineers when approaching train order offices, shall have their trains under control, and if the order signal is against them, they must not assume that it will be changed."

Of the various efforts to locate blame for this wreck, where circumstances combined in such a way as to give the engineer on the high-speed train no chance whatever to avoid the collision, the trumping up of that "caution rule" by the officers, a rule which need and custom had long since made obsolete, was the most unfair thing imaginable, for, because of it, the engineer of the flyer was made to suffer the penalty of discharge. The rules, which like the general system of operating high-speed trains in that territory, were charged by the Commission as being "decidedly inadequate," also required that engineers approaching order stations must see the order block changed from red to green after the whistle call is sounded, but the fact that the operator's duties prevented his always being where he could attend to the signal promptly, as was proven at the investigation, and conceded by the officers, had made that rule obsolete also, and the engineer of the high-speed train was doing just what the general practice of the engineers had all found to be necessary in order to meet the demands for time with fast trains, and the failure of the officers of the company to enforce that rule, which to their knowledge was so generally disregarded, was practically an acknowledgment of the need of disregarding it Yet the engineer of the fast train, doing as the Commission reported, "all that was possible for one not endowed with superhuman intelligence could do," was dismissed from the service.

Brothers, take this lesson home to yourselves. Very many of you are doing the same today as this Brother who was giving the fullest measure of his accumulated experience of a lifetime to do what he knew was demanded of him, and on a safety margin that was fearfully narrow at times, due to conditions over which he had no control. Doing the thing which the general practice of the engineers—as was brought out in the investigation-was proven absolutely necessary to meet the company's demands for train dispatch, on that particular part of the road.

The writer met a Brother engineer recently who had just finished a trip pulling one of the fast passenger trains on a prominent trunk line road, and in answer to the question as to how things were with him, he replied, "It is getting to be so that in order to deliver the goods on our fast trains, nowadays, a man must put aside his better judgment and run like a damn fool."

When a wreck like that at Shepherdsville, Ky., takes place, conditions are brought to light that are apparently amazing to the State Inspectors, and the public in general, but the men in the service are facing these conditions every day and night in many places, fully conscious of the possibilities, even surprised that the inevitable disaster does not take place more often, and the nerve-racking effect of it all is reflected in the careworn look of the engineer at the end of a trip on one of these so-called "flyers," on roads where the mechanical aids and general system of train operation are wholly inadequate for that class of train service.

The great lesson of it all certainly furnishes one more illustration of the failure of private control of railroads, and that if we are to gain any relief from such conditions we must look to the National Government for it, the source from which has come the 8-hour day; the 16-hour service law; the patent coupler; the block system and practically every safety measure introduced into railroad train operation in recent years.

Appendix H
Report of the
Kentucky Railroad Commission
January 30, 1918, pages 101-132.

The following is taken from the *Thirty-Ninth Annual Report of the Railroad Commission of Kentucky for the Year 1918*, in the section titled "Formal and Informal Complaints, Petitions and Hearings, Railroad Commission Office.

To Hon. A. O. Stanley, Governor of Kentucky, and to the Honorable Members of the General Assembly of the Regular Session of the Legislature for 1918.

Gentlemen :

The Railroad Commission of Kentucky herewith submits for your consideration its Report upon the wreck which occurred on the Louisville & Nashville Railroad at Shepherdsville, Kentucky, on December 20, 1917.

Said Report contains the opinion, findings and recommendations of the Commission.

Respectfully submitted,

Laurence B. Finn, Chairman.

Sid T. Douthitt, Commissioner.

H. G. Garrett, Commissioner.

BEFORE THE KENTUCKY

RAILROAD COMMISSION.

IN RE: INVESTIGATION OF THE CAUSE OF THE WRECK AT SHEPHERDSVILLE ON DECEMBER 20, 1917, BETWEEN PASSENGER TRAINS NO. 7 AND NO. 41 ON THE LOUISVILLE & NASHVILLE RAILROAD COMPANY.—OPINION, FINDINGS, AND RECOMMENDATIONS OF THE COMMISSION.

On December 20, 1917, passenger train No. 7 ran into the rear of passenger train No. 41 at Shepherdsville, Ky., causing the death and injury of more than fifty of the most prominent people of the State. Within five days thereafter notice of the accident and its results was given to the Commission by the management of the Louisville & Nashville Railroad Company and thereafter the Commission fixed January 10, 1918, as the date for hearing testimony concerning the cause of the accident. The hearing was held at the Seelbach Hotel in Louisville, Kentucky.

Before entering into the investigation the Commission made the following statement:

"In pursuance to the authority vested in the Railroad Commission, we have met for the purpose of investigating the cause of the accident which occurred on the Louisville & Nashville Railroad at Shepherdsville, Ky., on December 20, 1917. The section of the Kentucky Statutes under which this investigation is held is Section 777, which reads:—

"'Notice of every accident which may occur and be attended with loss of life shall be given within five days thereafter by the company operating the road on which the accident occurred to the Railroad Commission, and such company shall furnish the Commission all information requested by it concerning the cause of the accident.'

"The object of this meeting is to request the Louisville & Nashville Railroad Company to give the Kentucky Railroad Commission the information necessary to ascertain the cause of this accident.

"It is not a part of our official duty to institute or assist in the prosecution of acts of negligence committed by railroad employes; neither is it our purpose to add to the sorrow or discomfort of those whose negligent acts may have contributed to this horrible accident; nor can we in any way hope to alleviate the anguish of the friends and relatives of those who were victims of this tragedy. We merely hope by this investigation to ascertain the cause of the accident and if the facts warrant, to recommend:

"1. Changes in the rules of the company so that the employes will not be required to do or perform conflicting duties.

"2. To inspire employes to do their full duty under reasonable rules.

"3. To propose legislative enactments that will prohibit or prevent the recurrence of such accidents.

"Such a task certainly demands the serious consideration of the common carriers, the Railroad Commission and the general public."

The attitude of the company towards this investigation is best evidenced by the following statement made by Mr. Edward S. Jouett, Attorney for the Company:

"In response to this request, the Louisville & Nashville Railroad states that it has caused to attend this meeting today all of the witnesses suggested by the Chairman of the Kentucky Railroad Commission and that it will be glad to have any others attend whose presence may be desired, as it is the wish of the company that the fullest possible hearing may be had."

Chairman Finn:

"The Commission wishes to state that the management of the Louisville & Nashville Railroad Company has manifested every disposition necessary to make this investigation thorough and complete, for which we thank the company."

The following witnesses were examined by the Commission:—D. M. Starks, General Manager of the Louisville & Nashville Railroad Company; W. F. Sheridan, Division Superintendent of the Main Stem Division, and various branch roads; J. W. Sams, Trick Train Dispatcher. Mr. Sams was dispatcher upon the evening of December 20th, and upon this occasion it was his duty "to direct the movement of trains." W. J. Haylow, Superintendent of Transportation; A. R. Fugina, Signal Engineer of the Louisville & Nashville Railroad Company; J. B. Keyer, Locomotive Engineer on train No. 41; Ernest Chase, colored porter on No. 41; W. E. Sanders, Telegraph Operator at Brooks Station; Jesse Weatherford, Telegraph Operator at Shepherdsville; W. T. Carter, Telegraph Operator at F. X. Tower; W. N. Wolfenberger, Engineer on train No. 7; John Ford, an engineer who was a passenger on No. 41; H. R. Johnson, Freight Engineer, who was standing at the depot at Shepherdsville at the time the wreck occurred.

A stenographic report of the evidence was taken by the Official stenographer and the record of the evidence contains 196 pages.

No 41 is a passenger train which does local work between Louisville, Bardstown Junction and Lebanon Junction. The line of the Louisville & Nashville is double tracked from Louisville to Lebanon Junction. No. 7 is a fast passenger train running fiom Cincinnati to Nashville and South. The stations where telegraph operators are employed, and which are known as "Train-order stations," are F. X. Tower, 3.2 miles from Louisville; Strawberry, 5.9 miles from Louisville; Brooks Station, 13.3 miles from Louisville; Shepherdsville, 18.3 miles from Louisville, and Bardstown Junction, 22.1 miles from Louisville. The ordinary schedule of No. 41 requires it to leave Louisville at 4:35 p. m.; to reach F. X. Tower at 4:47; Strawberry at 4:53; Brooks Station at 5:06; Shepherdsville at 5:18; Bardstown Junction at 5:27. The regular schedule for No. 7 is as follows: It leaves Louisville at 3:00 p. m.; passes F. X. Tower at 3:12; passes Strawberry at 3:16; passes Brooks Station at 3:25; passes Shepherdsville at 3:31 and reaches Bardstown Junction at 3:35. From this statement the normal schedule of 41 requires it to execute the following distances in the following time:—

From Louisville to F. X. Tower
3.2 miles, 12 minutes;

From F. X. Tower to Strawberry
2.7 miles, 6 minutes;

From Strawberry to Brooks
7.4 miles, 13 minutes;

From Brooks to Shepherdsville
5 miles, 12 minutes;

From Shepherdsville to Bardstown Junction
3.8 miles, 9 minutes.

The ordinary schedule of No. 7 requires it to run:

From Louisville to F. X. Tower
3.2 miles, in 12 minutes;

From F. X. Tower to Strawberry
2.7 miles, in 4 minutes;

From Strawberry to Brooks
7.4 miles, in 9 minutes;

From Brooks to Shepherdsville
5 Miles, in 6 minutes;

From Shepherdsville to Bardstown Junction
3.8 miles, in 4 minutes.

41 is required to execute the distance between Louisville and Shepherdsville in 43 minutes; while No. 7 is required to execute the same distance in 31 minutes. 41 is required to execute the distance between Louisville and Bardstown Junction in 52 minutes; while No. 7 must execute the distance in 35 minutes.

On the afternoon of December 20th, No. 41 left Louisville at 4:35. No. 7 left Louisville 18 minutes later, at 4:53, with an order to run 1 hour and 30 minutes late to Bowling Green. A Book of Rules is issued by the company prescribing the various duties of employes. Under Rule 222, it is the duty of operators to "promptly record and report to the train dispatcher the time of the arrival and departure of all trains," and from these reports a record is made by the train dispatcher. The record of the train dispatcher shows 41 at F. X. Tower at 4:51; at Strawberry at 4:56; arrived at Brooks at 5:12, departed at 5:13; that it arrived at Shepherdsville at 5:24. The record shows that No. 7 left Louisville at 4:53, passed F. X. Tower at 5:08, passed Strawberry at 5:11, passed Brooks at 5:23 and that it reached Shepherdsville at 5:26. That this record is not correct, the following analysis will conclusively show.

The record shows that No. 7 executed the distance between Louisville and Strawberry, 5.9 miles in 18 minutes, which is not improbable on account of yard delays; that it executed the distance between Strawberry and Brooks, 7.4 miles, in 12 minutes, which is not improbable; but that it executed the distance between Brooks and Shepherdsville, 5 miles, in three minutes, which is admitted by all concerned to be most improbable. As these records cannot be relied upon with accuracy, we must, therefore, adopt some reasonable rule to ascertain how these trains actually executed their schedules upon the evening of December 20th.

The record least to be relied upon is the record at Shepherdsville; for the operator at Shepherdsville testifies that the date of the arrival of No. 41 and No. 7 were not sent to the Train Dispatcher until long after the wreck had happened. It is manifest also that No. 41 was losing time. Its regular schedule after leaving Louisville at 4:35, required it to be at F. X. Tower at 4:47; but the record at F. X. Tower shows 4:51, 4 minutes late. The record at Strawberry shows 4:56, 3 minutes late. The record at Brooks, arrived at 5:12, left at 5:13, therefore it arrived at Brooks 6 minutes late. The record at Brooks may or may not be correct; but in all probability it is fairly accurate as it shows an additional loss of about four minutes from Strawberry until it left Brooks at 5:13. However, we do not ascribe to the accuracy of the record that 41 arrived at Brooks at 5:12 and left at 5:13, thereby unloading and reloading and leaving in one minute.

There is no evidence warranting the conclusion that 41 was losing time between stations as no complaint was made that the engine of 41 was not working right; and, as Christmas crowds were traveling, the delay must have been at the stations in letting off and taking on the passengers; and besides the schedule time of 41 was very slow between stations.

The ordinary time that it required of No. 41 to execute the distance between Brooks and Shepherdsville, a distance of 5 miles, is 12 minutes (a very reasonable schedule), and if the ordinary time between stations had been taken, No. 41 would have reached Shepherdsville about 5:25; which is the time we believe 41 did reach Shepherdsville.

No. 7 left Louisville at 4:53 and passed F. X. Tower at 5:08. The record shows that it passed Strawberry at 5:11, which required 3 minutes to execute the distance between F. X. Tower and Strawberry, a distance of 2.7 miles. If this is true,

No. 7 executed the distance in 1 minute less than the usual or schedule time, the schedule time being 4 minutes. Mr. Wolfenberger, the engineer, doubts that he executed this distance in the time the record indicates: for he says, 'We are supposed to run 20 miles an hour through a short space out there."

The record shows that No. 7 passed Brooks at 5:23, which required No. 7 to execute the distance between Strawberry and Brooks, 7.4 miles, in 12 minutes. The usual time that it requires No. 7 to execute this distance is 9 minutes. There is no explanation why No. 7 executed the distance between F. X. Tower and Strawberry in 1 minute less than its usual time (if it did do so), or why No. 7 executed the distance between Strawberry and Brooks in 3 minutes more than its usual time (if it did do so). If, as a matter of fact, No. 7 did execute the distance between Strawberry and Brooks in its usual schedule time, towit, 9 minutes, then it passed Brooks at 5:22, which was less than 10 minutes behind No. 41; but we believe the proof fairly warrants the conclusion that for some reason No. 7 did not execute its regular time and that it passed Brooks approximately at 5:23. This time is corroborated by Mr. Wolfenberger, the engineer of No. 7, who says that he passed Brooks "nearer 5:24 than 5:23." Assuming then that the record at Brooks is fairly accurate and that No. 7 passed Brooks at 5:23, just 10 minutes behind No. 41, the interesting question is—At what minute did No. 7 strike No. 41 at Shepherdsville?

There is nothing in the record or the evidence which shows anything unusual about the speed of No. 7 between Brooks and Shepherdsville. The usual time required by No. 7 to execute the distance between Brooks and Shepherdsville is 6 minutes. If the usual time was taken upon this occasion (and we are warranted in believing from the evidence that such was the case) No. 7 must have reached Shepherdsville not sooner than 5:29 and not later than 5:30. This is corroborated by the testimony of Mr. Wolfenberger, who looked at his watch as he passed Gap-in-the-Knobs, which is near 2 miles north of Shepherdsville: "I looked at my watch," says he, "and it was 5:27 and some seconds." If this is true, No. 7 almost executed the distance between Brooks and Shepherdsville in its normal time and the accident must have occurred between 5:29 and 5:30. Therefore, No. 41 must have been at the station at Shepherdsville between 5 and 6 minutes before it was struck.

The accident happened between 5:29 and 5:30. No. 41 was due by schedule to leave Shepherdsville at 5:18. At the time this accident occurred No. 41 was between 11 and 12 minutes behind its schedule time. Thus 41 lost at least from 4 to 5 minutes additional time at Shepherdsville. In the distance covered by the two trains from Louisville to Shepherdsville No. 41 lost 11 or 12 minutes on the schedule time and No. 7 gained 6 or 7 minutes over the schedule time of 41, which inevitably brought the trains together at Shepherdsville. The proof, therefore, warrants the conclusion that the two trains were 18 minutes apart at Louisville, 17 minutes apart at F. X. Tower; 15 minutes apart at Strawberry; 10 minutes apart at Brooks, and that between 6 and 7 minutes after No. 7 passed Brooks at 5:23 the accident occurred. It also occurred between 16 and 17 minutes after No. 41 passed Brooks at 5:13.

When No. 41 left Brooks at 5:13, under its normal schedule it should have reached Shepherdsville 12 minutes later, at 5:25. When No. 7 left Brooks at 5:23, normally it should have reached Shepherdsville 6 minutes later, at 5:29, with just 4 minutes difference between them.

When No. 41 left Brooks at 5:13, under its normal schedule, it should have reached Bardstown Junction 18 minutes later, at 5:31. When No. 7 left Brooks at 5:23, under its normal schedule it should have reached Bardstown Junction 10 minutes later, at 5:33, with just 2 minutes difference between them.

When No. 41 left Louisville at 4:35, under its normal schedule, it should have reached Bardstown Junction 52 minutes later, or at 5:27; and when No. 7 left Louisville at 5:43, under its normal schedule, it should have reached Bardstown Junction 35 minutes later, at 5:28, with only 1 minute's time between them.

With these narrow margins of time between the two trains some precaution should have been taken by the one whose duty it was "to direct the movement of trains." Unless 41 executed its schedule to the minute, No. 7 was sure to overtake it before it reached Bardstown Junction. Judgment and discretion dictated that a suitable passing point should have been designated where No. 7 should pass No. 41 between Louisville and Bardstown Junction. It required but little thought to fix Shepherdsville as the place. The normal schedules of the two trains should have settled this question. Both trains should and could have been notified; No. 7 when it left Louisville and No. 41 either at Strawberry or Brooks.

Here we quote the testimony of Train Dispatcher Sams (See page 81).

Q. Now, when it is known that a local train is to be passed by a fast train, whose duty is it to give the orders to designate the passing point?

A. The dispatcher.

Q. Your duty, is it not?

A. Yes, sir.

Q. What orders did you give No. 41 and No. 7 that afternoon with reference to passing each other?

A. I did not give them any orders at all. They are both of the same class of trains and it was not necessary to give them orders.

Q. How were they to pass each other?

A. They could very easily pass each other; one man could get in a siding and the other could go by.

If an order had been given Conductor Campbell for 41 to take the siding at Shepherdsville, we do not believe the accident would have occurred. At Shepherdsville, Campbell first did his train work, then left the train and went to the telephone, called up Mr. Sams, the dispatcher, to ascertain the whereabouts of No. 7 and to find out what he should do. After the conversation, he concluded he would take the siding and the colored porter was instructed to notify the engineer to back in. The unnecessary time thus spent by Campbell in ascertaining what to do at Shepherdsville would have been sufficient to have permitted 41 to take the siding before No. 7 reached Shepherdsville. The time thus spent by Campbell would not have been necessary if 41 had been ordered, either at Strawberry or at Brooks, to take the siding at Shepherdsville.

The testimony relating to the information received by 41 as to the whereabout of No. 7 is as follows: (See record of evidence, page 115). Sanders, the agent at Brooks, testified: "I told him (Campbell, conductor of 41) Mr. Sams, the dispatcher, told me to tell the conductor of No. 41 that No. 7 was by F. X. at 5:08 and if he could not go to Bardstown Junction on time it would be at good idea to go in at Shepherdsville."

At page 82 of the evidence Sams, the dispatcher, testifies: "I told the operator at Brooks to tell No. 41 that No. 7 at that time was by F. X. Tower. I did it merely for his information. Told him if he could not go to Bardstown Junction on time it would be better to let them by at Shepherdsville in order to avoid delaying No. 7, the fast train.

Q. Didn't you talk to Campbell at Shepherdsville?

A. Yes sir. Campbell came in at Shepherdsville.

Q. Didn't you tell Campbell then that No. 7 had left F. X. Tower at 5...?

A. 5:08.

Q. At 5:08?

A. Yes, sir.

Q. That showed then that at F. X. Tower No. 7 was running 17 minutes behind No. 41?

A. Yes, sir.

Q. The station at Strawberry is a train-order station?

A. Yes, sir.

Q. You had an operator there?

A. Yes, sir.

Q. At the time you were talking to Campbell at Shepherdsville No. 7 had already passed Strawberry?

A. Yes, sir; but I did not have the report of it in.

Q. Was it not the duty of the agent at Strawberry to report to you exactly when they passed?

A. They don't do it just as soon as they are by; sometimes they wait until we call on them for it.

Q. Why didn't you call on them that afternoon?

A. I had something else to do. My attention or my time was with some other trains out in different territories.

Q. When the operator at Brooks called you up and told you that No. 7 had passed Brooks, what time did he tell you it had passed?

A. At 5:23. I don't know what time it was; they told me that but it was after that that he told me it was by there at 5:23. That was after I had been talking to Campbell.

Q. Then you tried to get?

A. Then I rang Shepherdsville to tell him that No. 7 was by Brooks.

Q. And you did not get Shepherdsville?

A. No, they did not answer.

Q. Under the rules of the company, is it his duty (referring to the operator) to respond to telephone calls?

A. Not necessarily. It would be if he were within hearing distance, but, if he had other duties to perform, he could not hear the bell.

Q. If he happens to be at the telephone, it is his duty to answer it?

A. Yes, sir.

Q. But it is his duty to be elsewhere if he has other business?

A. Yes, sir."

Here we call attention to Rule 343, which provides:

"The proper place for an operator, when trains are due or standing at his station, is in the office; and at such times he must not leave his office, unless the Company's business actually requires his presence elsewhere."

and to Rule 344, which provides:

"Operators are required to devote themselves exclusively to the Company's business while on duty. Those having other duties to perform must not allow them to interfere with their telegraph and telephone duties. The telegraph and telephone service must always be regarded as first in importance."

Thus we see from the testimony that when Campbell talked from Shepherdsville to the Dispatcher that he received information calculated to mislead him. He was only told by the Dispatcher when No. 7 passed F. X. Tower at 5:08, 17 minutes behind 41. At the time of this conversation No. 7 had passed Strawberry and had evidently passed Brooks. It must have been approximately 3 minutes after Campbell talked to Sams when 41 was struck. Such is evidently the impression of Mr. Jouett, Attorney for the company, as shown by a question propounded Weatherford on page 119.

Q. Then he went in and talked "with Mr. Sams?

A, Mr. Campbell?

Q. Yes, Sir?

A. I met him coming out.

Q. He had already talked when you met him?

A. Yes, sir.

Q. How long after that before No. 7 struck 41?

A. I don't know.

Q. Was it 2 or 3 minutes?

A. I could not say, etc.

If it required No. 7, 6 or 7 minutes to run from Brooks to Shepherdsville; and if No. 7 passed Brooks at 5:23 and the accident occurred between 5:29 and 5:30, No. 7 was past Brooks 3 or 4 minutes when Sams told Campbell about No. 7 passing F. X. Tower; for No. 41 must have been struck about 3 minutes after Campbell left the telephone.

After the telephone conversation, Campbell went back to his train and Sams, the dispatcher, did not know what Campbell intended to do. After Campbell left the telephone, the agent at Brooks notified Sams that 7 had passed Brooks, whereupon Sams endeavored to ring Shepherdsville, but no one answered the phone. Campbell concluded to take the siding and his train had pulled up beyond the semaphore signal about 40.8 feet, where it was struck by No. 7.

From this recital of the evidence, those who were responsible for the operation of these two trains were the Train Dispatcher, the Operator at F. X. Tower, the Operator at Strawberry, the Operator at Brooks, the Operator at Shepherdsville, the Conductor and Flagman of No. 41, the Engineer of No. 7, those who framed the Book of Rules, and those whose duty it is to equip the system with adequate safety appliances.

We have no criticism of the conduct of the operator at F. X. Tower. Evidently he promptly reported the passing of trains 41 and 7. Under these rules, it was the duty of the operator at Strawberry to have promptly reported the arrival and departure of trains 41 and 7. No. 41 passed Strawberry 3 minutes after No. 7 left Louisville. Therefore, the Train Dispatcher could have notified 41 at Strawberry to take the siding for No. 7 at Shepherdsville. If the operator at Strawberry had promptly notified the Train Dispatcher when No. 7 passed Strawberry, the Train Dispatcher could have told Campbell at Shepherdsville that No. 7 was by Strawberry. If the operator at Brooks had promptly notified the Train Dispatcher when No. 7 passed Brooks, the Train Dispatcher would have been able to accurately answer Campbell at Shepherdsville when he asked the question, "where is No. 7 now?" (See testimony, page 84). Any and all of which, if it had been done, would have avoided the wreck.

If the operator at Shepherdsville had remembered Rule 344, "that the telegraph and telephone service must always be regarded as first in importance and that those having other duties to perform must not allow them to interfere with the telephone and telegraph duties," he would have been at the telephone when Sams called Shepherdsville. If the operator had been at the telephone, he would have received information that No. 7 had been past Brooks 3 minutes, which would have given the operator ample time to have warned 41 of the approach of No. 7. It would also have prompted him to display the red or "stop" signal to No. 7, if necessary. Either or both of which, we believe, would have avoided the wreck.

We shall not discuss the different constructions placed upon the same rules by different officials and employes of the company; but it demonstrates the necessity of a complete revision of the rules and a more thorough understanding of their meaning by all employes. Illustrative of this we will cite Rule 91, which provides "that operators must keep trains in the same direction at least ten minutes apart." This rule, when construed by some, means that an operator who holds a stop signal on a train when the preceding train has passed ten minutes violates his duty. Others hold that it is discretionary with the operator whether he displays the stop signal after a preceding train has passed exceeding ten minutes. The last construction is the only reasonable construction to be placed upon the rule. It gives an operator a discretion if the train has passed ten minutes or more. It gives him no discretion if the trains are less than ten minutes apart.

When the operator at Brooks knew that the slow train, 41 was losing time and that the fast train, No. 7, was passing just ten minutes behind 41, which had four flagstops before it reached the next train-order station, Shepherdsville, which was only five miles, it appears that in the exercise of good judgment he should have exposed the stop signal "red" to No. 7 when it passed Brooks.

Under a "supplement" we will quote all the rules cited by all the officials and witnesses, so that none of these rules will be omitted in this report; but for the purpose of discussing the evidence and the duties of employes, we will only quote those rules which, in our judgment, particularly relate and are applicable to the duties of the employes who were responsible for the movement and operation of the two trains, No. 7 and No. 41. As to the Train Dispatcher, the following rules show his duty:

RULE 317: They will issue orders governing the movement of trains, and must see that all such orders are transmitted and recorded according to the prescribed forms and rules.

RULE 319: They must keep a record showing the time of arrival and departure of trains at train-order offices, and such record must be carefully filed for future reference.

RULE 201: For movements not provided for by Timetable, train orders will be issued by authority and over the last name of the Chief Train Dispatcher. They must contain neither information nor instructions not essential to such movements. They must be brief and clear; in the prescribed forms when applicable; and without erasure, alteration or interlineation.

Other rules applicable to operators are as follows:

RULE 330: Should a train be delayed in leaving a station, the operator will promptly notify the train dispatcher.

RULE 91: Unless some form of block signals is used, trains in the same direction must keep at least ten minutes apart, except in closing up at meeting and passing stations.

RULE 222: Operators will promptly record and report to the train dispatcher the time of arrival and departure of all trains, including the direction of extra trains.

As to the train crew of 41, the evidence shows that at F. X. Tower it was four minutes late, at Strawberry three minutes late, at Brooks six minutes late, and that when it was struck it was between eleven and twelve minutes late on its schedule time. No fusees were placed upon the track, no torpedoes were placed upon the track, no flagman was sent to the rear to protect 41. Therefore, No. 41 violated the following rules of the Company:

RULE 11: A fusee on or near the track burning red must not be passed until burned out. When burning green it is a caution signal indicating that train ahead is not making its usual speed.

RULE 85a: A train which has fallen back and is running on the time of another train of the same class, as provided in Rule 85, must at all points where stops are made, or in case it is not making running time, be promptly protected as prescribed by Rule 99.

RULE 99 is as follows:

"When a train stops or is delayed, under circumstances in which it may be overtaken by another train, the flagman must go back immediately with stop signals to stop any train moving in the same direction. At a point fifty rail lengths, or fifteen hundred feet, from the rear of his train, he must place one torpedo on the rail; he must then continue to go back at least one hundred rail lengths, or three thousand feet, from the rear of his train, and place two torpedoes on the rail, thirty feet, or one rail length apart, when he may return to a point seventy rail lengths, or twenty-one hundred feet, from the rear of his train; and he must remain there until recalled by the whistle of his engine; but if a passenger train is due within ten minutes, or if an approaching train is within sight or hearing, he must remain until it arrives. If the view is obstructed or if on descending grade, he must go as much farther as may be necessary to reach a point where he is absolutely sure that he can be seen by the expected train at a sufficient distance in which to stop. When he comes in, he must remove the torpedo nearest to his train; but the two torpedoes must be left on the rail as a caution signal to any following train. When protecting at night, the flagman must, the last thing after being recalled, place a lighted red fusee upright between the rails at the point where the one torpedo was removed."

RULE 85b: If, for any cause, the speed of a train is so much reduced as to endanger the rear, the conductor will be held responsible for fully protecting it by the use of the proper signals.

The record shows conclusively that all of these rules were violated by the crew of No. 41.

MR. WOLFENBERGER.

Mr. Wolfenberger, the engineer of No. 7, left Louisville at 4:53, with orders to run one hour and thirty minutes late to Bowling Green. All he knew about No. 41 from the time he left Louisville until No. 41 was struck, was that 41 left Louisville eighteen minutes before his own train. When he passed F. X. Tower at 5:08 he had lost three minutes on his schedule time. If he passed Strawberry at 5:11 he was two minutes behind his schedule time. If he passed Brooks at 5:23, he was running five minutes behind his schedule time. Although No. 7 was running late on its own schedule, it was gaining upon the actual schedule made by 41. 41 was due to leave Brooks at 5:06, which was 17 minutes before No. 7 actually passed Brooks; but as a matter of fact No. 41 did not leave Brooks, according to the record, until 5:13. This, however, was not known to Wolfenberger. So, without notice to him from either the train dispatcher or the operators or the train crew of 41, he had the right to presume that No. 41 was executing its regular schedule.

Therefore, he had a right to presume that No. 41 left Brooks 17 minutes before his train arrived at Brooks.

The history of the wreck and the part enacted by Wolfenberger as gleaned from his testimony is as follows:

He was engineer on train No. 7 on the afternoon of December 20th, when this accident occurred at Shepherdsville. He received an order from the train dispatcher to run one hour and thirty minutes late from Louisville to Bowling Green. It is 114 miles to Bowling Green. The schedule on the time card is three hours and five minutes. To execute this schedule he is required to run sixty miles an hour between some stations. If he approached all train-order stations with train under control, he could not execute the schedule from Louisville to Bowling Green. From Shepherdsville to Bardstown Junction is about four miles. He has four minutes for the four miles; and from Bardstown Junction to Belmont he has three minutes for the three miles.

Interrupting the trend of this recital for a moment, we wish to cite the fact that in the testimony of Mr. Sheridan he left the impression upon the Commission, and those who heard the evidence, that prior to the wreck, he (Sheridan) had issued an order that no train should exceed 45 miles an hour; but upon page 195 of the record, Mr. Sheridan corrected that impression and stated that the bulletin restricting trains to a speed of 45 miles an hour was issued after the wreck at Shepherdsville.

Continuing the narrative: Mr. Wolfenberger knew that he left Louisville 18 minutes behind 41. As he was running late on his own schedule he could not anticipate that he would pass 41 before it reached Bardstown Junction, if 41 was maintaining its schedule. 41 had the same speed limits as No. 7 and the same rights on the time card. Dispatcher Sams, and the operators at the various train-order stations, and the train crew of 41 knew that 41 was losing time and, therefore, No. 7 would have to pass it before reaching Bardstown Junction. They also knew what time No. 7 was making.

When Wolfenberger passed Brooks he did not know that he would overtake No. 41 before 41 executed its schedule to Bardstown Junction. He received clear boards which indicated that he was ten minutes or more behind 41. Before reaching stations, he usually examined his watch. When he passed F. X. Tower, to the best of his recollection, it was some seconds past 5:08. He had no recollection what time he passed Strawberry. The record shows 5:11. He was operating his train about as usual. When he reached Brooks he examined his watch and it was nearer 5:24 than 5:23. From Strawberry to Brooks, 7.4 miles he ran in 12 minutes, which, under the conditions that day and the train he had, was normal. As to the duty of the operator at Brooks he said, "I don't know what was the duty of the operator at Brooks; but, if 41 had been told to head in to let No. 7 pass 41, the wreck would not have happened. The way I look at it, it was his duty to notify me that I would pass 41 at Shepherdsville and that they were not making running time."

When he reached Gap-in-the-Knobs, near two miles north of Shepherdsville, his watch showed 5:27 and some seconds, indicating that he had lost a little time. When he got to the whistle board, he sounded the station alarm with one long blast of the whistle. Then there is a little sharp curve. When he got off of the curve he saw the light was green and called for the signal. About that time of evening it is hard to see the light. For a second he could see it and for a second he could not. After he called for the board, the first time, he believed that between these intervals the board changed; but having some doubt he made a reduction in air, drawing off from six to eight pounds. He called for the board again, running, of course, all the while against the board. The second time he must have been about three hundred yards from the board, after which, it was pulled up "red."

He went into full emergency with the brake valve. It was a heavy train, six cars of steel and three wooden. He did not have time to sand the track. The brakes must have picked up the wheels, causing the train to slide on the track. Either smoke or steam evidently came from 41's engine, which got between his view and the board long enough to make him believe that the board had been changed. He did not see the markers on the end of No. 41. No fusees were seen. No torpedoes exploded. If, as a matter of fact, the board at Shepherdsville had shown red, instead of green, when he blew for the signal; and if the red had not been changed to green immediately after he whistled, he says, he would have brought his train under control and that he would not have struck 41. He says that he thought the operator was in his office. He had a right to presume that he was there. He says that he knew that "green stationary" was not the proper signal "to proceed;" that the proper signal to proceed "was a change from red to green," which meant of course, that there were "no orders" for him at the station; and that he must execute his schedule according to original orders. He says, however, that it is a common occurrence with engineers for operators to change the board, or station signal, before they call for it. He says that Weatherford, before the Coroner's Jury, agreed with him upon this fact. He said that this custom made him believe that Weatherford had changed the signal when he sounded the whistle for the station.

Mr. John Ford, engineer, who was a passenger on No. 41, on page 189 of the testimony, in speaking of this custom, said: "That he had seen the semaphore down before it was called for and that sometimes he had to blow twice before getting the signal." He said that engineers did not always get their engines under control when going into train-order stations.

Mr. Wolfenberger testified that No. 7 did not stop at Shepherdsville once in a hundred times and, when it did stop, specific orders were received at Louisville. The stop was usually for the purpose of picking up passengers. No. 7 is a fast train and the purpose of those who direct the movement of trains is to clear the track to prevent No. 7 from losing time.

On page 175, Mr. Wolfenberger was asked the following question and made the following answer:

Q. If any member of your family had been on that train, and you knew it, could you have done other than you did?

A. No, sir; I could not have done anything more than what I did. I was simply led into a trap.

In analyzing the testimony as it relates to Mr. Wolfenberger, it must be remembered also that whatever he did in connection with this accident involved a risk to his own life.

If Weatherford had been at the semaphore when No. 7 sounded the station whistle or blew for the signal, it is a reasonable presumption that he would have changed the "imperfect signal, green," to "red" which, Wolfenberger says, would have avoided the accident. The rules of the company require that the semaphore should display green until the train at the station has proceeded 200 feet beyond the semaphore, when it should be changed to "red." There is a strong presumption based upon the speed of the two trains that 41 had proceeded 200 feet from the semaphore when No. 7 sounded the whistle for the signal at Shepherdsville.

This presumption is strengthened by the testimony of Mr. Sheridan, who says at page 64 of the evidence: "that when No. 7 reached a point 2,256 feet from the semaphore signal Wolfenberger saw the signal showing green. At that point he sounded four blasts, which were intended for the operator."

While there is no evidence to show the exact speed of No. 41, in going the distance of 408 feet beyond the semaphore, yet we may fairly assume that its speed was approximately five miles an hour. At this rate in one-half minute it would go 220 feet. If another half minute was consumed by No. 41 otherwise, in standing or backing, one minute in time elapsed after 41 had gone 200 feet beyond the semaphore before it was struck.

No. 7 was running at about the rate of forty miles an hour. Each minute it would go about 3,520 feet. A minute before No. 7 struck No. 41 it was then about 3,500 feet from the semaphore, about the place where Sheridan says Wolfenberger whistled. Thus there is a strong presumption that, at the time Mr. Sheridan said Wolfenberger sounded the signal whistle, No. 41 had passed 200 feet beyond the semaphore and Weatherford should have answered by changing the signal from green to red.

The rules cited as governing the conduct of Wolfenberger are: Rules 106-ll-27-85-119-221-221a-221b-221c-221d-221e and the second paragraph of 221f (See Supplement). Some of these rules we think advisable to quote with comment. In order that the signals may be understood,

Red indicates Stop—Danger;

Green indicates Proceed; but before proceeding under the rules the engineer must see the signal changed from red to green at train-order stations.

RULE 106: "In all cases of doubt or uncertainty the safe course must be taken and no risks run."

RULE 85: "When a train of one schedule is on the time of another schedule of the same class in the same direction it will proceed on its own schedule."

That is to say, No. 41 should proceed on its own schedule. But No. 41 was not executing its schedule, and yet No. 7 had never reached the schedule upon which No. 41 was to proceed. No. 7 knew the schedule of No. 41 and No. 41 had the right to proceed on its own schedule and No. 7 had no right to run on the schedule of 41. But No. 7 had not reached the schedule of No. 41 at Shepherdsville. The accident occurred between 5:29 and 5:30, at which time the schedule of No. 41 required it to be at Bardstown Junction. The schedule of 41 shows that it should arrive at Bardstown Junction at 5:27.

RULE 221: Provides "that a fixed signal must be used at each train-order office which shall indicate 'stop' when there is an operator on duty except when changed to 'proceed' to allow a train to pass for which there are no orders."

The fixed signal to indicate "stop" is "red" where an operator is on duty. Shepherdsville was a place where an operator was on duty; but the signal showed "green" which, under the above rule, literally construed, indicated, "proceed," "there are no orders."

RULE 221a: provides, "That when a train is approaching a train-order office and has reached 600 feet from the signal or nearer, if the signal cannot be plainly seen that far, the engineer will give four short sounds of the whistle; if there are no orders for the train the signal must be changed to 'proceed.' Enginemen will acknowledge this change by two short sounds of the whistle, or if the signal is not changed to 'proceed' give one short sound. If there are no orders for the train the signal must be held at 'proceed' until the rear end of the train has passed 200 feet beyond the signal when it must again be changed to 'stop.' Conductors

must know that signal is properly changed as herein directed."

RULE 221b: "No train must pass a train-order office where 'stop' is indicated so long as the signal remains at 'stop' without an order addressed to it, or a clearance card, etc."—"when an operator has an order for a train he must not change the signal to 'proceed' for another train running in the same direction as the train for which he holds the order, until after he has delivered it. The fixed signal must only be fastened at 'proceed' when there is no operator on duty. This signal must also indicate 'stop' to hold trains running in the same direction the required time apart."

RULE 221c: "Operators having business at trains must not neglect to change the signal back to 'stop' immediately after their return to the office."

RULE 221d provides, "that when conductors and enginemen approach train-order offices they must have their trains under control and must not assume that the signal will be changed from stop indication when within the distance prescribed."

Attention is called to this last rule. The signal displayed was not the regular "stop" signal. It was an imperfect signal. The "stop" signal is red; and if the "stop" signal, red, had been displayed and Wolfenberger had run into 41, he would have violated Rule 221d; because he would have assumed that the signal would have been changed from "stop" to green, which means "proceed."

RULE 221e provides, "That if the proper signal is not displayed at an open train-order office, or if it is not changed from stop indication in full view of the engineer as prescribed by Rule 221a the train must be brought to a stop and must not proceed without a clearance card."

This is the rule which Mr. Wolfenberger violated. But if he had not violated this rule under the circumstances he would have been possessed of more than human judgment and prophetic wisdom; for this rule itself presumes that something unusual has happened to the operator.

The rule continues as follows:

"If the office is found' to be closed and no operator on duty, trains must stop and inquire the cause and before proceeding satisfy themselves that there are no movement orders for them, and report the facts to the Chief Train Dispatcher from the next open train-order office."

Second paragraph of Rule 221f reads as follows:

"A fixed train-order signal must never be passed if kept stationary, regardless of its position or the color it displays, without the cause being first investigated."

This rule being almost identical with 221e was also, of course, violated.

From the evidence and these rules we conclude that Mr. Wolfenberger did violate a rule of the company; but, in so doing, so many other employes violated duties which they owed to him under the rules, that, as expressed by him, "he was led into a trap."

Wolfenberger had a right to anticipate that a normal signal would be displayed to him at Shepherdsville. He had a right to anticipate that the train crew of 41 had performed its full duty. He had a right to anticipate that the operator at Strawberry had performed his duty. He had a right to anticipate that the operator at Brooks had performed his duty. He could not have presumed that 41 was running 11 or 12 minutes behind its schedule time. He had the right to

presume that when he ran into Shepherdsville that 41 was at Bardstown Junction.

COST OF WRECK.

To say nothing of the precious lives that were lost, the suffering experienced and the sorrow felt, this wreck will cost the Louisville & Nashville Railroad Company, in our judgment, more than $750,000.00, although one of the witnesses for the company estimated it at about $500,0000.00.

The record shows that an automatic, block signal system could have been installed on this division of the Louisville & Nashville Railroad Company between Louisville and Bowling Green at a cost of about $320,000.00, placing the blocks at approximately one mile apart.

In the operation of railroads man-power is an important factor. A great deal of dependence must be placed on it; but realizing that the human equation is not infallible, the more devices which can be obtained to supplement this man-power, the less liability will there be for accidents. Devices, such as block signals, must be of such a character as will best serve the particular traffic on any given railroad. On some railroads, and on parts of some railroads, the manually operated block signal (with passenger trains operated under an absolute block and freight trains under a permissive block) might serve the purpose. On other railroads, perhaps, the most practical block signal system would be automatic. Such questions are to be determined by a careful investigation and a study of the physical and transportation conditions of the road.

In manually operated block signal systems the blocks run from station to station. In the automatic block signal systems the blocks, generally speaking, vary from 2,000 feet to two miles depending on the grade, curvature and other physical characteristics. As heretofore stated, while a great deal of dependance must be placed on man-power in the operation of railroads, and while this is even true in the use of block signals; nevertheless, the liability for accident is so much lessened that it justifies the expenditure necessary to install and equip a road with these safety devices and appliances. Generally speaking, if every employe connected with the operation of trains rigidly carried out well formulated rules and instructions, there would be extremely few accidents; but it is the duty of transportation companies to provide such safety appliances and devices as will eliminate to the maximum degree the fallibility of man-power.

With this opinion as a basis we find the following facts:

(a)—That the train dispatcher at Louisville did not perform his full duty; in that he did not specifically order trains No. 41 and No. 7 to pass each other upon the evening of December 20th, at Shepherdsville.

(b)—That the operator at F. X. Tower did his duty in that he promptly reported the passing of Trains No. 41 and 7.

(c)—That the operator at Strawberry failed in his duty in that he did not promptly report the passing of trains No. 41 and No. 7 to the train dispatcher.

(d)—We find that the operator at Brooks failed in his duty; in that he did not promptly report the passing of trains No. 41 and No. 7 by the station at Brooks.

(e)—We find that Weatherford was confused, no doubt, by the complicated rules relating to his duty as operator; Rule 343 providing:

"The proper place for an operator, when trains are due or standing at his station, is in the office, and at sucfh times he must not leave his office (unless the Company's business actually requires his presence elsewhere),"

and Rule 344 providing:

"Operators are required to devote themselves exclusively to the Company's business while on duty. (Those having other duties to perform must not allow them to interfere with their telegraph and telephone duties.) (The telegraph and telephone service must always be regarded as first in importance,"

and that being confused he exercised woefully bad judgment in looking after the baggage instead of staying in his office "when trains were due and standing at the station." But we find that the rules were calculated to mislead him. Also his conduct seems to have the approval of the officials of the company, notwithstanding the fact, the rules provide that "the telephone and telegraph service must always be regarded as first in importance.

We find also that the strong presumption is that at the time No. 7 sounded the station whistle he should have been in his office and that the signal green should have been changed to red.

(f)—We find that the conductor and flagman of train crew 41 failed in their duty; in not placing fusees on the track, or torpedoes on the track, or protecting the rear of train 41, when 41 was running late under such circumstances that it might be overtaken by No. 7.

(g)—We find that Wolfenberger failed in his duty; in that he did not bring his train under control at Shepherdsville, when he was "in doubt" as to whether or not the signal had been changed from "red to green" in his sight; but we find that his failure to do so was under such circumstances as were calculated to mislead any engineer of extraordinary prudence and skill; and that it would have required more than human intelligence for him to have anticipated that the green signal thus displayed at Shepherdsville indicated a danger signal which should require him to stop.

(h)—We find that the rules of the Company in many instances are too vague and indefinite and that employes on some occasions are permitted such latitude in their discretion that it is not compatible with safety; and that under the rules of the company the same acts may either be commended or condemned.

(i)—We find that the management of the Louisville & Nashville Railroad Company has not adequately equipped its system with necessary safety devices.

Therefore we recommend:

1st—A revision of the rules of the company;

2nd—That official tests be made by the management;

3rd—That for immediate safety a manual block be established for trains going south from Louisville to Bardstown Junction similar to the block now maintained between Bardstown Junction and Louisville for trains going north.

4th—We recommend that the Legislature pass the following proposed measures:

It shall be the duty of every carrier to adopt reasonably adequate safety measures and install, operate and maintain reasonably adequate safety devices for the protection of life and property. If, after investigation, the Railroad Commission shall determine that public safety requires the installation, operation and maintenance of a block system or other safety devices or measures by any carrier, the Commission may, after due notice and hearing order such carrier to install, operate and maintain a block system or other safety devices or measures as may be necessary to render the operation of such carrier reasonably safe, and the Commission may establish reasonable rules, regulations,

specifications and standards for the installation, operation and maintenance of all safety devices and measures.

The foregoing was Section 20 of a proposed act suggested by the Railroad Commission in its Annual Report for 1914.

5th—We also recommend the following additional legislation in the interest of public safety.

Whenever complaint is filed with the Railroad Commission to the effect that a public highway and railroad cross one another at the same level and that such grade crossing is unsafe and dangerous to the travelers over such highway or railroad, it shall be the duty of said Commission to give notice to the railroad company in interest of the filing of such complaint and to furnish copy of same to the railroad company and to order a hearing thereon in the manner provided in Section 820a, Carroll's Edition, 1909, Kentucky Statutes. If, upon such hearing, it shall appear to the satisfaction of the Commission that the crossing complained of is unsafe and dangerous to human life, said Commission may order and direct the railroad company to erect gates at said crossing and place an agent in charge to open and close the same when an engine or train passes, or that a flagman be stationed at such crossing, who shall display a flag when an engine or train is about to pass, or that such crossing shall be provided with an electric signal or other device as the Commission determines; and such railroad company shall comply with the terms of such order.

The above was Section 19 of an act proposed by the Railroad Commission and presented to the Legislature of 1916.

Respectfully submitted,

Laurence B. Finn, Chairman,

Sid T. Douthitt, Commissioner,

H. G. Garrett, Commissioner.

January 30, 1918.

Attest: Richard Tobin,

Sec'y Kentucky Railroad Commission.

SUPPLEMENT.

The following contains all the rules for the Operating Department issued by the Louisville & Nashville Railroad Company cited at the hearing by officials and witnesses who testified before the Commission:

RULE 11: A fusee on or near the track burning red must not be passed until burned out. When burning green it is a caution signal, indicating that train ahead is not making its usual speed.

RULE 27: A signal imperfectly displayed, or the absence of a signal at a place where a signal is usually shown, must be regarded as a stop signal, and the fact reported to the Superintendent.

RULE 83: A train must not leave its initial station on any division (or sub-division), or a junction, or pass from double to single track, until it has been ascertained whether all trains due, which are superior, or of the same class have arrived or left.

RULE 85: When a train of one schedule is on the time of another schedule of the same class in the same direction, it will proceed on its own schedule. Trains of one schedule may pass trains of another schedule of the same class, and extras may pass and run ahead of extras, provided their train orders do not conflict. On double track a section may pass and run ahead of another section of the same schedule, first exchanging orders, signals and number with the section to be passed. A train or section passing another between train-order offices must report the case to the Chief Train Dispatcher from the next open train-order office.

RULE 85a: A train which has fallen back and is running on the time of another train of the same class, as provided in Rule 85, must at all points where stops are made, or in case it is not making running time, be promptly protected as prescribed by Rule 99.

RULE 85b: If, from any cause, the speed of a train is so much reduced as to endanger the rear, the conductor will be held responsible for fully protecting it by the use of the proper signals.

RULE 91: Unless some form of block signals is used, trains in the same direction must keep at least ten minutes apart, except in closing up at meeting and passing stations.

RULE 99: When a train stops or is delayed, under circumstances in which it may be overtaken by another train, the flagman must go back immediately with stop signals to stop any train moving in the same direction. At a point 50 rail lengths, or 1,500 feet, from the rear of his train, he must place one torpedo on the rail; he must then continue to go back at least 100 rail lengths, or 3,000 feet, from the rear of his train, and place two torpedoes on the rail, 30 feet, or one rail length apart, when he may return to a point 70 rail lengths, or 2,100 feet, from the rear of his train; and he must remain there until recalled by the whistle of his engine; but if a passenger train is due within ten minutes or if an approaching train is within sight or hearing, he must remain until it arrives. If the view is obstructed, or if on descending grade, he must go as much farther as may be necessary to reach a point where he is absolutely sure that he can be seen by the expected train at a sufficient distance in which to stop. When he comes in, he must remove the torpedo nearest to his train; but the two torpedoes must be left on the rail as a caution signal to any following train. When protecting at night, the flagman must, the last thing after being recalled, place a lighted red fusee upright between the rails at the point where the one torpedo was removed.

RULE 100: When the flagman goes back to protect the rear of the train, the conductor must, in the case of passenger trains, and the next brakeman or the conductor in the case of other trains, take his place on the train.

RULE 106: In all cases of doubt or uncertainty the safe course must be taken and no risks run.

RULE 118: Special bulletin order, form 49, will be used as prescribed to notify trains by wire of defects in tracks, switches, bridges and other structures, also of obstructed passing sidings, and for any other purpose where the safety of trains is involved.

RULE 119: Register books will be maintained at points designated in the time table. Conductors and enginemen must examine register books before starting on each trip, and, unless otherwise provided, at points where trains of the same or superior class start or terminate, also at other points indicated by special instructions. Register books must invariably be checked against the time table. (See rule 83.)

RULE 201: For movements not provided for by timetable, train orders will be issued by authority and over the last name of the Chief Train Dispatcher. They must contain neither information nor instructions not essential to such movements. They must be brief and clear; in the prescribed forms when applicable; and without erasure, alteration or interlineation.

RULE 221: A fixed signal must be used at each train-order office, which shall indicate "stop" when there is an operator on duty, except when changed to "proceed" to allow a train to pass for which there are no orders.

RULE 221a: When a train approaching a train-order office has reached a point 600 feet from the signal, or nearer if the signal cannot be plainly seen that far, the engineman will give four short sounds of the whistle; if there are no orders for the train the signal must be changed to "proceed." Enginemen will acknowledge this change by two short sounds of the whistle, or if the signal is not changed to "proceed," give one short sound. If there are no orders for the train, the signal must be held at "proceed" until the rear end of the train has passed 200 feet beyond the signal, when it must again be changed to "stop." Conductors must know that the signal is properly changed as herein directed.

RULE 221b: No train must pass a train-order office where "stop" is indicated so long as the signal remains at "stop," without an order addressed to it, or a clearance card, form 456, stated over the operator's signature that he has no orders for it, except as prescribed by rules 221 (d) and (e). When an operator has an order for a train, he must not change the signal to "proceed" for another train running in the same direction as the train for which he holds the order, until after he has delivered it, unless authorized by the train dispatcher. The fixed signal must only be fastened at "proceed" when there is no operator on duty. This signal must also indicate "stop" to hold trains running in the same direction the required time apart. Operators must be prepared with other signals to use promptly if the fixed signals should fail to work properly.

RULE 221c: Operators having business at trains must not neglect to change the signal back to "stop" immediately upon their return to the office. After the signal has been changed to "proceed" for a train, the operator must not take an order for that train until after the conductor and engineman have come to the telegraph office.

RULE 221d: Conductors and enginemen, when approaching train-order offices, must have their trains under control and must not assume that the signal will be changed from "stop" indication when within the distance prescribed, as, if any portion of a train runs beyond the signal before it is so changed, an infraction of these rules will have been committed.

RULE 221e: If the proper signal is not displayed at an open train-order office, or if it is not changed from "stop" indication in full view of the engineman, as prescribed by rule 221 (a), train must be brought to a stop and must not proceed without a clearance card, form 456, or movement order; if, however, the office is found to be closed and no operator on duty, trains must stop and inquire the cause, and before proceeding satisfy themselves that there are no movement orders for them, and report the fact to the Chief Train Dispatcher from the next open train-order office.

RULE 221f: Where two-position train-order signals are used, the arm to the right, when horizontal, indicates "stop"; when in a diagonal or vertical position it indicates "proceed." See diagrams for indications and instructions covering the three-position block and train-order signals. (Page 90-92.)

A fixed train order signal must never be passed if kept stationary, regardless of its position or the color it displays, without the cause being first investigated.

These rules are in effect continually at continuously operated train-order offices, and during such hours at other train-order offices at may be designated by the superintendent.

When the train-order offices are closed, the fixed signal must be changed to "proceed" and remain in that position until the office is opened, when it must be returned to "stop."

RULE 222: Operators will promptly record and report to the train dispatcher the time of arrival and departure of all trains, including the direction of extra trains.

RULE 317: They will issue orders governing the movement of trains, and must see that all such orders are transmitted and recorded according to the prescribed forms and rules.

RULE 319: They must keep a record showing the time of arrival and departure of trains at train-order offices, and such record must be carefully filed for future reference.

RULE 328: In matters pertaining to the telegraph and telephone service, operators report to and receive instructions from the Chief Train Dispatcher; in other matters they report to and receive their instructions from the agent.

RULE 329: They must hold the fixed signal at "stop" and keep trains the required distance apart, as provided in rule 91; and in such cases the clearance cards must state why the trains are held.

RULE 330: Should a train be delayed in leaving a station, the operator will promptly notify the train dispatcher.

RULE 340: Operators must be in their respective offices at least ten minutes before trains are due, and those whose duties require them to sell tickets must be governed by rule 412.

RULE 343: The proper place for an operator, when trains are due or standing at his station, is in the office; and at such times he must not leave his office unless the company's business actually requires his presence elsewhere.

RULE 344: Operators are required to devote themselves exclusively to the company's business while on duty. Those having other duties to perform must not allow them to interfere with their telegraph and telephone duties. The telegraph and telephone service must always be regarded as first in importance.

RULE 412: Ticket offices and baggage rooms must be opened for the sale of tickets and receipt and delivery of baggage not less than half an hour, or the time required by law, before the departure of passenger trains.

Agents must use all diligence to have passengers purchase tickets before entering trains.

They must not sell tickets to persons who are intoxicated, or otherwise calculated to be a source of danger or annoyance to others on the train. They must not sell tickets for extra trains without instructions to do so.

View of Shepherdsville from the south side of Salt River, with signal tower on the right.

Appendix I
Interstate Commerce Commission Report
January 28, 1918.

REPORT OF THE CHIEF OF THE BUREAU
OF SAFETY COVERING THE INVESTIGATION
OF AN ACCIDENT WHICH OCCURRED ON
THE LOUISVILLE & NASHVILLE RAILROAD
AT SHEPHERDSVILLE, KY.,
ON DECEMBER 20, 1917

JANUARY 28, 1918.

To the Commission:

On December 20, 1917, there was a rear-end collision between two passenger trains on the Louisville & Nashville Railroad at Shepherdsville, Ky., resulting in the death of 46 persons and injuries to 52 persons. After investigation as to the cause and nature of this accident, I beg to submit the following report:

The Louisville division of the Louisville & Nashville Railroad, on which this accident occurred, extends between Louisville and Bowling Green, Ky., a distance of 113.6 miles. It is for the most part a single-track line, but from Louisville to Lebanon Junction, a distance of 29.7 miles, the track is double. It was on this double-track section, about 18 miles south of Louisville, that the collision occurred. On this division trains are operated under a time interval and dispatching system, no block system being used.

The trains involved in this accident were southbound passenger train No. 41, consisting of engine 18 with three cars, in charge of Conductor Campbell and Engineman Keyer, en route from Louisville, Ky., to Springfield, Ky., and southbound passenger train No. 7, consisting of engine 230 and nine cars, in charge of Conductor Ogle and Engineman Wolfenberger, en route from Cincinnati. Ohio. to Montgomery, Ala.

Train No. 41 is a local train which leaves the main track of the Louisville division at Bardstown Junction, 22 miles south of Louisville. On the date of the accident this train left Louisville on time, at 4:35 p.m., but was unable to make schedule time on account of holiday travel. At Brooks, a station 5 miles north of Shepherdsville, the train dispatcher told Conductor Campbell, through the station operator, to let train No. 7 pass at Shepherdsville if he could not go to Bardstown Junction on time. The train left Brooks at 5.13 p.m., seven minutes late, and arrived at Shepherdsville at 5.24 six minutes late. After doing the station work, Conductor Campbell notified Engineman Keyer, through the train porter, to move ahead beyond the south passing track switch, located about 400 feet south of the station, and back into the sidetrack to permit train No. 7 to pass. It was after the passing track switch had been opened, and the train was about to back in, that its rear end was struck by train No. 7, moving at a speed estimated at 25 miles per hour. The collision occurred about 5:30 p.m., at which time it was dark, but the weather was clear.

Train No. 7 left Louisville at 4:53 p.m., 1 hour and 53 minutes late. It passed Brooks at 5:23, 10 minutes behind train 41, and collided with that train about 400 feet south of Shepherdsville station about 5:30 p.m., as above stated.

The force of collision drove train No. 41 forward a distance of 800 feet, completely telescoping the rear coach and crushing the rear compartment of the compartment car next to the rear coach Figures Nos. 1 [see page 24] and 2 [see below] are views of the rear coach and compartment coach, respectively, of train No. 41 after the accident. All of the wreckage was shoved ahead with train No. 7 unit it came to a stop. The engine and baggage car of train No. 41 remained coupled together and were driven ahead about 150 feet beyond where the wrecked cars stopped. All of the cars in this train were of wooden construction.

On train No. 7 the express car next to the engine was crushed in for 8 or 10 feet and the sides of the car were bulged. The baggage car was not damaged with the exception of a broken steam pipe and no other cars in the train were damaged. The engine of train No. 7 had its front end crushed and some other parts broken, as shown by figure No. 3 [see page 17], but was not derailed. Five of the cars on this train were of wood with steel underframe, and three were of all-steel construction.

Conductor Campbell and Flagman Greenwell were on the platform between the rear coach and the compartment car at the time of the collision, and both were killed.

Approaching Shepherdsville station from the north the track is level for a distance of 2,100 feet, and is straight for 8,400 feet north of the point of collision. In this distance of more than 8,000 feet there is nothing to obstruct the view of the engineman of an approaching train.

At a point 2,500 feet north of Shepherdsville station the main tracks are spread to provide for a middle passing track, 2,900 feet long and extending 400 feet south of the station. The station itself is on the west side of the tracks and adjacent to the southbound main track.

Train order signals are used for the purpose of maintaining a time interval of 10 minutes, at open telegraph offices, between trains running in the same direction. The signals are of the two-arm type, operating in two positions in the lower right hand quadrant. The night indications are green for proceed and red for stop. The signals are normally held in the stop position, and the rules require enginemen of trains, when approaching a train order office, to sound four short blasts of the whistle, whereupon, if it is proper for the train to proceed, the operator is required to clear the signal; and hold it in the clear position until the rear end of the train passed 200 feet beyond the signal, when it must again be changed to the stop position. Enginemen are required to see the position of the signal change. If it is not changed in full view of the engineman he is required to bring his train to a stop and not proceed without an order or a clearance card.

Train Dispatcher Sams stated that he knew train No. 41 was not making schedule time and he instructed the operator at Brooks to notify Conductor Campbell that if he could not go to Bardstown Junction on time to let train No. 7 pass at Shepherdsville. He said he talked with Conductor Campbell of train 41 at Shepherdsville, and repeated these instructions to him over the telephone, but he does not remember what reply was made. Later the operator at Brooks reported train 7, but Dispatcher Sams said he was unable to get Shepherdsville again. The collision was reported to him over the telephone, but he is not sure by whom. Dispatcher Sams further said there were no blocking rules in effect between train 41 and 7, and under the rules it was permissible for train 41 to leave Shepherdsville close ahead of train 7, and the information that train 7 was close was given to the conductor of train 41 to aid the conductor in flagging and in order to avoid delay to train 7. While it is the custom to give this information no record is made of such messages, and he expected the conductor of train 41 to protect his train against train 7.

Agent Thompson, in charge of Shepherdsville Station, stated that after he had the mail and baggage unloaded from train 41 he started with the truck toward the station and met Operator Weatherford coming out of the office with a red lantern. There was more than the usual amount of work to do and more passengers to get off, so that train 41 laid at this station a minute or a minute and a half. He did not know whether Conductor Campbell went to the office or not to consult the dispatcher, and did not know where the conductor or flagman were when train 41 pulled away from the station. He noticed that the markers on train 41 were burning brightly, but he did not observe the order board and did not see it change. When he first saw train No. 7 it was at the crossing north of the station, but he heard no whistle. When that train passed the station he judged it was running at 35 or 40 miles per hour, its usual speed, and there were no signs of the brakes being applied.

Operator Weatherford, on duty at Shepherdsville, stated that when train 41 arrived at Shepherdsville he went out to assist the agent in unloading mail, baggage, and express. After the packages were unloaded he jumped from the truck and started for the telegraph office door, a distance of 80 or 90 feet, without waiting to help handle the mail and baggage from the truck into the station. On his way he met Conductor Campbell, asked him what he was going to do, and he replied that he was going to back in for train 7. Immediately after that he saw train 7 coming, ran into the office, threw the signal to stop, and ran out again with his lantern to flag the train. When the train was first seen by him it was 600 or 700 feet north of the office and 300 or 400 feet from the signal when it was put to the stop position. He said he heard no whistle from train 7, and saw no indications of the brakes being applied as the train passed him. He had talked with the dispatcher and had been told to report when train 41 cleared; he also saw Conductor Campbell in the office talking with the dispatcher. He had no conversation with the operator at Brooks regarding either train and saw no protection given to train 41. He said the markers on train 41 and the switch light were red and were perfectly clear, as there was no smoke or fog to interfere. He said the rules require the signal to be left in clear position until after the rear of a train has passed it 200 feet, and as the rear of train 41 while at the station was north of the signal he had left it clear. In this position it was an imperfect signal for an approaching train and the engineman should have stopped and come to the office to see why the signal was not changed when he called for it.

Operator Sanders, on duty at Brooks, stated that train 41 arrived at 5:12 p.m. and departed at 5:13 p.m., and train 7 passed between 5:23 and 5:24 p.m. The dispatcher told him to tell the conductor of train 41 that train 7 has passed FX tower at 5:02 p.m., as he remembered it, and for him to stay at Shepherdsville if he could not get to Bardstown Junction on time, which message was delivered to the conductor, who replied "All right." He had no conversation with the operator at Shepherdsville regarding either train and did not know of the accident until he heard it reported at 5:30 or 5:31 p.m.

Engineman Keyer, of train 41, stated that he did not know that train 7 was following his train closely, although he knew it was behind him. He said he left Brooks about on time, made three stops, and reached Shepherdsville at 5:21 p.m., remaining there about two minutes, long enough to unload six sacks of mail and more than the usual number of passengers. As he pulled away from the station the train porter got on the engine and said the conductor wanted to back in, as train 7 had just left Brooks. He had just stopped south of the switch and the porter had jumped off to throw the switch when train 7 struck them. He looked at his watch and compared its time with this fireman, which was 5:24 p.m. Approaching Shepherdsville he could see the semaphore without difficulty from a point north of the siding, called for the signal, and got it promptly. He had no advice as to train No. 7, nor any instruction to let it pass until the porter came to the engine at Shepherdsville. He did not see either his conductor or brakeman at Shepherdsville and did not know whether any protection had been given the train, but he depended on the semaphore and the flagman for protection when backing in. When he found the conductor and flagman after the accident they were between the two coaches. Brakes were not applied at the time he was hit. At the time of the collision it was clear and calm, and he did not think his engine was making any smoke.

Fireman Masden, of train 41, said it was dark, but he had no trouble in seeing the switch or other lights, and thinks he saw the Shepherdsville signal from the north switch. He had no information of train 7 until the porter came up to the engine just after they received the signal to go ahead, and he did not see the train approaching. Just before the accident he had stepped to the engineman's side to help him reverse the engine, but the collision occurred before they had reversed the lever.

Porter Chase, of train 41, said that the conductor told him, leaving Brooks, that he had an order to run ahead of train 7 to Bardstown [Junction] if they could get there on time; if not, they were to head in at Shepherdsville. At Gap-in-Knob he asked the conductor if the engineman knew they were to head in, and was told they would go on to Shepherdsville, and the operator could tell them where train 7 was. He did not deliver any instructions to the engineman before they got to Shepherdsville, because he had no orders to do so. At Shepherdsville he was told by the conductor to tell the engineman to back in, and reached the engine after it had started. He got off, threw the switch, and looked back to see if the flagman had thrown the inside switch, but he did not see either him or the conductor. About that time he heard train 7 whistle, saw it approaching at a high rate of speed, and jumped over the fence at the side of the track. He stated that neither the conductor nor flagman went back to flag train 7, and he did not know where they were. The engineman of his train did not signal for the flagman to go out, nor did he hear him give any signal. His markers were showing red.

Engineman Wolfenberger, of train No. 7, stated that he had orders to run 1 hour and 30 minutes late, Louisville to Bowling Green, but actually left Louisville at 4.53, 1 hour and 53 minutes late. Stops were made at Oak Street and the Southern Railway crossing, due to other trains in the way, and he passed Brooks close to 5:24 p.m. He knew that train 41 was ahead of him and knew of the local work which that train had to do. He thought it was 600 or 700 yards north of Shepherdsville when he first saw the train-order signal. The signal was green when he first saw it and he called for the signal with four blasts of the whistle, but the signal was not changed so he called again, after he had gone about 200 yards. It was then changed to red and he applied the brakes in emergency; previous to that time had had only made a slight application, or enough to bring the brake shoes up against the wheels. He said there was fog or smoke which caused the light to disappear for an instant and then to reappear, so he was not certain when he first saw the signal whether it had been cleared for him or not, but he believed that the operator would find it had not been cleared after he called the second time and would return it to clear before he got by. He estimated that he was running 40 or 45 miles per hour when the brakes were applied the first time, but that the speed had been reduced to 20 or 25 miles at the time of the collision. He further stated that he understood the rules require that he approach a train-order office prepared to stop before any portion of the train had passed the train order signal, and that it was required that he should see the signal change from red to green, any other indication being an improperly displayed signal, requiring him to stop. When he saw the markers on train 41 he was within 100 yards of the train, as he was looking at the train-order signal and smoke from train 41 was blowing his way, causing the lights to appear dim. He said he saw no flagman from train 41 and met no flag, saw no fusees, nor heard any torpedoes between Louisville and Shepherdsville; neither did he see the operator at Shepherdsville attempt to flag him. It did not occur to him that not getting the signal at Shepherdsville was due to train 41 being close ahead, although he knew he left Louisville 18 minutes behind it, as he had been losing time himself and had received clear signals at the other stations. The fireman was on his seat but did not say anything to him about the signal. The brakes were tested before leaving Louisville and were in good order and worked properly at the stops he made at Oak Street and the Southern Railway crossing, but the rail appeared to be a little slippery. He said that if he had made a

heavy service application of the brakes when he first saw the signal he thought he could have stopped.

Conductor Ogle, of train No. 7, said he had an order to run 1 hour and 30 minutes late and left Louisville at 4:53 p.m., 1 hour and 53 minutes late. He examined the register and knew that train 41 had gone. He knew when they passed Gap-in-Knob, and noticed the curve just south of that point, at which time he was working in the second passenger coach, the sixth car from the engine. He heard the engineman call for the signal approaching Shepherdsville, but was not in a position to see the signal and did not look out when he heard the engineman call the second time. There were two applications of the brakes, one between the two calls for the signal and the other, a heavier one, he thought before the station was passed, and speed was reduced to 20 or 25 miles per hour. It did occur to him that they might be overtaking train 41, but as it was 12 minutes late on that train's time, he thought they would be protecting themselves. He said it was not customary to watch out for a preceding train, as they were expected to be protected. He stated the accident occurred at 5:30 p.m., as given by his watch, and that the weather was clear.

Flagman Bowman, of train No. 7, stated that he heard the engineman sound the station whistle approaching Shepherdsville. He also heard the second signal very soon after the first, the rear of the train then being about half way between the north switch and the station. He felt the brakes applied when the train was some distance south of the north switch and it appeared to be an emergency application. He noticed only the one application, but as the brakes are often applied slightly at the curve where the tracks are thrown for the middle track, it may have been done in this case and so not noticed. Very little time elapsed between the brake application and the shock of the collision.

Fireman Gossom, of train No. 7, stated that he got his first view of the train-order signal at Shepherdsville about at the north switch and it then showed green. The engineman called for the signal the first time at the north switch, again between that point and the north switch of the house track, and it changed to red almost as they were at that switch. He said the engineman was applying the air when he called for the signal, and apparently put the brakes into emergency position as he passed the north house track switch. He first observed the markers at the house track switch, and it was smoky and foggy so that he could not see them before. The speed of the train had been considerably reduced after applying the air and the brakes seemed to take hold well. He saw no flagman, nor did they run over any torpedoes or see any flags between Louisville and Shepherdsville, and all train-order signals were given promptly. He saw the orders leaving Louisville and knew train 41 was running ahead of them. He had no conversation with the engineman about the position of the signal at Shepherdsville as they were approaching, and the rules do not require that they announce the position of signals to one another.

Operator Morrison, first-trick [daytime shift] operator at Shepherdsville, stated he was not on duty at the time of the accident, but had been to the station to get a paper from train 41, and had started back home when he heard train 7 whistle. He stepped back to see where train 41 was standing and saw it just south of the middle track switch. Train 7 was approaching at a speed which he estimated to be 40 or 45 miles per hour, and did not seem to decrease speed until it struck train 41. There was no evidence of brakes being applied as the head end of the train passed him, and he did not see anyone protecting the

rear of train 41. The weather was clear and calm, and there was no smoke to obscure the view. He could see the markers and switch light clearly, saw the train-order signal was green and the light burning brightly, but did not see it changed. He did not see the conductor or flagman of train 41 at any time, saw no fusees, nor heard any torpedoes explode.

Engineman Johnson, an employee not on duty, said he was standing on the Shepherdsville Station platform at the time of the accident. He saw the work done while train 41 was at the station, heard the conductor instruct the porter to tell the engineman to back in, and saw the conductor and flagman get on the steps between the two coaches as the train pulled out, there was no one on the rear end when it passed him. The markers on train 41 were burning brightly, and he said there was nothing to interfere with the view, except it was smoky. When he first saw train No. 7, he judged it to be about at the north switch of the passing siding. When the train passed him the brakes had been applied and steam was shut off, and he estimated the speed to be 20 or 25 miles per hour. He did not see the flagman or conductor of train 41 make any effort to flag train No. 7, saw no fusee, and did not see the operator come out and attempt to flag.

Conductor Willett, of train No. 13, which was waiting on the siding at Brooks, stated that he took the time when both trains 41 and 7 passed him, it being 5:13 p.m. for the former and 5:23 p.m. for the latter. He did not see the conductor of train 41. He did not think there was anything to obstruct the view of the signals, and it did not appear to be in any way foggy.

The direct cause of this accident was the failure of the conductor and flagman of train 41 properly to protect their train. Knowing that they were on the time of train 7, and that it could not be far behind, the action of these two experienced employees in failing to protect their train is inexcusable.

A material contributing cause of the accident was the failure of Engineman Wolfenberger properly to observe the train order signal at Sheperdsville and so control his train as to stop before passing the signal, as required by rule.

A large measure of responsibility for this accident must rest with the operating officers of the Louisville & Nashville Railroad for their failure to provide proper means of spacing trains in this territory.

Between South Louisville and Lebanon Junction, which territory embraces the scene of this accident, there are 44 scheduled trains in both directions daily. Traffic of such density can not be safely handled under the rules and practices of the time-interval system. For the prevention of similar accidents the operating officers of the Louisville & Nashville Railroad should take immediate steps to provide an adequate block system for the protection of trains on this section of road.

Rules 221 (a) and (d), which assume to provide means for the proper spacing of trains in this territory, are grossly inadequate, if not positively unworkable. Rule 221 (a) required that when an approaching train has reached a point 600 feet from the signal, "or nearer if the signal can not be seen that far," the engineman will call for the signal, and if it is not changed to the proceed position at once the train must be brought to a stop before the signal is reached, as required by rule 221 (d), which reads as follows:

Conductors and enginemen when approaching train-order offices must have their trains under control and must not assume that the signal will be changed from "stop" indication when within the distance prescribed, as if any portion of a train runs beyond the signal before it is so changed an infraction of these rules will have been committed.

Rules 221 (a) and (d) establish a maximum braking distance of 600 feet, which is entirely inadequate for the safe movement of high-speed passenger trains. The schedule rate of speed of train No. 7 between Brooks and Shepherdsville is 50 miles per hour, and had the signal been in its normal position the engineman of train No. 7 could not have stopped short of the signal without having reduced speed very materially at a point considerably farther away then 600 feet. In short, compliance with this rule means that, irrespective of their schedules, trains must approach all open train-order offices prepared to stop within a distance of 600 feet.

The method of operation also by which trains are informed through verbal messages of the whereabouts of following trains which may be expected to pass them is not a safe one to follow, except where a proper block system is in use. Rule 103 requires that message directing the movement of trains must be in writing. This rule was violated by the dispatcher in his handling of train 41.

The Louisville & Nashville Railroad in its annual reports to the Interstate Commerce Commission has repeatedly stated that this section of the road from Louisville to Bardstown Junction was operated under manual-block rules. It is clearly disclosed by this investigation, however, that such protection is not afforded, and furthermore it is evident that such protection was not intended to be given. Several witnesses stated that it was the practice to space train 10 minutes apart. This is provided for in rule 91, which reads as follows:

Unless some form of block signals is used, trains in the same direction must keep at least 10 minutes apart, except in closing up at meeting and passing stations.

This rule is found among the general rules for movement of trains, and there is no rule among those providing for train movement under the manual block which permits this method of operating trains. It is therefore apparent that the manual block system is not in force on this portion of road, notwithstanding the Louisville & Nashville Railroad Company's reports to that effect.

During the past 5 years about 700 miles of road of the Louisville & Nashville Railroad have been protected by automatic block signals. most of which is on single tracked portions of the road. According to its reports for 1916, 132 miles of road are worked under the manual block system. With 4,700 miles of road operated, this gives about 20 per cent of its passenger mileage protected by some form of space interval, and of its principal main lines about 45 per cent is so protected. While this shows commendable progress, the fact remains that there are still long sections of its main lines carrying heavy traffic without adequate protection.

All the employees involved in this accident were experienced men. The engine crew on train 41 had been on duty 5 hours and 45 minutes and the train crew about 12 hours previous to the accident. The crew of train 7 had been on duty about 1 hour and 30 minutes.

Respectfully submitted.

H. W. BELNAP,

Chief Bureau of Safety

A week after the wreck, President Wilson nationalized the railroads to support the war effort.

The immediate effect was seen in the next day's headline.

Appendix J

MUIR v. LOUISVILLE & N. R. CO.

(District Court, W. D. Kentucky. March 2, 1918.)

1. CITIZENS ☛2—CORPORATIONS.

A corporation Is a citizen of the state under whose laws It was organized.

2. REMOVAL OF CAUSES ☛95—EFFECT OF FILING PETITION AND BOND.

Where defendant appeared in an action in the state court, and tendered therein and prayed leave to file a petition for removal of the cause to the federal court, at the same time tendering a bond in the terms prescribed by law, with good and sufficient sureties, the cause was effectively removed to the federal court, notwithstanding the state court refused to enter the removal order sought.

3. COURTS ☛508(8)—REFUSAL TO ENTER ORDER OF REMOVAL—INJUNCTION.

Where defendant's filing of a petition for removal of a cause to the federal court and tender of a bond effectually removed the cause, though the state court declined to enter an order of removal, the federal court may protect its jurisdiction by injunction order, restraining the plaintiffs and their attorneys from further prosecuting the action in the state court.

4. EVIDENCE ☛46—JUDICIAL NOTICE—PRESIDENTIAL PROCLAMATIONS.

The courts will take judicial notice of the proclamation of the President of December 26, 1917, declaring the necessity to take possession and control of certain systems of transportation in the United States, including railroads.

5. UNITED STATES ☛58.5—PROPERTY—SEIZURE—LITIGATION.

Where property of the United States has been seized or impleaded in litigation between individuals, the government, through the suggestion by the district attorney, in a form showing title to the property in the United States, may secure release of the property without becoming a party, in which event the litigation must cease.

6. UNITED STATES ☛125—JURISDICTION—ACTIONS AGAINST UNITED STATES.

Where by proclamation of December 26, 1917, the President, under Act Aug. 29, 1916, c. 41S. § 1, 39 Stat. 645 (Comp. St. 1916, § 1974a), providing that the President is empowered, through the Secretary of War, to take possession and assume control of any system or systems of transportation, or any part thereof, and to utilize the same for the transfer or transportation of troops, war material, and equipment, or for such other purposes connected with the emergency as may be needful or desirable, took possession of and assumed control of every system of transportation within the United States, including railroads, the Secretary of the Treasury being appointed Director General, actions thereafter begun against a railroad company for causes arising prior to the proclamation cannot, despite the extremely broad war-making powers of Congress under Const, Art. 1, § 8, be defeated on the ground that, as the United States had taken over the property of the railroad company and had not given its consent to be sued, the courts were without jurisdiction, the actions in effect being against the sovereign, for the doctrine that, where property of the government is seized or impleaded in litigation between individuals, the government may secure its release by suggestion of that fact, In which case the litigation must end, applies only where property has been actually seized or impleaded, and the mere institution of actions against railroad companies was not a seizure of property of which the government had taken control.

7. REMOVAL OF CAUSES ☛19(1)—FEDERAL COURTS—JURISDICTIONS—"ACTIONS ARISING UNDER CONSTITUTION OR LAWS OF UNITED STATES."

In such case, as Act Aug. 29, 1916, does not authorize the President to make any proclamation of any character in taking possession and assuming control of transportation systems, and thus the presidential proclamation is without force of law, actions begun in the state court against a railroad company after the President had taken possession of railroads, which were based on the negligence of the railroad company occurring prior to the executive action, cannot be removed to the federal courts, under Judicial Code (Act March 3, 1911, c. 231) § 28, 36 Stat. 1091 (Comp. St. 1916. § 991 [1]), on the ground that they were actions arising under the Constitution and laws of the United States, for the cause of action was not based on any act of Congress, and the proclamation of the President, though It might have afforded basis for the actions, was without effect as law.

8. UNITED STATES ☞28—LEGISLATIVE DEPARTMENT—EXECUTIVE REGULATIONS—STATUTE.

While Congress may authorize heads of executive departments or other officials to make regulations within certain limits, and when made within those limits such regulations have the force and effect of law, the delegation of authority to make regulatory orders gives no power to add to, take from, or modify the limitations prescribed by Congress, and, as Act Cong. Aug. 29, 1916, authorizing the President to take possession of and assume control of transportation systems through the Secretary of War, made no provision for presidential proclamation providing an elaborate scheme of control, such proclamation has no force as law.

9. CONSTITUTIONAL LAW ☞105—VESTED RIGHTS—RETROACTIVE LEGISLATION.

Where, as a result of a railroad wreck, plaintiffs acquired causes of action against a railroad company arising out of the relation of carrier and passenger, such rights were then vested, and they cannot be taken away or divested by authority exerted thereafter, either by a legislative body or by an executive officer; and hence, though the President thereafter took possession of and assumed control of railroads under Act Aug. 29, 1916, such vested rights of action could not be interfered with.

10. REMOVAL OF CAUSES ☞25(1)—ACTIONS ARISING UNDER LAWS AND CONSTITUTION OF UNITED STATES—RIGHT OF REMOVAL.

To remove from the state to the federal court an action on the ground that it arose under the Constitution and laws of the United States, such fact must appear from the initial pleading of the plaintiff; and, where it did not appear, such cause cannot be removed, though the action was one against a railroad company, and it was contended that, because the President, under Act Aug. 29, 1916, had taken possession of and assumed control of railroads before the initiation of the action, the cause was one removable, as arising under the laws of the United States.

Actions by J. W. Muir, administrator of George S. Muir, by Jasper W. Muir, administrator of N. W. Muir, by Thomas J.

Miller, administrator of Mabel Brown Miller, by H. H. Mashburn, administrator of Emily Mashburn, by R. H. Miller, administrator of Lillian Miller, and by J. E. Smith against the Louisville & Nashville Railroad Company, which were begun in the state court and removed by defendant to the federal court. On motion to remand. The proceedings were also consolidated with suits in equity by the Louisville & Nashville Railroad Company against Jasper W. Muir, administrator of George S. Muir and others, and against the other plaintiffs and their attorneys, to enjoin proceedings in the state court, which had declined to enter an order for the removal sought. Motions for remand sustained, and the temporary restraining order issued on the several bills set aside and the bills dismissed.

Nat. W. Halstead and J. D. Wickliffe, both of Bardstown, Ky., and Frank P. Straus and Howard B. Lee, both of Louisville, Ky., for plaintiffs.

Helm Bruce, H. L. Stone, E. S. Jouett, and B. D. Warfield, all of Louisville, Ky., for defendant.

WALTER EVANS, District Judge. The first six of the above-styled suits are actions at law, which have been removed to this court, while the other six of them are suits in equity, brought in this court, seeking to enjoin separately the prosecution in the state court of each of the others.

[1] The Louisville & Nashville Railroad Company (which will be called the Railroad Company) is a corporation organized under the laws of this state, and therefore is a citizen of Kentucky. On December 20, 1917, there occurred at Shepherdsville, Ky., an accident to a passenger train of the Railroad Company which brought instant death to at least 45 passengers, ultimate death to not less than 4 more of them, and suffering and injury to 47 others. They were all at the time passengers on a train operated locally between Louisville, Ky., and Bardstown,

Ky., which cities are about 40 miles apart. The disaster was the most distressing which had ever happened in the long life of the Railroad Company, and brought from its president, Mr. Milton H. Smith, a published statement, notably commendable in spirit and tone (which we are much tempted to insert in full), admitting liability and offering to make settlements in the fairest spirit. No adjustment of damages, however, could be reached in these cases.

At various dates between January 9, 1918, and February 2, 1918, the six actions at law first above styled were commenced by the respective plaintiffs therein against the Railroad Company in the Nelson circuit court of Kentucky. The amount sued for ranged from $100,000 to $35,000 in those five of the suits where death had occurred, and $20,000, the amount sued for in that one of the actions where death did not result from the injuries received.

[2] The term of the Nelson circuit court, then next, began on the second Monday (the 11th day) of February, 1918. At that time the Railroad Company appeared therein and tendered to that court and asked its leave to file in each of the cases its petition for the removal thereof to this court. It also with each petition tendered a bond in the terms prescribed by law, with good and sufficient surety thereon. Upon consideration of the motions for leave to file the several petitions for removal the Nelson circuit court denied each of them, and declined to enter an order for the removal sought, though in each case the court found the bond tendered to be sufficient. Obviously each of the suits was effectively removed to this court by what had been done. Traction Co. v. Mining Co., 196 U. S. 239, 244, 25 Sup. Ct. 251, 49 L. Ed. 462; Marshall v. Holmes, 141 U. S. 595, 12 Sup. Ct. 62, 35 L. Ed. 870, and cases cited; Stevenson v. Illinois Central R. R. Co. (C. C.) 192 Fed. 958.

A transcript of the record in each case was filed in this court on the 16th day of the same month. In no one of the six actions at law thus removed was there any person sued as a defendant, except the Railroad Company. Each plaintiff in the six actions was a citizen of Kentucky, and his action was against another citizen of the same state. Each plaintiff in his pleading alleged in clear and explicit terms that the injured person, at the time of the accident, had been a passenger on the train then owned and operated by the Railroad Company, and that while such passenger, and by the gross and inexcusable negligence of the defendant in operating its train, the injury complained of had been inflicted. These averments in substance stated the whole cause of action, and nothing else was relied upon by the respective plaintiffs as a basis for the recovery sought.

[3] In this condition of the record the plaintiff in each of the actions thus removed entered a motion to remand it to the state court; but as that court had refused to remove the cases, and as each of them was upon its docket for trial at the term then in session, the Railroad Company filed in this court its separate bill in equity against each of the several plaintiffs in the actions at law and his attorneys therein, and thereby sought a separate injunction against the plaintiffs severally and their respective attorneys to prevent them from further prosecuting in the state court their respective actions which had been removed to this court. Pursuant to the prayer in its several bills, the Railroad Company moved in each case for an injunction pendente lite. Those motions and the motions to remand were all heard together, and must be determined upon the same propositions of law, and it is therefore convenient to embrace all of them in one opinion; it being apparent, we think, that, if this court has no jurisdiction, the actions at law must all be remanded to the state court, while, if

the jurisdiction is here, that jurisdiction must be protected through the injunctions sought by the Railroad Company. This course is abundantly supported by the decision of the Supreme Court in Madisonville Traction Co. v. St. Bernard Mining Co., 196 U. S. 239, 256, 25 Sup. Ct. 251, 49 L. Ed. 462, which affirmed the judgment of this court in 130 Fed. 794.

Section 24 of the Judicial Code (Act March 3, 1911, c. 231, 36 Stat. 1091 [Comp. St. 1916, § 991(1)]) among other things, provides that:

"The District Courts shall have original jurisdiction as follows: "First. Of all suits of a civil nature, at common law or in equity * * * where the matter in controversy exceeds, exclusive of interest and costs, the sum or value of three thousand dollars, and arises under the Constitution or laws of the United States."

And section 28 of the Code (Comp. St. 1916, § 1010) provides that "any suit of a civil nature, at law or in equity, arising under the Constitution and laws of the United States, * * * of which the District Courts of the United States are given original jurisdiction," may be removed by the defendant or defendants therein to the District Court, if brought in a state court.

Under these provisions the Railroad Company in its petitions claims the right to remove the cases. It is entirely clear, from the petitions of the several plaintiffs filed in the state court, that the amount in controversy in each case exceeds the sum or value of $3,000, exclusive of interest and costs, and equally is it clear that the cause of action stated by each plaintiff is not one which appears from the plaintiff's pleading itself to arise under the Constitution or laws of the United States. This being so, the Railroad Company admits at the outset that it is confronted with many adverse rulings of the Supreme Court. Only one of these need be cited, for in its opinion in In re Winn, 213 U. S. at page 465, 29 Sup. Ct. 516, 53 L. Ed. 873, the court fully covered the subject when it said:

"It is the settled interpretation of these words, as used in this statute conferring jurisdiction, that a suit arises under the Constitution and laws of the United States only when the plaintiff's statement of his own cause of action shows that it is based upon those laws or that Constitution. It is not enough, as the law now exists, that it appears that the defendant may find in the Constitution or laws of the United States some ground of defense. Louisville & Nashville Railroad v. Mottley, 211 U. S. 149 [29 Sup. Ct. 42, 53 L. Ed. 126], and cases cited. If the defendant has any such defense to the plaintiff's claim it may be set up in the state courts, and if properly set up, and denied by the highest court of the state, may ultimately be brought to this court for decision."

Nevertheless the Railroad Company seeks to maintain the jurisdiction of this court upon the general proposition that the facts stated in its petitions for removal are such as, if true, will authorize a departure from the general rule. We are thus brought to the novel, interesting, and important questions presented for determination. Aided by the able, ingenious, and energetic arguments of counsel for the various parties, we have given them very careful consideration.

The sole ground upon which the right of removal in each case is claimed is that the suit arises under the Constitution or laws of the United States; but obviously, as no one of them arises under any express clause or provision of the Constitution itself, the right to remove must be regarded as asserted upon the single proposition that each of the several actions arises under the "laws of the United States." Accordingly in each of its petitions for removal the Railroad Company states that in the act making appropriations for the support of the army for the then current fiscal year, approved August 29, 1916, there was a clause which reads as follows:

"The President, in time of war, is empowered, through the Secretary of War, to take possession and assume control of any system or systems of transportation, or any part thereof, and to utilize the same, to the exclusion as far as may be necessary of all other traffic thereon, for the transfer or transportation of troops, war material and equipment, or for such other purposes connected with the emergency as may be needful or desirable." 39 Stat. 645, 4 Comp. Stat. p. 3778, § 1974a.

Each petition for removal also states that on December 26, 1917, the President, therein reciting that previously in 1917 Congress had declared war, first against Germany, and afterwards against the Austro-Hungarian government, and that it had become necessary, under the legislative provision just copied, to take possession and control of certain systems of transportation for the transfer or transportation of troops, war material, and equipment therefor, and for other useful and desirable purposes connected with the prosecution of the war, had made proclamation that he, as President, through Newton D. Baker, Secretary of War, would take possession of and assume control at 12 o'clock noon on the 28th day of December, 1917 (though for accounting purposes such taking possession should only operate as from midnight on the 31st day of December, 1917), of every system of transportation within the United States, including railroads.

[4] It also appears in the proclamation, of which we take judicial notice, that while, nominally, possession and control of the systems of transportation are to be taken through the Secretary of War, in that document in plainly expressed language it is "directed that the possession, control, operation and utilization of such transportation systems hereby by me undertaken shall be exercised by and through William G. McAdoo, who is hereby appointed and designated Director General of Railroads," and as such is given all the power and authority fully set forth in the proclamation, although this was done in "time of war" and obviously in a war emergency. As all know, Mr. McAdoo was then and is now the Secretary of the Treasury. It is also shown that at the time appointed in the proclamation he, as the Director General of Railroads, took full possession and control of such of the defendant's property as is designated in the proclamation, and yet holds the same.

In these circumstances the Railroad Company contends: (1) That as all its property has been taken from it in the manner stated, as the government cannot be sued without its consent, and as such consent has not been given, the courts have no right to proceed against the defendant in these cases; (2) that, as matter of law, it results from the facts shown that the actions which have been removed must be considered as having arisen under the laws of the United States, no one of them having been commenced in the state court until on or after January 9, 1918; and (3) that these facts bring about a situation which must be held to justify a ruling that these cases present an exception to the general rule that a removal cannot be sustained unless the plaintiff's own pleading shows on its face that his cause of action arises under the Constitution or laws of the United States.

[5, 6] These contentions involve questions of momentous importance, which, in the great crisis now upon the country, will only be discussed to the extent necessary to a proper determination of the rights demanded under them by the Railroad Company. Our decision must and will be limited to ascertaining what those rights are in these cases.

By article 1, section 1, of the Constitution, all the legislative power of the government is vested in the Congress. By the same article, section 8, Congress is given power to declare war, to raise and support armies, and to make all laws which may be necessary and proper for carrying into execution all the powers given by the section. All agree, and the courts hold, that in time of war the Congress has wide discretion in determining what is "necessary and proper" to make good its declaration of war against the enemies of the country. These provisions, in this connection, become all the more important because, in his proclamation, the President declared in express words that in taking control and possession of the railroads of the country he was acting by virtue of that statutory provision and the resolutions declaring war. This being true, and the Railroad Company making claim to the right of removal of these cases from the state court upon the same statutory provisions and the action of the President thereunder, we are brought to the necessity of analyzing the provisions of that enactment. While by no means comprehensive, nor possibly adequate to the great emergency which subsequently arose, they are nevertheless, so far as they go, neither doubtful nor ambiguous. In order that they may serve the great purposes which they were intended to accomplish, they necessarily must be construed to carry the implied right, when control and possession of the transportation systems are taken under them, to have those systems utilized and operated in the most efficient manner. We shall yield full effect to these propositions in what we say concerning the proper construction of the provisions themselves, so far as these cases demand it.

The statute authorizes the President (a) in time of war, (b) through the Secretary of War, (c) to take, possess, and assume control (d) of any system of transportation, to the exclusion, if necessary, of any other transportation thereon, (e) for the transfer or transportation of troops, war material, and equipment, and for such other purposes connected (f) with the emergency as may be needful or desirable. Under no established rule of interpretation can it be doubted that it was the intention of the legislative body to authorize, in time of war, the

War Department and no other to take over the railroads for war purposes, such as transportation of troops and war material, and for such other purposes as might be desirable in the emergencies of war. Besides being an appropriate function of the War Department, it was the plain meaning of the statute which Congress enacted that the War Department should have authority over it, and even if we assume (which is inconceivable) that the Secretary of War declined for that department to take up the war work indicated, we find nothing in the statute which authorizes it to be taken up by the Treasury Department, nor by a Director General of Railroads; Congress not having intrusted the work to either. And the situation, if strict rules were to operate, might involve consideration of the question whether the rule stated by the Supreme Court in Smith v. Black, 115 U. S. at page 319, 6 Sup. Ct. 56, 29 L. Ed. 398, to the effect that, "where there is a statute requiring a thing to be done by a known and responsible public officer, it may well be held that he must do it in person," would not apply.

But the Railroad Company in this case makes no objection to the taking over of its property under the proclamation, and we are no further concerned with the situation than to inquire whether there is anything in the entire record from which we may fairly draw the legal conclusion, either upon the statute or the President's proclamation, or upon anything done under either, that the several actions which have been removed arise under the Constitution or laws of the United States, and especially as all that has been done by the government was done after each of the causes of action had become perfect as against the Railroad Company.

True, as the Railroad Company insists, the law is that the United States cannot be sued without its consent; also it is true that the government has not consented to being sued in these cases, though, if ownership and title to the property of the Railroad Company has passed to the United States, the authorities establish the proposition that, if that property has been seized or impleaded in a litigation between individuals, the government, through the district attorney, may secure its release by suggestion to the court without making the government a party. In such cases, when the district attorney makes the suggestion in a form which shows the United States to have title, the litigation must end. Stanley v. Schwalby, 147 U. S. 512, 513, 13 Sup. Ct. 418, 37 L. Ed. 259; Carr v. United States, 98 U. S. 438, 25 L. Ed. 209; The Siren, 7 Wall. (74 U. S.) 153, 154, 19 L. Ed. 129. This doctrine, however, applies only where the property of the United States has been seized or is impleaded in some litigation. So far nothing of that sort has occurred or appears here, and we conclude that the first of the contentions of the Railroad Company above stated cannot be maintained.

[7-9] The second of the contentions of the Railroad Company, briefly stated, is that the actions were all brought in the state court after the promulgation of the President's proclamation and the taking possession thereunder of property of the Railroad Company. Much of what we have already said is applicable to this contention, but it requires further and somewhat more radical treatment, and especially must we ascertain what, if any, effect upon the rights of the plaintiffs in the litigation the proclamation of the President can have.

Certainly the proposition is so well established as to be elementary that Congress may authorize heads of departments or other officers to make regulations within certain limits, and, when made within those limits, such regulations have the force and effect of law, and may be enforced as such; but it has often been held that the delegation of authority to make regulatory orders gives no power to add to, take from, or modify the limitations prescribed by Congress. United States v. 200 Barrels Whisky, 95 U. S. 576, 24 L. Ed. 491; United States v. 11,150 Pounds Butter, 195 Fed. 663, 664, 115 C. C. A. 463. In many instances proclamations by the President, authorized by the Constitution or by statute, have been given great effect. Notably was this so in United States v. Klien, 13 Wall. 129, 20 L. Ed. 519, and Armstrong v. United States, 13 Wall. 154, 20 L. Ed. 614, and other cases.

On its face the act of August 29, 1916, does not give authority to the President to make or promulgate a proclamation of any character. No one, however, could or would contend that he had not abundant authority to issue such documents whenever he thought it proper to give notice or information to the public. But such papers cannot have any effect as laws, in the absence of express constitutional or congressional authorization. We cannot say that the President had any view to the contrary of this when he issued the proclamation in question; but the second contention of the Railroad Company, which demands consideration, is and necessarily must be based upon the idea that that document did have the force and effect of law, and should, as such, be enforced to the extent that it therefrom be made to result that any suit subsequently brought against a railroad company whose property had been taken into possession under the statute (even if such suit were brought upon a cause of action which had been perfected on or before December 20, 1917) arose under the laws of the United States. While the statute is silent upon the subject of litigation of any character, it by no means follows that causes of action might not arise thereunder. The vital question here is not that, but is this: Did the causes of action of the several plaintiffs, as stated in their petitions, so arise, or did they arise under the proclamation of the President?

In the familiar and oft-cited case of Tennessee v. Davis, 100 U. S. at page 264, 25 L. Ed. 648, the Supreme Court said:

"Cases arising under the laws of the United States are such as grow out of the legislation of Congress, whether they constitute the right or privilege, or claim or protection, or defense of the party, in whole or in part, by whom they are asserted."

This language was repeated in the case of Bock v. Perkins, 139 U. S. at page 630, 11 Sup. Ct. 677, 35 L. Ed. 314, and, when we subject the cases before us to this authoritative test, can we properly say it is met? We think clearly not, because obviously these cases arose out of the facts stated in the pleadings of the several plaintiffs, and not out of the legislation of Congress. Nevertheless, in effect it is urged that, when the statute is read in connection with the proclamation of the President, the test is met. There possibly might be great force in this view, were it not, first, that the statute does not authorize the proclamation, and therefore leaves that document without force as legislation of Congress or as a law of the United States; and, second, that the causes of action arose upon facts plainly stated by the plaintiffs, and consequently, even if it could by any possibility be said that they arose under the proclamation, they nevertheless would not arise under any law of the United States—the proclamation not being such. The statute is silent upon the subject of litigation of any character, and does not attempt to close either the state or federal courts to any person who might already have an existing cause of action against any railroad company upon the mere ground that the property of the company had been taken over for a temporary though most important use. The proclamation designates Mr. McAdoo as Director General of Railroads. This position being unknown to the law, its powers are not fixed; but we suppose it was the intention to make him, not only a member, but the head, of the board of directors of each railroad company, the property of which was taken into possession—thus giving him, instead of the Secretary of War, the control of all operations under the statute. Many rules for him to enforce appear to be prescribed in the proclamation, but we pass over all of them as having no bearing upon the cases before us, except that one of them which is in this language:

"Except with the prior written assent of said Director, no attachment by mesne process or on execution shall be levied on or against any of the property used by any of said transportation systems in the conduct of their business as common carriers; but suits may be brought by and against said carriers and judgments rendered as hitherto until and except so far as said Director may, by general or special orders, otherwise determine."

We find no statutory warrant for this provision in the proclamation, and especially none for the exception mentioned in the last clause of it. We may, however, ignore that exception, because nothing appears to show any attempt to carry it into effect; but, even if we suppose that the other limited interruption of the rights of litigants while the war goes on should be patriotically accepted by all good citizens, litigant and otherwise, it by no means follows that the law authorizes any interference with the course of judicial procedure between litigants before the time arrives when there might be attempts to seize, under execution issued upon final judgments, property in the temporary possession of the United States under the proclamation. Nor can we see how even a right to prevent interruption of such temporary possession after final judgment has been rendered can, per se and independently of the nature of the cause of action, support the theory of the Railroad Company that the suits in which judgments may be rendered arise under the Constitution or laws of the United States.

The non sequitur becomes apparent when we recall the exact nature of the cause of action declared upon by the respective plaintiffs. Upon the allegations of his pleading each plaintiff seeks a money judgment and nothing else. Neither of the plaintiffs has made any claim in his pleading to be entitled, under our Code of Practice, to any provisional remedy like an attachment or other similar writ under which any part of defendant's property could be seized pendente lite. When, if ever, judgments shall be rendered in favor of the plaintiffs, the question of means for their enforcement shall arise, it may demand the consideration of the trial court; but at present we are concerned only with the question of whether we have jurisdiction—not, indeed, to seize property, but "to hear and determine a cause." The question of jurisdiction here must be determined upon the nature of the cause of action, and from that we ascertain whether it arises under any law of the United States.

Furthermore, it is obvious from the averments of his pleading that the cause of action of each plaintiff arose and was perfected immediately after the infliction of the injuries complained of. At once thereafter each plaintiff had a clear right to sue upon that cause of action. Each one of them promptly exercised that right and commenced his action at law in the state court. As it is quite obvious from the pleadings of the plaintiffs that each of the causes of action arose out of what occurred while the relationship of passenger and common carrier existed, and not out of any law of the United States, the right of each plaintiff to sue became a vested right on December 20, 1917, and cannot be taken away or devested by any authority exerted, ex post facto, either by a legislative body or by an executive officer of any degree. This proposition was clearly announced by the Supreme Court when, in Angle v. Chicago, St. Paul, etc., Railway, 151 U. S. at page 19, 14 Sup. Ct. 247, 38 L. Ed. 55, it said:

"A right of action to recover damages for an injury is property, and has a Legislature the power to destroy such property? An executive may pardon and thus relieve a wrongdoer from the punishment the public exacts for the wrong; but neither executive nor Legislature can pardon a private wrong or relieve the wrongdoer from civil liability to the individual he has wronged."

After the plaintiffs' causes of action had all arisen, the President's proclamation was promulgated, and in pursuance thereof possession and control of the Railroad Company's property was taken. Upon this state of fact as its sole basis the Railroad Company contends that each of the separate causes of action arose under the laws of the United States. After most careful consideration we have, upon the grounds stated, concluded that this contention has not been maintained and is not maintainable.

[10] The third contention of the Railroad Company is that the facts here justify the conclusion that these cases present an exception to the general rule that in order to remove the plaintiff's petition on its face must show how the action arises under the Constitution or laws of the United States, and in support of this suggestion the counsel for the Railroad Company cite cases like Pacific R. R. Removal Cases, 115 U. S. 1-24, 5 Sup. Ct. 1113, 29 L. Ed. 319; Texas & Pacific R. Co. v. Cody, 166 U. S. 606, 17 Sup. Ct. 703, 41 L. Ed. 1132; Texas & P. R. Co. v. Cox, 145 U. S. 593, 12 Sup. Ct. 905, 36 L. Ed. 829; Macon Groeery Co. v. Atlantic Coast Line, 215 U. S. 501, 30 Sup. Ct. 184, 54 L. Ed. 300; Toledo R. R. v. Penna. Ry. (C. C.) 54 Fed. 730, 19 L. R. A. 387.

Careful consideration of each of these cases has failed to convince us that any one of them has any tendency in the direction suggested. It is an everyday construction of the Removal Act that the diverse citizenship of the parties may be shown for the first time in the petition for removal, for the reason that in stating a cause of action an allegation of citizenship is not material, and need not be made by the plaintiff; but it is different as to the amount in controversy. In respect to that the plaintiff must, in an action at law, state the amount he seeks to recover, and ordinarily the case is not removable unless the amount in controversy exceeds the sum or value of $3,000 and is claimed by the plaintiff in his pleading. So, in stating the nature of his claim, the plaintiff's pleading should show, and, if well constructed, does show, the nature of his claim and how it arises, and in this way, if he seeks to recover under the Constitution or laws of the United States, it will inevitably so appear. These propositions are the basis of the rule stated in the Winn Case, supra, and in the extract we have made from the opinion in that case the Supreme Court has pointed out that, if the defendant has any defense based upon the claim that the action is one arising under the Constitution and laws of the United States, he can set it up in the state court, and, if it is denied, he can carry the case to the Supreme Court.

The several motions of the plaintiffs to remand to the Nelson circuit court will be sustained for want of jurisdiction in this court. In each of the equity suits the temporary restraining order made at the hearing will be set aside, the motions for temporary injunctions will be each overruled, and each of the bills in equity will be dismissed, with costs.

Orders accordingly may be entered.

NAT MUIR'S ADMINISTRATOR SUES L. & N. FOR $170,000

DAMAGES ASKED FOR DEATH OF WEALTHY FAMILY IN SHEPHERDSVILLE WRECK.

Headline in *The Courier-Journal*, Saturday, 26 Jan 1918.

Appendix K
Louisville & Nashville Railroad Company v. Commonwealth.
Decided October 22, 1918.

Reports of Civil and Criminal Cases Decided by the Court of Appeals of Kentucky
Robert G. Higdon, Reporter
Volume 181, Kentucky Reports
containing cases decided from
June 7, 1918, to November 1, 1918, pages 671-5.

Appeal from Bullitt Circuit Court.

Railroads— Operation— Nuisance— Indictment—Sufficiency.—in the absence of an ordinance prescribing a reasonable maximum speed through an incorporated town, it is essential to the validity of an indictment charging a railroad company with maintaining a common nuisance, by habitually running its trains at such a dangerous and excessive rate of speed as to jeopardize the lives of the public, to allege that such running of such trains was without the customary and necessary warnings of their approach.

MOORMAN & WOODWARD, J. F. COMBS and BENJAMIN D. WARFIELD for appellant.

CHARLES H. MORRIS, Attorney General, J. LEWIS WILLIAMS, T. C. CARROLL and CHARLES CARROLL for appellee.

OPINION OF THE COUBT BY WlLLIAM ROGERS CLAY, COMMISSIONER—Affirming as to Commonwealth and reversing as to Louisville & Nashville Railroad Company.

The Louisville & Nashville Railroad Company and B. M. Starks, its general manager, W. F. Sheridan, its superintendent, and F. J. Fishback, its trainmaster, were indicted by the grand jury of Bullitt county for the offense of maintaining a common nuisance in the city of Shepherdsville, the county seat of Bullitt county. On a trial before a jury the railroad company was found guilty and its punishment fixed at a fine of $8,420. Pursuant to a peremptory instruction, Starks, Sheridan and Fishback were acquitted. From the judgment of conviction, the railroad company appeals, while the Commonwealth appeals from the judgment acquitting Messrs. Starks, Sheridan and Fishback.

The indictment charges that appellant operated a double-tracked railroad through Bullitt county and Shepherdsville, a town of the sixth class, having a population of about five hundred inhabitants; that it had a station, switches and side tracks at which passengers boarded and alighted from trains, and to and from which freight was shipped; that at all hours of the day numerous persons were in and about said station; that the platforms thereat were on a level with the railroad tracks without any railings between the tracks and the platforms; that there is a street crossing over the tracks north of the station used by many persons, traveling on foot, in vehicles and on horseback; that the railroad runs through the corporate limits of Shepherdsville a distance of more than 200 yards; that immediately adjoining the right of way are many houses in which many persons reside; that there is on the east side of the right of way in Shepherdsville, within a short distance of the tracks, a common and high school, which is in session from September 1st to June 1st, with an average attendance of about 250 pupils, between the ages of six and twenty years, many of whom cross over the tracks at various points in Shepherdsville, including the crossing north of the station above referred to, and many of whom use appellant's trains in going to and from Shepherdsville to attend school; that about 100 yards south of the station, Third street approaches the railroad right of way over a footbridge erected and maintained by appellant, and that persons going to and from its station walk along the right of way between the station and the Third street footbridge. After specifying the offices held by the individual defendants and their respective duties, the indictment proceeds as follows:

"That said Louisville & Nashville Railroad Company now, and continuously for one year last past, has habitually, unlawfully, willfully, negligently and carelessly operated its trains at all hours of the day over its tracks through the corporate limits of the city of Shepherdsville, as aforesaid, at a great, excessive and dangerous rate of speed, and without having said trains under proper control; and it is now, and has continuously for more than one year last past, habitually, negligently, willfully and unlawfully run, at all hours of the day, its trains over the public streets and crossings in said town, at a reckless, excessive and dangerous rate of speed, without having same under proper control, or being able by use of ordinary care, to stop same to prevent injury to those passing or re-passing over the public crossings and streets in said city, or using the footpaths provided by said company, as aforestated; and has unlawfully, recklessly, carelessly and negligently caused its trains, within the time above stated and in the corporate limits of Shepherdsville, to run at such an excessive and dangerous rate of speed, and

without being under proper control, so as to, on numerous occasions, almost cause passenger trains to collide in the city of Shepherdsville, and did, on the 20th day of December, 1917, unlawfully, recklessly, carelessly and negligently operate its train of cars at a dangerous and excessive rate of speed in Shepherdsville, and thereby causing the death of many persons and serious injury to many others; and the said B. M. Starks, as general manager aforesaid of said company, and F. J. Fishback, master of trains of said company, and the said W. F. Sheridan, as superintendent of the first division of said company, have all and each unlawfully, willfully, wantonly and negligently continuously for one year last past before the finding of this indictment, suffered, permitted and caused the trains over which they have supervision and control, to be so managed and run as aforesaid through the corporate limits of the said city of Shepherdsville; and by reason of the aforesaid unlawful, willful, reckless and negligent conduct of the said Louisville & Nashville Railroad Company, and the said B. M. Starks, F. J. Fishback, and W. F. Sheridan, and all, and each of same, the lives of the citizens of Bullitt county and of the city of Shepherdsville and of other counties and cities of the state while in said city of Shepherdsville have been put in jeopardy and the aforesaid conduct of said parties and said company has caused terror and annoyance and placed in jeopardy the citizens of Bullitt county and Shepherdsville in said city and other persons having business in said city and persons on the trains of said railroad company in said city and at the said railroad station, and on the footpaths from the bridge of said railroad station, and those crossing the public streets and crossings in said city, and all to the common nuisance of all persons there being, passing and re-passing and having the right to be, to pass and repass, and against the peace and dignity of the Commonwealth of Kentucky."

The first error relied on, and the only one that we deem it necessary to consider, is the overruling of the demurrer to the indictment. The sufficiency of the indictment is assailed on the ground that it failed to allege that the running of the trains was without the necessary warnings to avoid injuring those using and crossing the company's tracks.

In the recent case of Cincinnati, N. O. & T. P. Ry. Co. v. Commonwealth, 126 Ky. 712, 104 S. W. 771, the railroad was indicted for maintaining a public nuisance by habitually running its trains through the incorporated town of Burgin at such an unreasonable and unsafe rate of speed as to endanger the lives and safety of persons using the crossing and without giving the customary and necessary warning signals of their approach. There it appeared that Burgin was an incorporated town of the sixth class with a population of about one thousand. The railroad ran through the town north and south. Its track was crossed by a turnpike which was the principal thoroughfare of the town. The main residence section of the town was on the west side, while the post office, school and churches and principal business houses were situated on the east side of the railroad. During the daytime there was a large amount of travel over the crossing. According to the Commonwealth's evidence, the company ran its trains through Burgin at a speed of from 40 to 70 miles an hour. However, the Commonwealth did not prove that the trains, in approaching and passing through Burgin, failed to give the usual and proper signals. On the contrary, the company showed that such signals were invariably given. After adverting to the fact that there was no state statute regulating the speed of trains through incorporated towns and that the town of Burgin had not, as it had the right to do, enacted an ordinance fixing a reasonable maximum speed, the court held that in order to find a railroad company guilty of committing a public nuisance by running its trains through an incorporated town at an unsafe rate of speed, without signals at a crossing therein, it was necessary not only to prove an habitual rapid running of the trains, but also that such running was without necessary warnings to avoid injuring those using the crossing. In laying down this rule, the court did not confine it to a case where a public crossing was being approached, but said:

"But, in order to sustain a penal prosecution against a railroad company for running its trains in city or country at a higher or even dangerous rate of speed, either upon a street or in approaching a crossing, it must be shown that such running of the trains was attended with a failure on the part of those operating them to give the necessary and usual signals of their coming."

That case cannot be distinguished from the case under consideration. The physical conditions surrounding the railroads in the two places are practically the same, with the exception that the town of Burgin is larger than Shepherdsville. Manifestly, if it is necessary to prove that the running of the trains was without the necessary warnings of their approach, it is essential to the sufficiency of the indictment that such fact should be alleged. We therefore conclude that in the absence of an ordinance fixing a reasonable maximum speed through an incorporated town, an indictment, charging a railroad company with the offense of maintaining a nuisance by habitually running its trains at such a dangerous rate of speed as to jeopardize the lives of those crossing its tracks, must also allege that such running of such trains was without the customary and necessary warnings of their approach. It follows that the demurrer to the indictment should have been sustained.

Since it was neither alleged in the indictment nor proved by the Commonwealth that the running of such trains was without the customary and necessary warnings of their approach, it is unnecessary to consider the appeal of the Commonwealth further than to say that the peremptory directing the acquittal of defendants, Starks, Sheridan and Fishback, was proper.

On the appeal of the Commonwealth the judgment is affirmed.

On the appeal of the Louisville & Nashville Railroad Company, the judgment is reversed and the cause remanded for proceedings consistent with this opinion.

Additional Frank Nunn Pictures

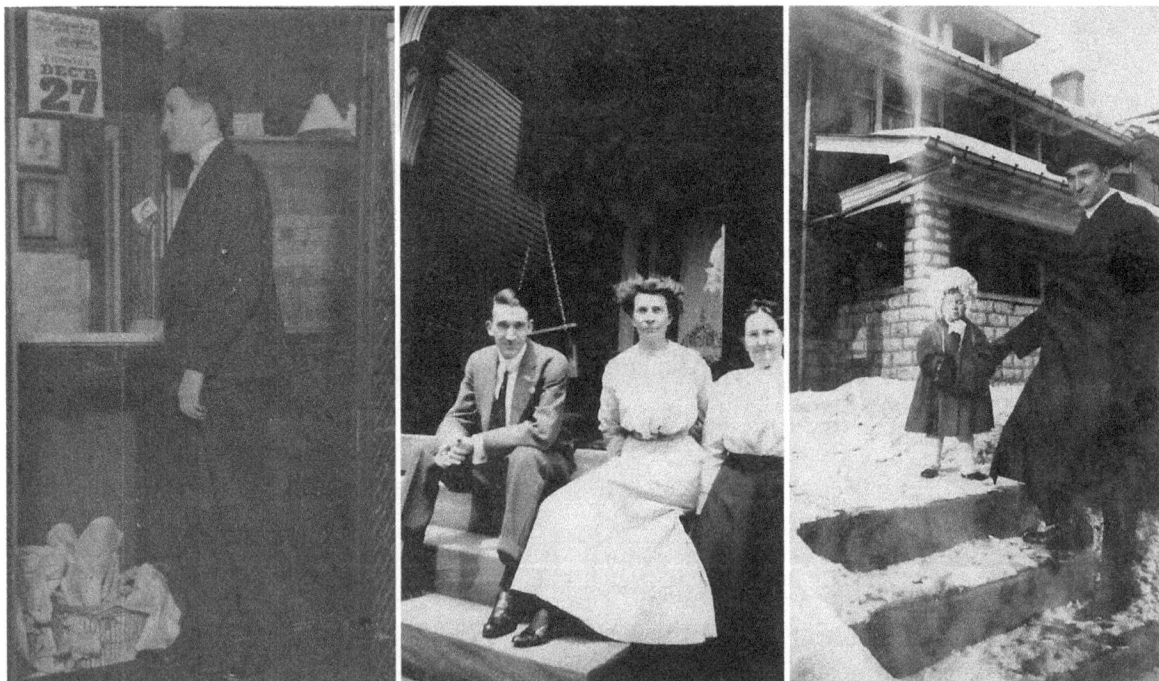

Left: Frank Nunn at the Masonic Theatre in 1904 where he worked as the assistant treasurer.

Center: Frank Nunn, his sister Anna, and their mother, Jennie Nunn.

Right: Frank Nunn with his daughter on the steps of their home, just weeks before the train wreck.

Photos provided by Joyce Toth, Frank Nunn's granddaughter.

Appendix L
Signaling and Manual Block System

The following excerpts are taken from chapter ten of *The Elements of Railroad Engineering* by William G. Raymond (1914). The entire volume is available online in various locations.

"As a term in railroading, signaling means informing the engineman of a train whether he is to proceed or stop. ... The information is given in daytime by the position of a blade or arm pivoted near one end on a vertical post, and at night by colored lights. The blade or arm signal is called a semaphore. ...

"Block signaling is the division of a railroad line into spaces of various lengths, called blocks, and the placing and operating of signals at the end of each block to tell the engineman of an approaching train whether or not the block ahead of him is clear, and hence whether or not he may proceed. Block signaling keeps trains separated by space intervals, which are much safer than time intervals. ...

"There are three principal methods of operating block signals: 1. Telegraphic. 2. Controlled manual. 3. Automatic.

"Let a double track be first supposed. By the telegraphic method of operating block signals, the signalman in the tower at the rear or entering end of a block informs the towerman at the forward or leaving end when a train enters the block, and the forward towerman informs the rear man when the train has passed out of the block. The rear towerman will not give the clear signal to an approaching train until the forward man has told him the last train through is out of the block.

"The signals are what are called 'mechanical,' that is, worked through levers by hand, and the normal position is danger, the signal being cleared by the signalman for each approaching train, provided he learns the block is clear. The signal is supposed to be held clear till the train has passed it and into the block, when it is at once restored to danger. The information from one tower to another is given by telegraphic code or a bell code, or both.

"In the controlled manual method the signals are worked by hand, as in the telegraphic method, but the signal levers are electrically interlocked, so that the forward operator must unlock the levers in the rear tower before the rear towerman can move the signals to the clear position. The locking mechanism is worked by an electric circuit. On the approach of a train toward any block, the towerman asks the towerman ahead to 'clear' him; if the block is clear, the forward towerman pushes a button or plunger and unlocks the rear operator's levers, after which that operator can give the clear signal. The advance towerman having once unlocked the levers of the tower at the entering end cannot again do so until his own signal has been cleared and again set at danger, which will not occur until the train he has admitted to the block shall have passed his own tower. The method is safer than the telegraphic, in that it requires a positive action on the part of two men to clear a signal, which having been cleared and moved again to danger cannot be again cleared till the block it controls is clear. The normal position of the signals is danger. In the automatic method an electric battery is placed near the forward end of a block and the current is run through the rail and through a relay, which, so long as the current flows, completes a circuit from a second battery that operates the signal mechanism. The device is so arranged that an accident to the apparatus would send the signals to danger, hence the automatic system must always be a permissive system; that is, the engineman finding a signal at 'stop,' does not know whether it is so because of a train in the block ahead or because of derangement of the mechanism; he therefore stops a prescribed time, and then goes ahead with caution. In the non-automatic system a signalman is always present to tell the engineman whether or not he may go ahead at speed, under control, or not at all; nevertheless, the automatic system is in growing favor.

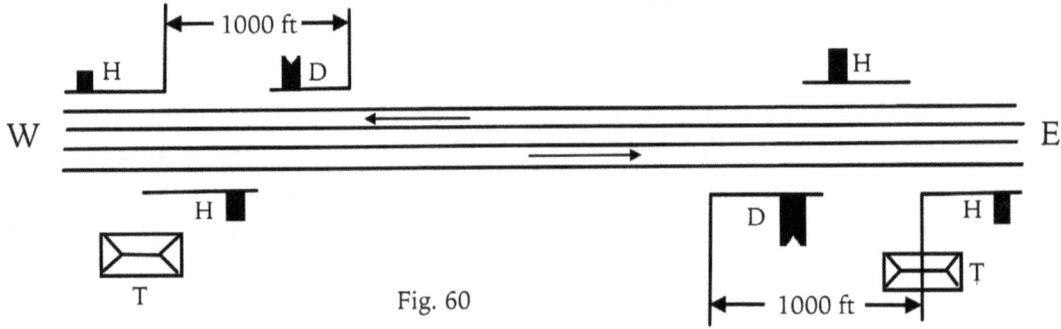

Fig. 60

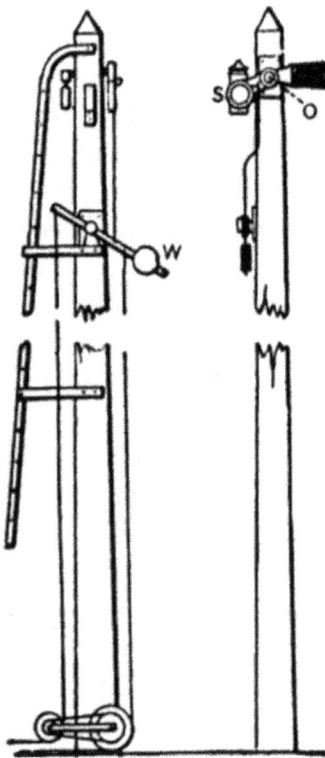

Fig. 61

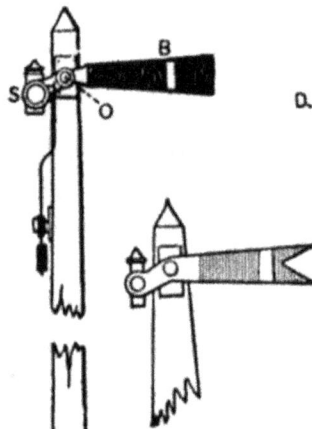

Fig. 62

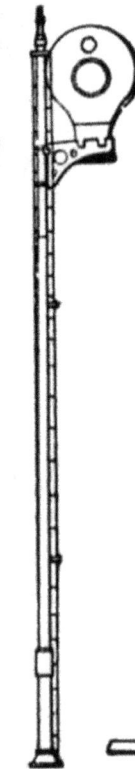

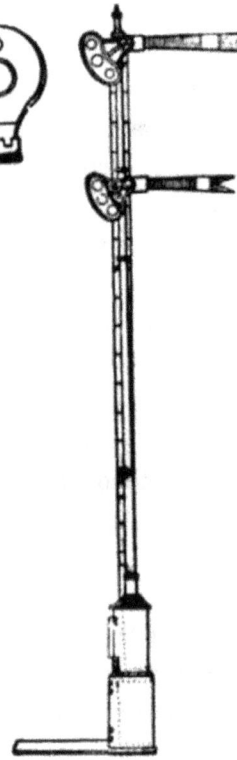

Fig. 63   Fig. 64   Fig. 65

"General Forms of Signals. — Figure 60 shows the relation of a semaphore signal and the track it governs. The blade is always to the right of an approaching train; if to the left, no attention is paid to it because it governs movement in the opposite direction. H is the home signal, D the distant signal, and T the tower.

"Figure 61 is a standard home semaphore, so called because it is located at the beginning of the block it governs near the signal cabin or tower; while Figure 62 is a distant signal, so called because it is located at some distance from the home signal toward an approaching train. The distance is not so great as to prevent operation from the same cabin, say, 1500 to 2000 feet. The distant signal is always in the same position as the corresponding home signal, and is used to tell the engineman in advance what information he may expect to find at the home signal, so that if it is 'clear' he need not reduce speed for a possible stop; and if it is 'stop,' he may approach the home signal under control. B is the blade pivotcd to the post at O; S is a frame carrying a red glass, and is called the spectacle. A lamp is on the bracket behind the spectacle, and when the signal is in the stop position shows its light through the red glass of the spectacle; when the blade is pulled down to 'clear' the spectacle rises, disclosing the white light of the lamp. When green is used for the clear signal, or when permission to go ahead under control is given by the signal, the spectacle is double or triple; if double, one glass is red, the other green; and if triple, a third opening is vacant for white, as in Figure 65. W is a counterweight which keeps the signal at stop except when the signalman pulls and holds the lever. The signal shown is worked by wires. The one difference between the home signal and distant signal is the notch in the end of the distance blade, though they are sometimes painted differently. The post is from 25 to 30 feet high. In yards, for slow movements, short posts with small arms and spectacles, called dwarf signals, are used. Usually where several parallel tracks are to be signaled, the signals are placed on an overhead bridge spanning the tracks, each signal over its own track.

"Figures 63 to 65 are forms of automatic signals. Figure 63 is the clockwork signal of the Union Switch and Signal Company. The disk D is turned by the weight of the clock within the hollow post; broadside means stop, edge means clear, go ahead; the lamp L shows the proper light by turning with the disk. These signals are not now being made, though some of them are in service.

"Figure 64 is the Hall banjo signal. A red disk appears at the larger opening for stop and disappears for clear, the proper light appearing at the small opening above. It is electrically operated, the connection being within the hollow post and banjo top. The disk in Figure 63 is exposed to the weather, but is protected in the signal shown in Figure 64. Figure 65 is a three-position automatic semaphore."

For more details on automatic blocking, see the original book online.

One source may be found at Archive.org at this address:

https://archive.org/stream/
elementsrailroa03raymgoog#page/
n2/mode/2up

Signaling Devices

Fusees

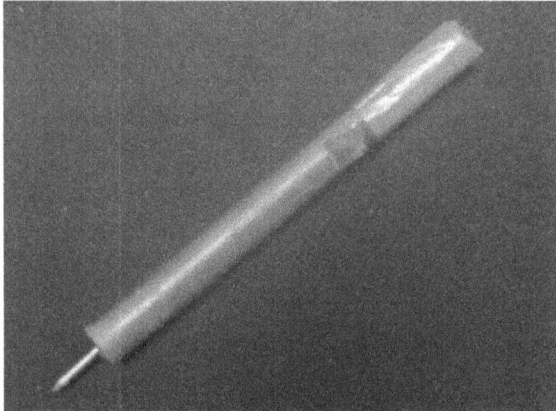

Fusees are similar to common highway flares, with some exceptions. They normally burn for just 10 minutes, and have a sharp spike in one end to enable the flagman to toss them into a railroad tie so they remain upright.

Torpedoes

Torpedoes were designed to be laid on a rail. When a locomotive ran over them, they exploded with a loud bang, alerting the engineer that there was danger ahead.

Either of these devices, properly placed, would have alerted Engineer Wolfenberger to the local train's presence on the tracks ahead. No explanation has ever been found to explain why Flagman Greenwell failed to protect his train with either of these devices.

Appendix M
Early Correspondence

Gary Gibson of Shepherdsville discovered a collection of papers and correspondence at an auction that date back to the time of the 1917 Shepherdsville train wreck. Through his and David Strange's efforts, these became part of the Bullitt County History Museum's collection.

We have included images of some of these documents in this section, along with explanations of their relevance to our research.

We begin with a list of fatalities prepared by Bullitt County Coroner C. A. Masden. He listed a total of 39 individuals for whom he had performed inquests, and divided them into two groups, those whose bodies were sent to Louisville and those who were handled by the local undertakers. This was a first attempt to identify those killed in the wreck.

He listed the 27 whose bodies were sent to Louisville in the first column, as shown here:

1. Josie Bridges
2. Hollie Bridges
3. Mrs. Nat Muir
4. Mr. Nat Muir
5. Mrs. Arch Pulliam
6. George Muir
7. Mrs. John Phillips
8. Mrs. Mac Miller
9. Mrs. Tom Moore, Sr.
10. Mrs. Joe Hurst
11. R. C. Cherry, Sr.
12. R. C. Cherry, Jr.
13. G. C. Duke
14. G. C. Duke's daughter Virginia
15. John Phillips
16. Mrs. H. H. Mashburn
17. W. Mac Miller
18. James Thompson
19. Ben Talbott
20. Mrs. R. H. Miller
21. Miss Althea Simms
22. Tom Spalding
23. David Phillips
24. Lucas Moore
25. Frank Nunn
26. Conductor Campbell
27. An unidentified woman
   (Elizabeth McElroy, Springfield)

In the second column, he listed those who remained in Shepherdsville at one of the two undertaking establishments there. They included the following:

28. Dave Maraman
29. Mrs. Katie Ice
30. Father Bertillo
31. N. H. Thompson [name marked through]
32. Mr. Greenwell (flagman)
33. Jimmie Morrison
34. Forest Overall
35. Mrs. Tom Moore [name marked through]
36. Mrs. Tom Miller [name marked through]
37. Emory Samuels
38. Mrs. Carrie Mae Simmons
39. Maggie Mae Overall
40. Thomas Schafer
41. James Stansbury, Jr.
42. Mrs. Dan Nutt

Written beneath the lists were these comments:

39 in all.

First line (27) sent to Louisville.

Second line (12) sent to Shepherdsville funeral

To holding inquests on 39 bodies @ $6.00 each = $234.

[signed] C. A. Masden, Coroner

Kindly notify me at once if the company refuses to pay this bill.

C.A.M.

An image of that document appears on the next page.

Coroner Masden's List of Dead

91380

LIST OF DEAD, wreck L. & N. R. R. Trains Nos. 7 and 4.

December 20, 1917.

1--	Josie Bridges	28-	Dave Maraman
2--	Hollie Bridges	29-	Mrs. Katie Ice
3--	Mrs. Nat Muir	30	Father Bertillo
4--	Mr. Nat Muir	31	N. H. Thompson
5--	Mrs. Arch Pulliam	32	Mr. Greenwell (flagman)
6--	George Muir	33-	Jimmie Morrison
7--	Mrs. John Phillips	34-	Forest Overall
8--	Mrs. Mac Miller	35-	Xxxxxxxxxxxx Mrs. Tom Moore
9--	Mrs. Tom Moore, Sr.	36-	Mrs. Tom Miller
10-	Mrs. Joe Hurst	37-	Emory Samuels
11-	R. C. Cherry, Sr.	38-	Mrs. Carrie Mae Simmons
12-	R. C. Cherry, Jr.	39-	Maggie Mae Overall
13-	G. C. Duke	40-	Thomas Schafer
14-	G.C.Duke's daughter Virginia	41-	James Stansbury, Jr.
15-	John Phillips	42-	Mrs. Dan Nutt.
16-	Mrs. H. H. Washburn		
17-	W. Mac Miller		
18-	James Thompson		
19-	Ben Talbott		
20-	Mrs. R. H. Miller		
21-	Miss Althea Simms		
22-	Tom Spalding		
23-	David Phillips		
24-	Lucas Moore		
25-	Frank Nunn		
26-	Conductor Campbell		
27-	An unidentified woman		

39 in all

Elizabeth McElroy Springf

First line (27) sent to Louisville
Second line (12) " " Shepherdsville line

To holding inquests on 39 bodies Dec. 1-28

G. A. Masden Co

Kindly notify me at once
if the Company refuses to
pay this bill.

A second list of fatalities, likely prepared by a railroad employee the day following the wreck, is shown below. A transcription of it is given on the next page.

LIST OF PEOPLE FATALLY INJURED IN WRECK AT SHEPHERDSVILLE
KY., DECEMBER 20th, 1917:

NAME	ADDRESS	UNDERTAKER.
Mahlon R. Campbell,	Conductor, train No. 41	Gralle
G. C. Duke,	Bardstown Jct., Ky.,	"
Virginia Duke, 13 years old	"	"
Frank Nunn,	L&N. employe,	"
Hollie Bridges,	Samuels, Ky.,	"
Miss Josie Bridges,	"	"
Mrs. N. R. Washburn,	Bardstown, Ky.,	"
Benj. Tabbott,	"	"
John Phillips,	"	"
Mrs. John Phillips,	"	"
Miss Elizabeth McElroy,	Springfield, Ky.,	"
Lucas Moore,	5th & Hill Sts., Louisville,	"
Davit Phillips,	(Address not known, no arrangements	"
Nat Muir,	Bardstown, Ky.,	Hoden
Mrs. Nat Muir,	"	"
George Muir, 11 years old	"	"
Mae Miller,	"	"
Mrs. Mae Miller,	"	"
R. C. Cherry, Sr.,	"	"
Mrs. R. C. Cherry,	"	"
R. C. Cherry, Jr., 11 years	"	"
Mrs. Joe Hurst,	"	"
7 months old baby of Mrs. Joe Hurst,		"
Mrs. Arch Pulliam,	"	"
Mrs. Tom Moore, Sr.,	"	"
Jos. Thompson,	Springfield, Ky.,	"
Tom Spaulding,	"	"
Miss Altha Simms,	"	"
Raymond Graves, 5 years old,	Taylor Boule., Louisville,	Al. Smith,
Mrs. Hattie J. Parman,	Shepherdsville, Ky.,	Fox
___ C. Johnson,	Bardstown, Ky.,	"
___ wife,	New Hope, Ky.,	Pierson
___ther Ballille,	Chinese, Ky.,	Trouthan Bros.
___ervison, 18 yrs.,	Bardstown Jct., Ky.	?
___ Hensbury, Jr.,		"
___ son,	Shepherdsville, Ky.,	Harages Bros.
___	Bardstown, Jct.,	"
___ C. Hadwell,	Pitman, Gr. No. 1,	"
___ Lovell,	High Grove, Ky.,	"
___ly Samuels,	Bee Lick, Ky.,	"
___ Simmons,	Shepherdsville, Ky.,	"
___ New Haven,	Nelson County, Ky.,	"
___ Wheeler,	Craig, Ky.,	"
___ mith,	___ Leachmont, Ky.,	"
Mrs. R. H. Miller,	Bardstown, Ky.,	Mass.

Name	Address	Undertaker
Mahlon H. Campbell	conductor, train No. 41	Cralle
G. C. Duke	Bardstown Jct.	Cralle
Virginia Duke	12 years old	Cralle
Frank Nunn	L&N employe	Cralle
Hollis Bridges	Samuels, Ky.	Cralle
Miss Josie Bridges	Samuels	Cralle
Mrs. H. H. Mashburn	Bardstown	Cralle
Benj. Talbott	Bardstown	Cralle
John Phillips	Bardstown	Cralle
Mrs. John Phillips	Bardstown	Cralle
Miss Elizabeth McElroy	Springfield	Cralle
Lucus Moore	5th & Hill Sts, Louisville	Cralle
David Phillips	(Address not known, no arrangements)	Cralle
Nat Muir	Bardstown	Boden
Mrs. Nat Muir	Bardstown	Boden
George Muir	11 years old, Bardstown	Boden
Mac Miller	Bardstown	Boden
Mrs. Mac Miller	Bardstown	Boden
R. C. Cherry, Sr.	Bardstown	Boden
Mrs. R. C. Cherry	Bardstown	Boden
R. C. Cherry, Jr.	11 years, Bardstown	Boden
Mrs. Joe Hurst	Bardstown	Boden
7 months old baby of Mrs. Joe Hurst		Boden
Mrs. Arch Pulliam	Bardstown	Boden
Mrs. Tom Moore, Sr.	Bardstown	Boden
Jas Thompson	Springfield	Boden
Tom Spaulding	Springfield	Boden
Miss Altha Simms	Springfield	Boden
Raymond Cravens	3 years old, Taylor Boule., Louisville	Al. Smith
Mrs. Mattie C. Harmon	Shepherdsville	Bax
W. C. Johnson	Bardstown	Bax
Mrs. Thos J. Miller	New Hope	Pierson
Father Bertillo	Chapeze	Troutman Bros.
Jimmy Morrison	15 yrs, Bardstown Jct.	Troutman Bros.
Jim Stansberry, Jr.	Bardstwon Jct.	Troutman Bros.
David Maraman	Shepherdsville	Maraman Bros.
Mrs. Katie Ice	Bardstown Jct.	Maraman Bros.
L. C. Greenwell	Flagman on No. 41	Maraman Bros.
Forrest Overall	High Grove	Maraman Bros.
Emory Samuels	New Hope	Maraman Bros.
Mrs. Wm. Simmons	Shepherdsville	Maraman Bros.
Maggie May Overall	Chapeze	Maraman Bros.
Mrs. Dan Nutt	Courier Journal says Leaches KY	Maraman Bros.
Mrs. R. H. Miller	Bardstown	Maas.

The railroad was aware that compensation costs would be high, and they were quick to try to get a handle on it.

The note below from A. M. Warren, Chief Law Agent for the railroad, to J. J. Donahue, railroad attorney, gives an early estimate of what those costs might be. As you can see from the stationery, Mr. Warren was already in Bardstown. The Kelly referenced in the note was likely John S. Kelley. We have transcribed the list from the second page below.

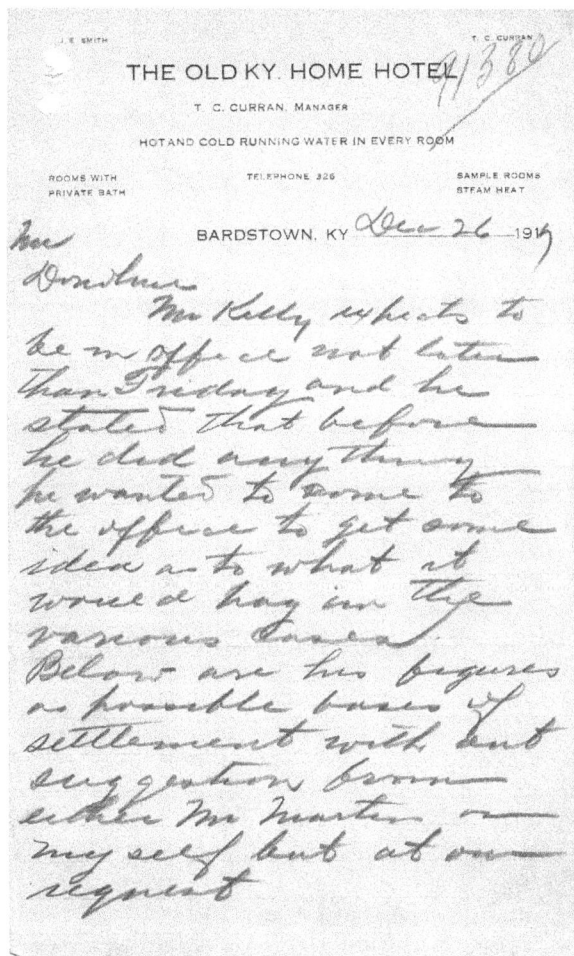

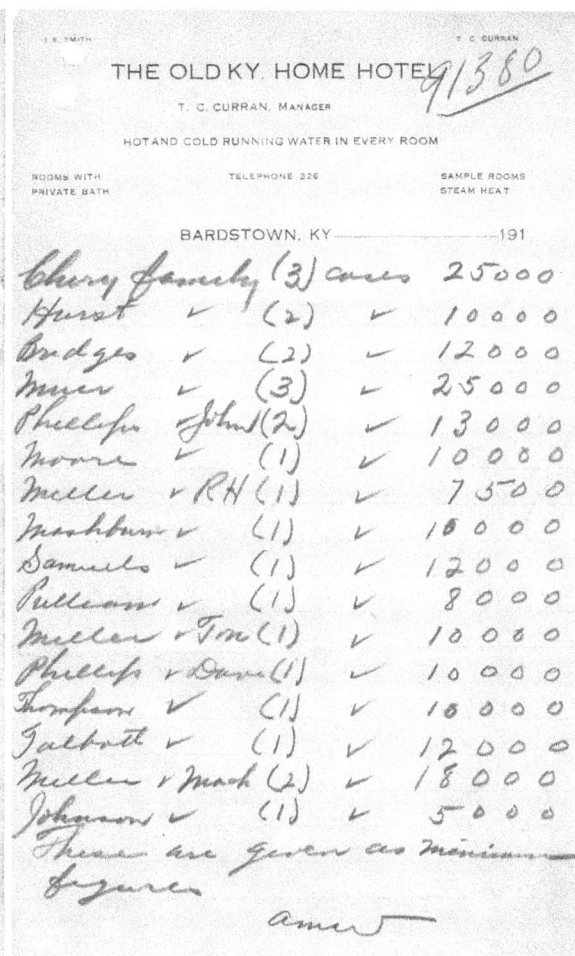

Cherry family	3 cases	$25000
Hurst family	2 cases	$10000
Bridges family	2 cases	$12000
Muir family	3 cases	$25000
Phillips family John	2 cases	$13000
Moore family	1 case	$10000
Miller family R.H.	1 case	$7500
Mashburn family	1 case	$10000
Samuels family	1 case	$12000
Pulliam family	1 case	$8000
Miller family Tom	1 case	$10000
Phillips family Dave	1 case	$10000
Thompson family	1 case	$10000
Talbott family	1 case	$12000
Miller family Mack	2 cases	$18000
Johnson family	1 case	$5000

Nashville, Tenn.
Jan 1 - 1918.

Mr. W. J. Dozohler,

Dear Sir:- My wife and
I were passengers on your
No. 7 Dec. 20-917 when it
collided with the accommodation
train at Shepardville, Ky.
We held tickets from
Albany, O. to Nashville, Tenn
on the Pennsylvania River
and L & N. R. R. My wife
was thrown forward against
the seat injuring her neck
and shoulders and has been
confined to her room ever since
on account of her injuries.

She was subjected to quite a
nervous shock and was compelled
to remain in the coacher for
some time in the cold in
which she contracted a very
bad cold adding to the strain
my explaining.

I am willing to adjust these
matters with you very reasonably.
I am a salaried man but
If you are with the N. C. & L. R. R.
We know that a well known
man to a railroad.

I am the large tall man
who was mentioned in your
paper as taking such an active
part in assisting in

every way possible to take
care of the dead and wounded.
Let to reference to me and a
man and a clergy man
gave to Mr. S. F. McConnell
(ticket agent) of N. C. & St
and the C. C. Steam Laundry
upon our personal reply
Yours Truly
J. Q. Black
197 Russell St
Nashville, Tenn.

Phone Main 332 K

This is typical of some of the inquiries the railroad received following the wreck. Some were legitimate, others not so much. This particular one was from John Quincy Black of Nashville regarding the injury his wife, Myrtle Lillian (Dale) Black was said to have received while they were aboard the express train at the time of the accident. He identifies himself as "the large tall man who was mentioned in your paper as taking such an active part in assisting in every way possible to take care of the dead and wounded." We have been unable to determine how the railroad responded to this inquiry.

H. T. Livey Letter to J. J. Donohue Regarding the Death of Silas Lawrence.

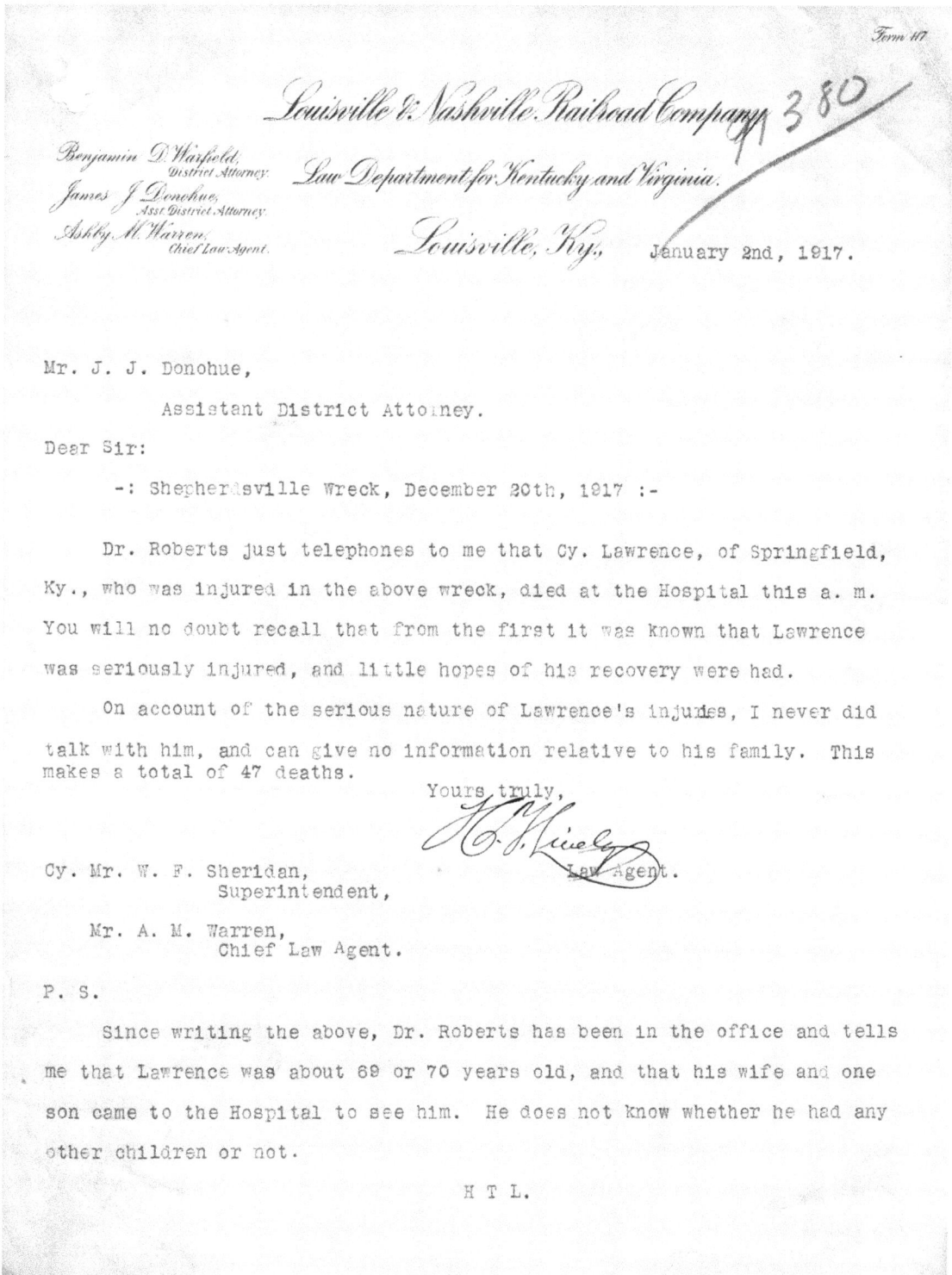

Louisville & Nashville Railroad Company 380

Benjamin D. Warfield,
    District Attorney.
James J. Donohue,
    Asst. District Attorney.
Ashby M. Warren,
    Chief Law Agent.

Law Department for Kentucky and Virginia.

Louisville, Ky., January 2nd, 1917.

Mr. J. J. Donohue,

      Assistant District Attorney.

Dear Sir:

    -: Shepherdsville Wreck, December 20th, 1917 :-

    Dr. Roberts just telephones to me that Cy. Lawrence, of Springfield, Ky., who was injured in the above wreck, died at the Hospital this a. m. You will no doubt recall that from the first it was known that Lawrence was seriously injured, and little hopes of his recovery were had.

    On account of the serious nature of Lawrence's injuries, I never did talk with him, and can give no information relative to his family. This makes a total of 47 deaths.

                 Yours, truly,

                                    Law Agent.

Cy. Mr. W. F. Sheridan,
       Superintendent,

    Mr. A. M. Warren,
          Chief Law Agent.

P. S.

    Since writing the above, Dr. Roberts has been in the office and tells me that Lawrence was about 69 or 70 years old, and that his wife and one son came to the Hospital to see him. He does not know whether he had any other children or not.

                H T L.

Correspondence between Walter Carter and H. T. Lively, law agent for the railroad. Walter was 18, and was working at Nazareth College as a dairyman, and was on his way to the college at the time of the wreck.

Shepherdsville Ky
Jany 24/1918

Dear Sir:

I had interview with Mr James Hardaway this evening & made him an offer of $10000. I was given to understand that they would not accept that sum. Said it was kindly bringing (foregone?) tion - so far as settlement was concerned and wanted to get all the other considerable folk I asked him could he that was right. He said he thought a jury would award $10,000. I told him the Company would not pay that sum & that it would take the chances rather than that sum.

Might be better done that out get all. He said it likely to be worse. Settled in next 2 or 3 days as he wished bring suit before to present such were filed. I told him there was enough funds on hand now to re- ... to affect any suit; the story all you will observe the paid $10000 in not met any would award $10000 in not met any of these cases. The impression I got was that less than $15000 - perhaps $12000 would settle but was positively in ... some $10000 would not be accepted.

yours truly
J. F. Combs

J. F. Combs, a Shepherdsville attorney acting on behalf of the railroad, inquired of James Hardaway, son of Henry Hardaway, as to what it would take for the Hardaways to settle with the railroad over the death of Henry in the train wreck. In this letter, Combs informs the railroad officials of the results of his effort.

Headlines

AKRON BEACON JOURNAL.

48 KILLED, MANY HURT IN WRECK

SANTA CRUZ NEWS

Forty-Six, Final Death Toll of Railroad Crash

41 KILLED IN L. & N. WRECK AT SHEPHERDSVILLE, KY.

Through Train No. 7 From Cincinnati Crashes Into Bardstown Accommodation Near Louisville.

ALL THE DEAD WERE ON KENTUCKY LOCAL

Thirty-Nine Are Reported Injured—Special Relief Party Is Rushed to the Scene.

NASHVILLE TENNESSEAN

THE PALM BEACH POST

SIXTY-SEVEN PERSONS KILLED, FIFTY INJURED IN TRAIN WRECK NEAR SHEPHERDSVILLE, KY.

CHAMPION PRESS AND LEADER

46 ARE KILLED IN WRECK ON L. & N. LINE

Fast Passenger Crashes Into Accommodation Train Just Leaving Station at Shepherdsville, Kentucky

MANY MORE ARE INJURED

46 KILLED BECAUSE ONE MAN TRIED TO DO TWO JOBS

Telegraph Operator Left Key to Handle Baggage and Collision of Trains Was the Result.

The Washington SUN

41 KILLED IN L. & N. WRECK

Twoscore Others Injured In Rear-End Crash At Shepherdsville, Ky.

EXPRESS TELESCOPES

The Courier-Journal.

VOL. CXXVIII. NEW SERIES—NO. 17,887— LOUISVILLE, FRIDAY MORNING, DECEMBER 21, 1917.—TWELVE PAGES. PRICE TWO CENTS

39 DIE IN CRASH OF L. & N. TRAINS AT SHEPHERDSVILLE

Train Wreck Headlines Dec. 21, 1917

The day following the wreck, the story made the front pages of newspapers across the nation, with varying degrees of accuracy regarding the number of people killed.

Index of Names

ASHBAUGH: Effie 44; Ross 44

ASHBY: William 15

ATHERTON: Clifton 55; Sue (Halstead) 55

BAILEY: Anna (See Anna Tucker)

BAIRD: W. J. 123

BAKER: Newton D. 169

BALL: B. B. 129-130

BARASS: Edward 69; Ernestine (Jones) 69; Nicholas 69

BARCLAY: Elizabeth (Thompson) 87; J. H. 87; Mary Jane "Mamie" (See Mary Jane "Mamie" Samuels)

BARDMAKER: Mary A. (See Mary A. Wolfenberger)

BARKHURST: Alice 48; Carrie Lucile (See Carrie Lucile Cherry); George 48; Mary Alice (Wood) 48

BARNES: Elizabeth (See Elizabeth Ice)

BATCHELOR: Mary Lee (Edwards) 101

BAXTER: Missy 77

BEALL: Elizabeth (See Elizabeth Phillips)

BEAM: Edward 97; John Henry "Jack" 97; Margaret (Thompson) 97-98; Maria (Nall) 97; T. D. 72

BEAN: Harriet Ann (See Harriet Ann Roby)

BEASLEY: Elizabeth Hanna (Jesse) 61-62; Sylvester 62

BELL: Amelia (See Amelia Tucker); Chrissie Lee 7; Donald

87; Dorothy Miriam (Samuels) 87; Henry Caleb 87; Kathryn 87; Lena (See Lena Sloss); Lera (See Lera Owens); Ottie (Satterfield) 52; Rufus 52

BELNAP: H. W. 33-34, 164

BERTELLO: Anna Eugenia Catterina 39; Eugenio 15, 22, 37, [39-40], 183, 186; Lucia (Ponzio) 39

BITNER: Ethel (See Ethel Ward)

BITTENBACK: Mary Amelia (See Mary Amelia Sanders or Mary Amelia Williams)

BLACK: John Quincy 188; Myrtle Lillian (Dale) 188

BLAKE: Juliann (See Juliann Wolford)

BLANTON: Anna (See Anna Showalter)

BOHLSEN: Henry 15

BOONE: Sarah "Sallie" (See Sarah "Sallie" Perkins)

BOOTS: Gillie (See Gillie Cundiff)

BOUCHER: Jack 10

BOWLES: Annie Fredericka (Pope) 40-41; Frederick 41-42; Fredericka (See Fredericka Lewis); Grace 40, 42; Isabelle (Williams) 42; James William 40-41; John Bethel 40; Joshua Bethel 25, 37-38, [40-42]; Julia 41-42; Margaret Eleanor (Nicholls) 40-42; Mary B. 38; Mary Caperton (See Mary Caperton Dale); Mary Elizabeth 40; Mary Guthrie 40; Nancy 40; Octavius Shreve 41

BOWMAN: Basil 42; Bertha (Hardin) 42; Charles 42; Emma (See Emma Maraman); Flagman 161; George 42-43; Henry [42-3]; Henry Clay 39, 64; Howard 42; John Henry 42-43; Mary (Shepherd) 64; Nellie (Simmons) 42; Susie Lillian (Murphy) 42; W. S. 124, 129-130

BOXLEY: Charlotte Ann 95; Jennie (Stansbury) 95; John 95

BRADBURY: Charles Preston 43; Della Mae (See Della Mae McClure); Evelyn May 43; Frances (Mathis) 43; Frances Vera 43; George Henry 43; James [43]; John 43; Margaret Belle (Patterson) [43]; Myrtle 43; William Oscar 43, 73

BRADY: Deborah 64; Debra Ann (See Debra Ann Lawrence); James 64

BREEDING: John 73; Mary Sue "Mamie" (Brown) 73

BRIDGES: Bessie (See Bessie Cotton); Fayette Hewitt 44; Hollie 11, 37, [44], 183, 186; Joel Thomas 44; John 44; Josie 11, 37, [44], 183; Laura (Fardette) 44; Miss Josie 186; Nannie (Lee) 44; Paulina (Tucker) 44; Robert Elwood 44

BROCK: Peggy (Troutman) 65

BROOKS: Margaret (See Margaret Craven)

BROWN: Alma (See Alma White); Carrie May (See Carrie May Simmons); Cecelia 110; Charles 70; Ethel (See Ethel Troutman);

CRAVEN: Annie 12, 20-21, 49-50; Edwin Melton 50; Eliza Marie (Montgomery) 12, 21, 35, [49-50]; Ella (See Ella Smith); George 49; Ival 50; Margaret (Brooks) 49-50; Mary 50; Raymond Thomas 12, 25, 37, 49, 186, 123-124; Thomas Washington 12, 20-21, 24, 49-50; Violet 50

CRAWFORD: Byron 77

CRIGLER: Arthur 89; Bill 89; Clyde 89; David 89; John 89; Lida 42; Lillian (Showalter) 89; Walter 89

CRIST: Irene (Conley) 77; John 77; Zilpah (See Zilpah Nutt)

CROAN: Ed 6; Gertrude (Showalter) 90; Hamlet E. 90

CROTHERS: Mary 93

CRUME: Beatrice (Losson) 59; Lillie (See Lillie McClure); Robert 59

CULVER: Catherine Ann (See Catherine Ann Greenwell)

CUNDIFF: Bertha (McClure) 68; Catherine "Kate" (See Catherine "Kate" Ice); Eliza E. (See Eliza E. Shelton); Elizabeth (See Elizabeth Shelton); Elmer 68; Eula (Ice) 60-61; George Etta (McClure) 68; George W. 60; Gillie (Boots) 89; Harvey 61; James B. 89; Jennie Bell (Moore) 60; Mary Jane (See Mary Jane Stansbury); Walter 68; William Morrow 61

CUNNINGHAM: Andrew 69; Annie (See Annie McElroy); Elizabeth (Bullock) 69

CURTSINGER: Armatha (See Armatha Pinkston)

DALE: Mary Caperton (Bowles) 41-42; Myrtle Lillian (See Myrtle Lillian Black); William 41-42

DALTON: Jack 24

DAUGHERTY: Daniel 50; Frank E. 6, 11, [50-51]; Sarah Ellen (Slevin) 50

DAVIS: Donna (Maraman) 65; James 102; John 6

DAVISON: Learner 5

DEACON: Ann (See Ann Harris); Rebecca (See Rebecca Lutes)

DEATS: Helen (See Helen Showalter)

DEMAREE: Ola (Johnson) 62; Stanley Raymond 62

DERRINGER: Mary Elizabeth (See Mary Elizabeth Perkins)

DICKEY: Ruby (See Ruby Nutt)

DODDS: Clara V. (Wolford) 51; John Gilmore 50, [51-52]; Josiah C. 51; Margaret Anne (Hutchison) 51-52

DOLAN: Charles Mark 73; Daniel 73; Dorothy 73; Frances Lucretia (Moore) 73; Jack 73; Ted 73

DONAHUE: James J. 98, 187, 189

DOOLAN: Anna (Nunn) 76, 178; William 76

DORCEY: Mary 105, 117-118

DOUTHITT: Sid T. 137, 153

DOWD: Charles Ferdinand 8

DOWNS: Addie (See Addie Mitchell); Catherine "Kitty" (Maddox) 83; John 83

DUDLEY: Garnette (McKay) 71; Lee Jouett 71; Mary (Jouett) 71; William Talbot 71

DUKE: George C. 11, 15, 37, [52], 58, 183, 186; J. Mills 52; Ottie (Satterfield) 11, [52]; Polina (Cooksey) 52; Virginia Frances 11, 24, 37, [52], 183, 186

DUNN: Elizabeth (See Elizabeth McClure); Mary Elizabeth (See Mary Elizabeth McClure)

DUTTON: John 97; Mary Francis (Nash) 97

EAKLE: Mary (See Mary Wolfenberger)

EDELEN: Texanna (See Texanna Marks)

EDWARDS: Clara (Ward) 100-101; Janice (See Janice Siler); John William 101; Mary Lee (See Mary Lee Batchelor); Mary Lou (See Mary Lou McCoppin); Mason 101; Ruth (See Ruth Shoemaker); Virginia Carolyn (See Virginia Carolyn Strain); William 101

EISENBACH: Annie Catherine "Kate" (See Annie Catherine "Kate" Saar)

ELLWANGER: Bertha (See Bertha Hoagland); Dorothy 58-59; John 59

ELZY: Solomon 15

EVANS: Charles Robinson 103; John Lewis 57; Lena (See Lena Hatfield); Lorraine (Williams) 103; Sarah Jane (Hatfield) 57; Walter 166

FARDETTE: Laura (See Laura Bridges)

FARRAR: William 6-7

FARRIS: Gillie (See Gillie Perkins)

FEATHERSTONE: John Walter F 55; Natalie (Halstead) 55

FIELDS: Charles 99; Rebecca (Garrett) 99

FINN: Laurence B. 31, 137-138, 152; Molly (See Molly Hurst)

HARRIS (continued): Mattie Lee (See Mattie Lee Overall); Sarah Elizabeth "Bettie" (Jones) 77; William Simeon 77

HARROD: Ellen Ann (See Ellen Ann Phillips)

HARTLEY: Betty 36

HATFIELD: Ben 58; Edith (See Edith Walker); Edith [57]; Elin (Tinnell) 57; Gilbert 57; Glendolin 57; John 57; Lena (Evans) [57-58]; Lennie Lee 57; Malinda (Hunt) 58; Marion 57; Nina (Perkins) 57; Sarah Jane (See Sarah Jane Evans); Stephen D. 58; Vesey 57; William Elias 57; Wilson 57

HATTER: Dudley 68; Martha (McClure) 68

HAYCRAFT: Emily (See Emily Mashburn); Hugh Chester 67; Julia (Arthur) 67; Samuel 67

HAYDON: J. D. 122

HAYLOW: W. J. 138

HAYS: Fannie (Lawrence) 64; Robert 64

HENDERSON: Annie (Combs) 92; Ralph 92-93, 95; Sarah Fletcher (See Sarah Fletcher Smith); Susan (See Susan Maraman); William 92

HICKERSON: Elizabeth (See Elizabeth Wright)

HICKS: Samuel 3

HIGDON: Robert G. 175

HILL: Caroline (Siler) 48; Robert 48; Susan (See Susan Lee)

HINKLE: Hurbert 81; William 81

HITE: Cora (See Cora Carrithers)

HOAGLAND: Bertha (Ellwanger) 58-59; Carrie 88; John Robert 9, 58, 74; Martha 58; R. I. 58; Sarah (See Sarah Samuels);

Thomas W. 9, 11, 25, 46, 52, [58-59]

HOBBS: Alpha (See Alpha Montgomery)

HOFFMAN: Benjamin F. 62; Eva (Johnson) 62; Margaret Geneva 62-63

HOOGE: Nell (See Nell Phillips)

HORRELL: Ermine (See Ermine Marks or Ermine Robinson or Ermine Webb)

HOSSELBACH: Susan (See Susan Schaefer)

HOUGH: James 15

HOUSE: Charles 28; Jerome 28; William 28

HOUSTON: William 4

HOVIOUS: Minnie (See Minnie Morrison)

HOWLETT: Ethel Lee 36; Lena (See Lena Smith)

HUBBUCH: Irene (See Irene Lell or Irene Tucker)

HUBER: John Henry 5

HUDSON: Effie (Jones) 69; Murray 69

HUMPHREY: Ella Alice (See Ella Alice Ford)

HUMPHREYS: Ethel (Showalter) 90; Jerome 90; Jerome Jr. 90

HUNT: Malinda (See Malinda Hatfield)

HURD: Eva (Johnson) 62; Fred 62

HURST: Family [59-60]; Gam 59; Harry 59; Joseph 21-22, 59-60, 83; Joseph Raoul Losson 24, 37, 123, [59-60], 186; Julian 59-60; Julian Jr. 59; Louisa (Losson) 11-12, 19, 24, 37, [59-60], 124, 183, 186; Mary (Spalding) 59; Molly (Finn) 59-60; Sarah Carolyn 59

HUTCHISON: Margaret Anne (See Margaret Anne Dodds)

ICE: Catherine "Kate" (Cundiff) 22, 24, 37, [60-61], 183, 186; Clara 60-61; Elizabeth (Barnes) 60; Eula (See Eula Cundiff); Jeff 60-61; Jenrose (Carby) 61; Joseph 60; Mamie (See Mamie Burns); Mamie 35; Norma Jean 61; Thomas C. 61; Thomas Robert 60

JELLISON: Byrd Mae (Wolfenberger) 104-105; Frank 104-105

JENKINS: Charles [61]; Charles Thomas 61; Charlie Parker 61; James Chester 61

JESSE: Charles Todd [61-62]; Eliza (Todd) 61; Elizabeth Ellen (Robertson) 61-62; Elizabeth Hanna (See Elizabeth Hanna Beasley); Gloria (Wollank) 62; James 61; James Henry 61-62; Mary Todd (See Mary Todd Fuller)

JOHNSON: Ada (See Ada Paulley); Albert 77; Charles W. [62-63]; Eva (See Eva Hoffman or Eva Hurd or Eva Parks); H. J. 129-130; H. R. 32, 138, 162; Kate (Whitesides) 62-63; Ola (See Ola Demaree); Susan (Nutt) 77; W. H. 98; William C. 25, 37, 123-124, 186

JONES: Dona (Roach) 69; Effie (See Effie Hudson); Elizabeth (Roby) 56, 77; Ernestine (See Ernestine Barass); Hattie 62; Iley 15; Lillian (See Lillian Miller); Martha E. "Mattie" (See Martha E. "Mattie" Harmon); Mrs. Mack 7; Oliver 69; Patrick 56; Patrick Henry 77; Sarah Elizabeth "Bettie" (See Sarah Elizabeth "Bettie" Harris);

MARKS: Anne 81; Dorothy 66; Edna 81; Elizabeth 81; Ermine (Horrell) 66; James Morgan 66; Joseph Edward 66; Joseph Edward III 66; Joseph Edward Jr. 38, [66], 81; Lovell Edelen 81; Maggie May (Phillips) 80-81; Texanna (Edelen) 66; William Gutherie 66

MARSHALL: Katherine (See Katherine Williams)

MARTIN: Matthew 51

MASDEN: C. A. 23, 91, 183; Charles 53; Eugenia (See Eugenia Stansbury or Eugenia Cash); Ezekiel John 12, 53, [66-67], 129-130, 160; Ezekiel John Sr. 66; Kate 53; Pearl (Wagner) 67

MASHBURN: Adelphia 67; Dorothy Elizabeth (McAdams) 67-68; Elizabeth Wilson (See Elizabeth Wilson Rodman); Emily (Haycraft) 24, 34-35, 37, [67-68], 166, 183, 186; Emily Bond 67; Forest C. 68; Henry Hamilton 35, 166, 67; Henry Hamilton Jr. 67; Henry III 68; Julia 67; Julia Rounsavall 68; Mariam (Wood) 68; Samuel Haycraft 67; Samuel Jr. 68; Theodosia (Tebbs) 68

MATHIS: Frances (See Frances Bradbury)

MATTINGLY: Lloyd 36; Susan (See Susan Carter)

MAY: Alice 6; Annie (Wakefield) 81; Bessie 81; Ernest 82; John S. 81; Lydia 82; Mary Alice (See Mary Alice Pulliam); Susie (See Susie Pulliam)

MAYES: T. Scott 73, 97; Virginia Kitura (See Virginia Kitura Thompson)

MCADAMS: Dorothy Elizabeth (See Dorothy Elizabeth Mashburn)

MCADOO: William G. 169, 172

MCALEER: Joseph 40

MCBRIDE: Ivy T. 39

MCCANDLESS: David A. 15, 58, 130

MCCARTY: Elizabeth (Hall) 79; James Nolia (See James Nolia Phillips); John Stapleton 79

MCCLAIN: W. D. 6

MCCLURE: Ada Belle (See Ada Belle Showalter); Annie (See Annie Overall); Bertha (See Bertha Cundiff); Clyde 43; Della Mae (Bradbury) 43; Elizabeth (Dunn) 90; George Etta (See George Etta Cundiff); James 89-90; John McKinley [68], 89-90; Lillie (Crume) 78; Martha (See Martha Hatter); Mary Elizabeth (Dunn) 68, 89; Mary Ellen 68; Maude H. (See Maude H. Shelton); Mildred Frances (See Mildred Frances Cornell); Thomas B. 43; William 78; Woodrow 43

MCCOPPIN: Mary Lou (Edwards) 101

MCCORD: Edna (Shelton) 89; J. L. 89; James 89

MCCUBBINS: Clyde 90; Clyde Jr. 90; Russell 90; Sara Jo 90; Sarah Elizabeth (Showalter) 90

MCCUE: Maggie (See Maggie Tucker)

MCDOWELL: Robert 59

MCELROY: Annie (Cunningham) 69; Elizabeth 12, 24, 37, [68-69], 183, 186; Hillary (See Hillary Reed); Howard B. 69; Josephine (See Josephine Gregory or Josephine Moore);

Sue (Calhoun) 69; William 69

MCFERRAN: Milton 4

MCGINNIS: Virginia (See Virginia Samuels)

MCGOVERN: Irene (See Irene Roby)

MCHUGH: James 4

MCKAY: Emily (See Emily Sturgis); Enoch Edwin 71; Florence (See Florence Shadburne); Garnette (See Garnette Miller or Garnette Dudley); Harry 71; Mary Sue (Loftin) 72; Ophelia (See Ophelia Robinson); Ophelia (Wilson) 71; Wallace A. 47

MCMAKIN: Lucy (See Lucy Grundy); Maggie (See Maggie Miller)

MCMANUS: Charles 96; Mary Ann (Robey) 96; Naomi (See Naomi Talbott)

MCNAULTY: Mary (See Mary Keyer)

MEIER: Erma (See Erma Ratliff)

MELTON: Fanny Bell 35

MEYERS: Mary (See Mary Klages)

MILES: Barbara Ann (See Barbara Ann Garrett); Geneva Betrix (Phillips) 79-80; Joseph Alton 80

MILLER: Amelia (Smith) 11, 24, 37, [70-71], 183, 186; Belle (See Belle Smith or Belle Tomlinson); Bernice Beatrice (Kelley) 70; Charles 70; Charles Howard 69; Dorothy 69; Edna (Smock) 69; Edward McMakin 71; Grover 112; Hazel 69; Humphrey 109, 112; Lillian (Jones) 24, 34, 37, [69-70], 183, 186; Lillie Lee (See Lillie Lee Ward); Lola (Prall) 69;

SHOWALTER (continued): Charlie 68, [89-90]; Debra 90; Della (See Della Kulmer); Earl 90; Ethel (See Ethel Humphreys or Ethel Sharp); Gertrude (See Gertrude Croan or Gertrude Walker); Helen (Deats) 90; Jacob Hite 89; John William 89; Lillian (See Lillian Crigler); Mary Jane 89; May (Roach) 89; Richard Thomas 89; Sara Lee (Phillips) 89; Sarah (Hall) 89; Sarah Elizabeth (See Sarah Elizabeth McCubbins); Sarah Ethel (See Sarah Ethel Gill or Sarah Ethel Noe); Sheila 90; Stella (See Stella Goodin)

SHOWALTERS: John [89-90]

SILER: Bess (Cherry) 48; Caroline (See Caroline Hill); Janice (Edwards) 48; Marshall Jr. 48; Marshall Mahan 48

SIMMONS: Carrie May (Brown) 11, 19, 22, 37, [90-91], 183, 186; Jennie (See Jennie Hardaway); Judy 50; Nellie (See Nellie Bowman); Sophronia (Shanklin) 55; Susan (See Susan Craik); William 62, 88, 90; William Peyton 55; Willie Maye (See Willie Maye Hackett)

SIMMS: Alethaire (See Alethaire Spalding); Benedict Francis 91-92; Benedict Francis Jr. 91; Frances (Reed) 83-84; James Edward 84; John Manning 92; Leo Godfrey 91; Mary Alethaire 12, 24, 37, 69, [91-92], 94, 183, 186; Mary Charlotte "Lottie" (Wall) 91-92; Mary Isabelle 91

SIMPSON: Susie 6

SIMS: Bertha Lee (Ford) 53; Henry 53

SINCLAIR: Kathryn (See Kathryn Malone)

SLEVIN: Sarah Ellen (See Sarah Ellen Daugherty)

SLOSS: Carolyn 52; Kelly 52; Lena (Bell) 52

SMITH: Addie (Patterson) 47; Albert 15; Alzo 49; Amelia (See Amelia Miller); Belle (Miller) 93; Benedict Joseph 85; Clara (Stovall) 93-94; Edward Clifford 93-94; Elizabeth (Langsford) 70-71; Ella (Craven) 49; Ellie (See Ellie Chase); Harriet (Rhodes) 85; Helen Anastasia "Annie" (See Helen Anastasia "Annie" Riney); Henry 93; James Everett 34, [92-93], 166; Lena (Howlett) 92; Leo 40; Mariah (See Mariah Chapeze); Mary (See Mary Adams or Mary Miller); Mary Inez (See Mary Inez Carrico or Mary Inez Moore); Mary Jane (Carrithers) 93; Michael 93; Mike [93-94]; Mikle S. 93-94; Milton H. 29, 129, 132, 167; Mitchell 93-94; Noah 92-93; Ophelia (See Ophelia Patterson); Perry L. 93-94; Sarah Fletcher (Henderson) 92-93; Thomas Jefferson 70; William 47

SMITHERS: Joseph 1

SMOCK: Edna (See Edna Miller)

SPALDING: Alethaire (Simms) 94-95; Benedict 94-95; George 95; Mary (See Mary Hurst); Nellie 59; William Thomas Simms 12, 24, 37, 59, 69, 92, [94-95], 183, 186

SPARROW: Anna Lou (See Anna Lou Lawrence)

SPIRES: Nellie (See Nellie Lawrence)

STAHL: Frances Martha (See Frances Martha Cherry)

STALLINGS: Sarah (See Sarah Thurman)

STANLEY: A. O. 29, 137

STANSBURY: Clarence 95; Ella (See Ella Hardy); Eugenia (Masden) 95; James Jr. 183, 186; James W. 22, 24, 37, [95]; Jennie (See Jennie Boxley or Jennie Carney); Lounetta (See Lounetta Williams); Mary Jane (Cundiff) 95; Nancy Jane (Carpenter) 95

STARKS: B. M. 31, 129-130, 132, 138, 175-176, 178

STONE: H. L. 166

STONER: Isabel (Newbolt) 78, 86; Martha (See Martha Samuels); Mary Frances (See Mary Frances Overall or Mary Francis Samuels); R. J. 78, 86

STOVALL: Amanda (Nall) 93; Clara (See Clara Carpenter or Clara Smith); Sam 93

STRAIN: Virginia Carolyn (Edwards) 101

STRANGE: David 183

STRAUS: Frank P. 166

STREBLE: Mary Lou (See Mary Lou Hackett)

STRUGAL: Louis 72

STURGIS: Effingham M. 71; Emily (McKay) 12, 71-72

SULLIVAN: Margaret (See Margaret Roby)

SUSIE: Frances (See Frances Sheckles)

SWEARINGEN: Fred 15; George 15

TABOR: Thomas T. 28

TALBOTT: Aimee (See Aimee Guthrie); Ben 6, 11-12, 24, 37,[96-97], 183, 186; Ben Johnson 96;

WHITTLE: David E. 65; Eva (Maraman) 65; Noah 65

WICKLIFFE: J. D. 166

WICKLYFFE: Margaret Logan (See Margaret Logan Halstead)

WIGGINTON: Betty Ann (See Betty Ann Robey); George W. 64; George W. Jr. 64; Mary Catherine (See Mary Catherine Harper); Sue Charles (See Sue Charles Jones); Susan Elder (Maraman) 64

WILHITE: Henry [102]

WILHOYTE: Hugh Berkley 102

WILLETT: Conductor John C. 15, 162

WILLHITE: Guy 102; James Manrow 102

WILLIAMS: Anna Louise 103; Bill 95; Carrie (See Carrie Ford); Clifford Marshall 103; Edgar Milton 103; Isabelle (See Isabelle Bowles); J. Lewis 34, 130, 133, 175; James Douglas 103; James Marvin [102-104]; James Marvin Jr. 103; John 103; Katherine (Marshall) 103; Lorraine (See Lorraine Burke or Lorraine Evans); Lounetta (Stansbury) 95; Margaret (Clay) 103-104; Martha 104; Marvin 11; Mary Amelia (Bittenback) 103; Mary Faith 104

WILLINGHAM: Elwood B. 97; Mary Francis (Nash) 97

WILSON: George 109; Ophelia (See Ophelia McKay); Rose (Buckner) 109-110; Sarah (See Sarah Losson); Woodrow 100

WOLFENBERGER: Anna Margaret 104-105; Birdie 104; Byrd Mae (See Byrd Mae Jellison); Ida 104; John 104; Mary (Eakle) 104; Mary A. (Bardmaker) 104-105; Michael 104; Nora (See Nora Hanley); William H. 16, 18, 29-34, [104-105], 120-124, 126-127, 129-130, 132, 138, 140-141, 146-151, 157, 160-161, 163

WOLFORD: Clara V. (See Clara V. Dodds); Eli 51; Juliann (Blake) 51

WOLLANK: Gloria (See Gloria Jesse)

WOOD: Mariam (See Mariam Mashburn); Mary Alice (See Mary Alice Barkhurst)

WOODS: Margaret 19, 117-118

WOODWARD: Ernest 15, 52, 58, 175

WORLEY: Eliza (See Eliza Gregory)

WRIGHT: Elizabeth "Bettie" (See Elizabeth "Bettie" Phillips); Elizabeth (Hickerson) 80; Morgan 80

ZIMMERMAN: J. R. 90